MW01515750

2010 SUPPLEMENT

MATERIALS ON

ACCOUNTING
FOR LAWYERS

UNABRIDGED AND CONCISE FOURTH EDITIONS

by

MATTHEW J. BARRETT
Professor of Law
Notre Dame School of Law

FOUNDATION PRESS
2010

THOMSON REUTERS™

© 2008, 2009 THOMSON REUTERS/FOUNDATION PRESS
© 2010 By THOMSON REUTERS/FOUNDATION PRESS

       1 New York Plaza, 34th Floor
       New York, NY 10004
       Phone Toll Free 1–877–888–1330
       Fax 646–424–5201
       foundation–press.com

Printed in the United States of America

ISBN 978–1–59941–852–0

Mat #41029182

PREFACE TO THE 2010 SUPPLEMENT

** Thank you for using our materials. In an effort to provide the most timely, accurate, and helpful materials possible, I want to highlight important developments occurring since the fourth editions went to press and to call to your attention a few typos and other glitches that appear in either the unabridged or concise versions of that edition. Double asterisks (**) note materials added or substantially revised since the 2009 Supplement.

** In the last four years, we have watched as the stock option scandals developed, the collapse in various subprime lending markets in the United States developed into a global financial crisis, and the Securities and Exchange Commission ("SEC") announced a proposed "roadmap" for adopting International Financial Reporting Standards ("IFRS"), then turned its attention to the credit crisis and the Bernard Madoff scandal, and then issued a statement in support of convergence and global accounting standard. Although far less publicized in the popular press, during the past year, the Financial Accounting Standards Board ("FASB") completed a multi-year project to develop a single authoritative source of generally accepted accounting principles for nongovernmental entities in the United States. Effective for financial statements for interim and annual periods ending after September 15, 2009, the FASB Accounting Standards Codification (the "Codification") assembles all authoritative guidance in one place and affects the way enterprises reference accounting policies in their financial statements and related notes.

** This 2010 Supplement highlights the most significant developments affecting our materials that have occurred between December 31, 2005, the cut-off date for the fourth editions, and April 30, 2010. Once again, however, I've tried to incorporate the most important "subsequent events," including the Supreme Court's decision holding unconstitutional those provisions in the Sarbanes-Oxley Act of 2002 ("SOx") that let the SEC remove members of the Public Company Accounting Oversight Board only for cause, but severing those removal provisions from the rest of the law, concluding that SEC can remove the PCAOB's member at will, and stating that SOx "remains fully operative as a law;" the Supreme Court's order denying a writ of certiorari in *Textron v. United States*; and the conference agreement on financial reform legislation.

The updates that follow provide cross references to the unabridged version of the fourth edition of our casebook, including chapter and section headings and page numbers, and where applicable, the concise version of that same edition.

** I again want to thank David R. Herwitz, who served for fifty years as author or co-author of *Accounting for Lawyer*, for his many kindnesses to me since I joined him on this text's second edition and his countless contributions to the field over a career in which he taught the subject to about 14,000 law students, primarily at Harvard Law School. I remain deeply grateful for the wonderful opportunity to collaborate on these materials, and I have thoroughly enjoyed working with him for almost fifteen years. He remains an invaluable mentor. I wish him the very best as he enjoys his emeritus status and devotes more time to his family, especially his grandchildren.

** I gratefully acknowledge the invaluable research and drafting assistance of John Berger, a Notre Dame law student in the Class of 2010; research assistance from Tom Geagan in the Class of 2009 and Kevin Musheno in the Class of 2011; and the efforts of my administrative assistant, Sharon Loftus.

** If you find any glitches, inaccuracies, or other significant developments that do not appear below, please let me know. You can reach me via e-mail at <Barrett.1@nd.edu>, phone at (574) 631-8121, or fax at (574) 631-8078. You will not offend me in any way because I want our materials to be as accurate and helpful as possible. Special thanks to Professors Steve Bradford, Wayne M. Gazur and Eric Halvorson for calling various glitches to my attention. I also welcome any other comments or suggestions that you might be willing to share. Thanks again.

Matthew J. Barrett

July 12, 2010

TABLE OF CONTENTS

Page references set forth the first item in this Supplement for that section.

TABLE OF ACRONYMS

AS	Public Company Accounting Oversight Board Auditing Standard
ASC	FASB Accounting Standards Codification
ASU	FASB Accounting Standards Update
CAQ	Center for Audit Quality of the American Institute of Certified Public Accountants
CON	Financial Accounting Standards Board Concept Statement
COSO	Committee of Sponsoring Organizations of the Treadway Commission
DPA	Deferred Prosecution Agreement
EFRAG	European Financial Reporting Advisory Group
FAS	FASB Statement of Financial Accounting Standards
FCAG	Financial Crisis Advisory Group of the Financial Accounting Standard Board and the International Accounting Standards Board
FRC	SEC Codification of Financial Reporting Policies
FTB	FASB Technical Bulletin
ICFR	Internal Control over Financial Reporting
IDEA	Interactive Data Electronic Applications
IFRSAC	IFRS Advisory Council
IFRSF	IFRS Foundation
IFRSIC	IFRS Interpretations Committee
ITAC	Investors Technical Advisory Committee of the Financial Accounting Standards Board
Libor	London Inter-Bank Offered Rate
NASBA	National Association of State Boards of Accountancy
MoU	Memorandum of Understanding between the International Accounting Standards Board and the Financial Accounting Standards Board
NPA	Non-Prosecution Agreement
OTTI	"Other than temporary" impairment
S-K	Regulation S-K
S-X	Regulation S-X
SMEs	Small- and medium-sized entities
TPA	AICPA Technical Practice Aid
WKSI	Well-Known Seasoned Issuer
XBRL	eXtensible Business Reporting Language

*

TABLE OF OFFICIAL ACCOUNTING AND AUDITING PROMULGATIONS

References are to Pages.

. . . .

TABLE OF CASES

Principal cases are in bold type. Non-principal cases are in roman type. References are to Pages.

*

CHAPTER I

INTRODUCTION TO FINANCIAL STATEMENTS, BOOKKEEPING, AND ACCRUAL ACCOUNTING

E. THE STATEMENT OF CHANGES IN OWNER'S EQUITY

1. THE SOLE PROPRIETORSHIP

On page 55 [omitted from the concise], Problem 1.4C assumes a $13,000 debit balance in Cash.

2. THE PARTNERSHIP

On page 56 [omitted from the concise], the word "Total" should appear at the top of the third column and the other headings for "Tutt" and "King" should move to the left one column in the Statement of Changes in Partners' Equity for King Tutt at the bottom of the page.

F. ACCRUAL ACCOUNTING

On page 69 [omitted from the concise], replace the second full paragraph with the following:

** The federal government's annual financial reports further illustrate the differences between the cash and accrual methods. Accruals for benefits that military and civilian employees earn, but that the government will not pay until a future fiscal year typically cause the government's "net operating cost" computed under the accrual method to exceed the cash-based federal deficit. For the fiscal year ending September 30, 2009, however, the federal deficit uncharacteristically exceeded net operating cost because the Veterans Administration substantially reduced its estimates for veterans' benefit liabilities and costs and the government reduced the estimated cost for the Troubled Asset Relief Program, usually called simply "TARP." From fiscal 2008 to fiscal 2009, the cash-based budged deficit increased from $455 billion to $1.4 trillion. By comparison, net operating cost under the accrual method increased from slightly more than $1 trillion in fiscal 2008 to about $1.3 trillion in fiscal 2009. U.S. DEP'T OF THE TREASURY, 2009 FINANCIAL REPORT OF THE UNITED STATES GOVERNMENT i, iv-v, 4, *available at* http://www.fms.treas.gov/fr/09frusg/09frusg.pdf. Based on recent history, fiscal 2008 provides the more common relationship between the measures. Under the cash method, the federal government reported a $455 billion budget deficit, while the accrual method produced a net operating cost exceeding $1 trillion. Regrettably, the typically larger net operating cost under the accrual method has historically received far less media attention than the usually smaller, but widely publicized cash budget deficit.

1. INTRODUCTION

b. BASIC PRINCIPLES

(7) An Emerging Fair Value or Relevance Principle

On pages 74 to 76, beginning with the carryover paragraph on the bottom of page 74 replace the remainder of the text in this section with the following text [on page 56 of the concise, insert the following text below the first full paragraph in section (7)]:

In December 1999, the leading body of accounting rulemakers in the United States published a document setting forth its preliminary views on measuring and reporting certain financial assets and liabilities at fair value. This document marked an important step in the seemingly inevitable move toward accounting standards that will eventually compel enterprises to use fair value to report all financial assets and liabilities. As we will read later in this text, more and more accounting standards, both domestically and internationally, require that enterprises report certain assets and liabilities at fair value. In their preliminary views, the rulemakers specifically stated that because they had not resolved all the conceptual and practical issues related to determining the fair values of financial assets and liabilities, they could not decide when, if ever, the basic financial statements should report such fair values. As possible alternatives, the rulemakers observed that they could require enhanced disclosures about fair values or a separate set of financial statements based upon fair value. Because market prices do not exist for many financial assets, enterprises would need to develop valuation models to determine fair value. Such valuation models would inherently depend upon subjective assumptions.

After starting a project in 2001 to require additional disclosures about the use of fair values in financial statements, the rulemakers later decided in mid-2003 to remove that project from their agenda so that they could concentrate first on issues related to fair value measurement. That project focused on *how* to measure fair value, not *what* to measure at fair value. The rulemakers decided to consider the latter question on a project-by-project basis. In 2006, the standard setters issued a final pronouncement on fair value measurements that codified and simplified the guidance that previously existed for developing fair value measurements, improved their consistency and comparability, and enhanced disclosures about those measurements.

** The new rules on fair value measurements took effect at about the same time that the credit crisis began. In response to criticisms that fair value accounting exacerbated the ongoing financial crisis by requiring enterprises to write-down assets in inactive markets, the standard setters announced significant clarifications to the rules in 2008, 2009, and 2010. The new rules, which this Supplement describes in more detail on pages 113 to 114 in the updates to Chapter VI, establish a uniform methodology for obtaining the fair value measurements that other standards require; offer guidance on calculating fair value for assets in an illiquid market and on determining whether an asset has suffered an other-than-temporary impairment in value; and require additional disclosures. Although controversial, the new rules do not obligate enterprises to measure any additional items at fair value. Not surprisingly, banks and other financial institutions have asked the rulemakers to suspend fair value accounting and have consistently objected to any rule that requires enterprises to use fair value accounting.

In response to certain developments in international accounting principles, the rulemakers in the United States began in 2004 another project that would permit, but not require, enterprises to account for financial instruments and similar instruments at fair value. The first phase culminated in early 2007 with a final pronouncement, described in more detail in the materials for Chapter V on pages 69 and 70 of this Supplement. In short, that pronouncement allows an irrevocable, one-time election to use fair value to measure and report certain financial assets and financial liabilities on a contract-by-contract basis, with any changes in fair value recognized in earnings as those changes occur.

4. PRACTICE PROBLEM

On page 82 of the concise [no adjustment needed in the unabridged version], insert "$810" as the balance on the last line in the credit column of the Profit and Loss T-account on the bottom of the page.

H.   THE STATEMENT OF CASH FLOWS

3. CASH AND CASH EQUIVALENTS

On page 131 at the end of the carryover paragraph at the top of the page, insert the following text [on page 106 of the concise, insert at the end of section 3]:

The credit crisis uncovered certain ambiguities in the requirements necessary to qualify as a "cash equivalent" for financial accounting purposes. After the relevant accounting rule's promulgation, new financial instruments, such as auction-rate securities and variable-rate demand notes, which typically offered higher returns than short-term commercial paper and Treasury securities, became very popular. Although these securities sometimes carried maturities up to thirty years, they also contained features, such as provisions allowing the holder to sell the securities back to the issuer every ninety days, designed to qualify as "highly liquid." As a result, numerous enterprises treated these securities as cash equivalents for financial accounting purposes. As the credit crisis worsened, some issuers defaulted and most securities in the $330 billion market suddenly became illiquid. Even before the crisis began grabbing headlines and in connection with an on-going project on financial statement presentation, accounting rulemakers had tentatively decided to eliminate the caption "cash equivalents" from financial statements and to revise the statement of cash flows to present information on movements of cash only. Steven D. Jones, *Firms Ponder What Constitutes Cash*, WALL ST. J., July 27, 2006, at C3.

4. CLASSIFICATION OF THE STATEMENT OF CASH FLOWS

On page 132 [omitted from the concise], delete the second full sentence that appears on the top of this page because Amazon.com's statement of cash flows does not appear in Appendix A.

5. THE OPERATING SECTION

On page 134 [page 110 of the concise], replace the first sentence in the carryover paragraph at the bottom of the page with the following sentence:

The scandals at Enron, Dynegy, Inc. ("Dynegy"), and Tyco International Ltd. ("Tyco") illustrate devious techniques that so-called "financial engineers" can use to manufacture fictitious operating cash flows.

On page 135 [page 111 of the concise] after the carryover paragraph at the top of the page, insert the following new paragraph:

Dynegy, another energy company, also developed a complex fraud to convert financing cash flows to operating cash flows. As mentioned earlier, entities can use "fair value" accounting for certain financial statement items and must "mark-to-market," or re-measure the fair value of these items, at each reporting date. Dynegy measured contracts for the future delivery of energy commodities at fair value, recognizing gains in income when the value of the contracts increased. Enterprises, however, may not treat these "unrealized gains" as operating cash flows because the actual transactions, and exchange of cash, have yet to occur. Analysts viewed the growing gap between Dynegy's net income and operating cash flow as a sign that Dynegy potentially overvalued its energy contracts. To reduce the gap, Dynegy employed "Project Alpha," a complex scheme similar to the "prepays" at Enron, using other entities as fronts in an attempt to disguise loans as commodity transfers. Through "Project Alpha," Dynegy fraudulently misclassified $300 million as operating, rather than financing, cash flows in 2001.

On page 135 [page 111 of the concise] after the first full paragraph and before the section heading, insert the following new paragraph:

Users of financial statements, including lawyers, should keep in mind that legitimate, but unsustainable, strategies for boosting operating cash flows for a particular accounting period involve selling receivables for quick cash or slowing down payments for goods and services purchased on credit. Michael Rapoport, *Quick Cash via Receivables Deals Can Leave a Blurry Fiscal Picture*, WALL ST. J., June 16, 2006, at C3.

I. CONSOLIDATED FINANCIAL STATEMENTS

On page 140 [page 113 of the concise at the end of the second full paragraph], replace the second paragraph with the following text:

** The Enron scandal caused the subject of consolidating controlled entities to explode in importance. Enron demonstrated that an enterprise could use contractual agreements, the entity's organizational instruments, or other governing documents to obtain or retain control or significant influence over an entity without holding a majority voting interest. In its "financial engineering," Enron designed a number of so-called "special purpose entities" ("SPEs"), which appeared independent, but which Enron or its officers controlled in fact. Enron used these SPEs to generate manipulated profits, to conceal poorly performing assets, and to hide large amounts of debt. Following Enron's collapse, accounting standard-setters in the United States issued rules that adopted a new model for consolidation, in addition to the so-called "voting interest model." For fiscal years that began on or before November 15, 2009, a quantitative "risk and rewards model" applied. Under that model, the primary beneficiary of a "variable interest entity" ("VIE"), a term that includes not only entities that the business community referred to as SPEs, but also other entities, must consolidate the VIE when the beneficiary receives a majority of the VIE's expected residual returns, absorbs a majority of the entity's expect losses, or both. Starting with fiscal years beginning after November 15, 2009, a primarily qualitative approach now applies to identifying a controlling financial interest in a VIE. The new rules require ongoing assessments as to whether an entity falls within the definition of VIE and whether a particular interest makes the holder the VIE's primary beneficiary. This newest approach focuses on which enterprise holds the power to direct a VIE's activities that most significantly effect the entity's economic performance and (1) the obligation to absorb the entity's losses or (2) the right to receive benefits from the entity, We will pursue this important topic in more detail in Chapter VI. For now, we need only an introduction to the process of consolidation. Please keep in mind, however, that this consolidation process applies to situations where an enterprise either owns a controlling voting interest or holds a controlling economic interest in another entity.

On page 144 at the end of the first full paragraph [page 117 of the concise at the end of the second full paragraph], please insert the following new text:

In an effort to improve comparability and converge accounting principles applying to consolidated financial statements globally, in December 2007 accounting standard setters in the United States issued a new pronouncement, effective for fiscal years beginning after December 15, 2008, regarding noncontrolling interests in consolidated financial statements. The pronouncement uses the term *"noncontrolling interests"* to describe what the previous paragraph refers to as "minority interests." The new standard provides that an enterprise should treat a noncontrolling interest in a subsidiary as an ownership interest in the consolidated entity that will appear as equity in the consolidated financial statements, albeit separate from the parent's equity. As a result, the new promulgation changes existing practice in the United States, which has typically classified minority interests as liabilities or reported such amounts in the "mezzanine" section between liabilities and equity on the balance sheet. Beginning with the financial statements for its fiscal year ending in 2010, Starbucks will need to adopt the new pronouncement and change the reporting for its "[m]inority interest liabilities."

On page 145 [page 118 of the concise], the word "Combined" should appear at the top of the far right column in the Combined Balance Sheet for X Corp. and Y Corp. at the bottom of the page.

CHAPTER II

THE DEVELOPMENT OF ACCOUNTING PRINCIPLES AND AUDITING STANDARDS

A. IMPORTANCE TO LAWYERS

On page 148 [page 122 of the concise], beginning with the third paragraph, and continuing throughout the chapter, please note that the Supreme Court of the United States upheld the PCAOB's existence in Free Enterprise Fund v. Public Company Accounting Oversight Board, 78 U.S.L.W. 4766 (2010). Although the Supreme Court concluded that the Board's structure violated the Constitution's separation of powers doctrine, the Court severed the unconstitutional provisions. Under the statutory scheme, the SEC could remove Board members only "for good cause shown," while the President could remove Commissioners only for good cause. As a result, the Supreme Court held that an impermissible two layers of tenure protection insulated Board members from Presidential control. Explicitly stating that "[t]he Sarbanes-Oxley Act remains 'fully operative as a law,'" the Supreme Court eliminated the unconstitutional tenure provisions, leaving the SEC able to remove Board members at will. Free Enter. Fund v. Pub. Co. Accounting Oversight Bd., 78 U.S.L.W. at 4776.

On page 149, delete the second and third sentences from the end of the second full paragraph near the bottom of the page, beginning with the words, "In addition, ..." [on page 123 of the concise, note the following development in regards to the carryover paragraph ending on the top of the page].

A new auditing standard for public company audits, described in this Supplement on pages 32 and 33, no longer requires auditors to express an opinion on management's assessment of the effectiveness of internal control over financial reporting. The auditor must, however, still express an opinion on whether the company maintained effective internal control over financial reporting.

C.   GENERALLY ACCEPTED ACCOUNTING PRINCIPLES

1.   THE ESTABLISHMENT OF ACCOUNTING PRINCIPLES

a. THE SECURITIES AND EXCHANGE COMMISSION

On pages 157 and 158 [omitted from the concise], the SEC has repealed Regulation S–B and eliminated the reporting forms for small business issuers, generally effective February 5, 2008, but subject to limited transition rules. Accordingly, replace the first sentence of the carryover paragraph at the bottom of page 157 with the following:

Shorter deadlines, however, apply to "accelerated filers," which means reporting companies that (1) have been subject to the SEC's periodic reporting requirements for at least twelve months and have filed one annual report and (2) have a "public float" that equals or exceeds $75 million.

On page 159 [omitted from the concise], replace the carryover paragraph at the bottom of the page with the following text that reflects Regulation S–B's repeal and the new system of disclosure rules for smaller companies filing periodic reports, effective February 5, 2008.

By regulation, the SEC imposes numerous reporting and disclosure requirements on registrants. Regulation S–X contains lengthy and detailed requirements prescribing the specific items which registrants must disclose or address in financial statements which they file with the Commission. 17 C.F.R. pt. 210 (2009). SEC officials have announced that the Commission will use amendments to Regulation S–X as a mechanism to attempt to protect the integrity of accounting standards in the United States. In addition, Regulation S–K presents standard instructions for filing forms under the Securities Act of 1933 and the Securities Exchange Act of 1934, including directions related to certain financial information which those forms require. *Id.* pt. 229.

In March 2005, the SEC organized the Advisory Committee on Smaller Public Companies to examine the effect of Sarbanes-Oxley and other federal securities laws on smaller companies. In its Final Report, the Advisory Committee offered several recommendations relating to scaling securities regulation for smaller companies. *See* SEC Notice of Establishment of the Advisory Committee on Smaller Public Companies, Final Report (2006), http://www.sec.gov/info/smallbus/acspc.shtml. In response to the Advisory Committee's recommendations, the SEC adopted a new system of disclosure rules for smaller companies filing periodic reports, effective February 5, 2008. Smaller Reporting Company Regulatory Relief and Simplification, 73 Fed. Reg. 934, 956 (Jan. 4, 2008) (codified at 17 C.F.R. § 229.10(f) (2009)). The new rules contain scaled requirements to reflect the characteristics and needs of smaller companies and their investors and replace the disclosure requirements formerly found in Regulation S-B. The new rules apply to all "smaller reporting companies," primarily "non-accelerated filer" companies, which generally means companies having less than $75 million in public equity float.

On page 160 [page 135 of the concise], insert the following text before the carryover paragraph at the bottom of the page:

Before the credit crisis and Madoff scandal captured the SEC's attention, the Commission devoted considerable energy to the convergence and advancement of international accounting principles. In December 2007, the SEC issued final rules that allow foreign private issuers to use international financial reporting standards ("IFRS") to prepare the financial statements that those companies must submit to the agency under the federal securities laws without any reconciliation to U.S. GAAP.

** Under the Administrative Procedure Act, the SEC must give formal notice and allow a period for public comment before adopting international accounting principles. About a year after issuing a 2007 concept release seeking public comment on a proposal to allow U.S. issuers to file financial statements prepared in accordance with IFRS, as published in English by the International Accounting Standards Board ("IASB"), the SEC announced a proposed "roadmap" for public companies to transition to IFRS for public filings. In November 2008, the SEC officially published its 165-page roadmap and sought public comments. Roadmap for the Potential Use of Financial Statements Prepared in Accordance With International Financial Reporting Standards by U.S. Issuers, 73 Fed. Reg. 70,816 (Nov. 21, 2008), *available at* http://www.sec.gov/rules/proposed/2008/33-8982fr.pdf. The Madoff scandal and the credit crisis, however, quickly shifted the SEC's focus away from global accounting principles.

** The 2008 proposed roadmap announced that the SEC expected to wait until 2011 to decide whether to require domestic issuers and registrants to switch to IFRS for financial reporting with the agency, and if so, by what date. At the time, the SEC proposal envisioned that public companies would file three years of audited financial statements prepared under IFRS. The new rules would have applied initially to the largest companies that file on an accelerated basis, beginning with their first fiscal year ending on or after December 15, 2014, which meant that calendar year enterprises would have needed to file financial statements prepared under IFRS for 2012, 2013, and 2014 in early 2015. The requirement would have expanded to other accelerated filers for fiscal years ending on or after December 15, 2015, and encompassed non-accelerated filers for fiscal years ending on or after December 15, 2016. The proposal also contained an early use option that would have allowed a limited number of qualifying U.S. issuers to use IFRS voluntarily for fiscal years ending on or after December 15, 2009, provided that such use would enhance comparability with non-U.S. competitors.

** More recently, in early 2010 the SEC issued Commission Statement in Support of Convergence and Global Accounting Standards ("2010 Statement"), 75 Fed. Reg. 9494 (Mar. 2, 2010), *available at* http://www.sec.gov/rules/other/2010/33-9109fr.pdf, to provide an update regarding the Commission's views and plans regarding global accounting standards. The 2010 Statement communicates at least six important messages.

** Perhaps most significantly, the 2010 Statement announced that the SEC still plans to evaluate IFRS through 2011. Before the end of that year, the SEC expects to decide whether to incorporate IFRS into the financial reporting system in the United States. Second, the 2010 Statement expressed the SEC's belief that, assuming a 2011 determination to incorporate IFRS into the financial reporting system, U.S. issuers would not report under such a system until "approximately 2015 or 2016." In response to the 2008 proposed roadmap, corporate commentators opined that U.S. issuers would need four to five years to implement a change in their financial reporting systems to incorporate IFRS. The 2010 Statement accepted these views.

** Third, the 2010 Statement expressed the SEC's continued support for efforts to converge U.S. GAAP and IFRS. More fundamentally, the Commission reaffirmed its belief that a single set of high-quality globally accepted accounting standards would benefit U.S. investors by both improving financial reporting in the United States and reducing country-by-country disparity in financial reporting. Fourth, the 2010 Statement recognized that IFRS enjoyed the greatest potential to function as global standards for the U.S. market. Earlier in the 2010 Statement, the SEC stated that the agency would consider progress by the FASB and the IASB in completing their convergence projects.

** Fifth, the 2010 Statement highlighted six factors especially important to the SEC as it continues to evaluate IFRS to determine whether to incorporate IFRS into the financial reporting system for U.S. issuers: (1) sufficient development and application of IFRS for the U.S. domestic reporting system, including comprehensiveness, auditability and enforceability, and consistent and high-quality application; (2) the independence of standard setting for the benefit of investors, specifically the IASB's governance structure and developments to secure a stable, broad-based funding source; (3) investor understanding and education regarding IFRS; (4) examination of the U.S. regulatory environment that would be affected by a change in accounting standards, including federal and state income taxes and the regulation of financial institutions, insurance companies, and public utilities; (5) the impact on issuers, both large and small, including changes to accounting systems, changes to contractual arrangements, corporate governance considerations, and litigation contingencies; and (6) human capital readiness.

** Finally, the 2010 Statement directs the staff of the Office of the Chief Accountant of the SEC, with appropriate consultation with other Divisions and Offices of the Commission, to develop and execute a work plan to enhance both the public's understanding of the SEC's purpose and overall transparency in the process, with periodic reports beginning no later than October 2010. The SEC included the initial Work Plan as an appendix to the 2010 Statement. *Id.* at 9500; see also Staff of the U.S. Sec. & Exch. Comm'n, Work Plan for the Consideration of Incorporating International Financial Reporting Standards into the Financial Reporting System for U.S. Issuers (Feb. 24, 2010), *available at* http://www.sec.gov/spotlight/globalaccountingstandards/globalaccountingstandards.pdf.

**   With more than 130 countries using or planning to use IFRS, most of the world, especially many non-U.S. based, multinational companies, have already adopted IFRS, but numerous countries have adopted local variations or special applications. In mid-2010, about 210 of the 500 largest companies in the world use IFRS for financial reporting. In the aftermath of the credit crisis, the SEC ultimately must decide whether the conversion to IFRS makes business sense, especially given the need to train preparers, auditors, investors, analysts, regulators, tax authorities, and educators. In its 2008 proposed roadmap, the SEC estimated that a transition to IFRS would cost the average public company about 0.125 percent of revenues. SEC Chairman Mary Schapiro has shared reports placing the cost for a single company to move from U.S. GAAP to IFRS in a range from $300,000 to $20 million. Of the 12,000-13,000 public companies in the United States, most do not raise capital internationally. Critics of the proposed transition have cited significant transition costs, adverse tax consequences, and inconsistent enforcement across countries and stock exchanges as reasons to reject IFRS in the United States. Numerous commentators have suggested that the SEC should instead allow FASB to continue its efforts to converge accounting standards as completely as possible before adopting IFRS. As discussed on pages 18 and 19, the European Union's threats to adopt its own accounting rules in response to the credit crisis have raised serious doubts about IASB's future, let alone its financial and political independence. Observers world-wide have increasingly voiced concerns as to whether moving to IFRS offers the best path for establishing a single set of high-quality accounting principles. Within the United States, opponents have asked whether regulators should allow an international body to create accounting standards for U.S. companies.

b.   THE PRIVATE SECTOR

On page 164 in the second paragraph in this section [on page 133 of the concise in the fourth paragraph], please note that effective May 18, 2008, the AICPA Council designated IASB as the body to establish international financial reporting standards for both private and public entities pursuant to Rule 203. *See* 1 Am. Inst. of Certified Pub. Accountants, Professional Standards AU § 9534.06 (July 2008).

On pages 166 and 167, substitute the following four paragraphs for the three paragraphs, including the chart on page 167, beginning with the third full paragraph on page 166, to reflect 2008 changes to

the oversight, structure and operations of the FAF and FASB [on pages 131 and 132 of the concise starting with the carryover paragraph beginning on the bottom of page 131, note the following developments]:

**   FASB differs from the CAP and the APB in one major respect: FASB exists independently from the AICPA. Effective July 1, 2008, the trustees of the Financial Accounting Foundation, an independent charitable corporation referred to simply as "FAF," appoint FASB's five full-time members to staggered five year terms. In the trustees' judgment, the Board's members shall possess "knowledge of and experience in investing, accounting, finance, business, accounting education and research and a concern for the investor and the public interest in matters of investing, financial accounting and reporting." Fin. Accounting Found. Bd. of Tr., Corporate Governance Changes to Oversight, Structure, and Operations of the FAF, FASB, and GASB (adopted Feb. 26, 2008), http://www.fasb.org/faf/FAFGovernanceResolutions02-27-08.pdf. In 2008, the FAF's trustees also gave FASB's chairman the authority to set the Board's agenda, project plans, and priorities. To assure independence, FASB's members must terminate all other employment ties in exchange for a generous salary, which amounted to $667,275 for the chairman and $542,500 for the other board members in 2008. In addition to appointing FASB's members, the trustees also select members for GASB, which sets accounting rules for state and local governments. Except on technical, standard-setting matters, the FAF oversees both FASB and GASB.

**   In 2009, FAF, in a joint initiative with the AICPA and the National Association of State Boards of Accountancy ("NASBA"), created a blue ribbon panel to examine how accounting standards can best meet the needs of users of private company financial statements in the United States. The panel hopes to reach some recommendation as to which generally accepted accounting principles should apply to private companies. At present, those companies that need audited financial statements can now typically choose between U.S. GAAP, IFRS, and IASB's new 230-page IFRS for small- and medium-sized enterprises ("SMEs").

Although FAF and FASB historically relied upon contributions and sales of publications to fund their operations, SOx section 109 included a mechanism that requires issuers to pay annual support fees to fund both FASB and PCAOB now that the SEC has designated FASB as the private standard setting body that may establish " 'generally accepted' accounting principles" for federal securities law purposes. Until that legislation, declining contributions to FAF, the potential loss of revenues from print publications, and increasing pressures to offer free, electronic access to FASB materials presented potentially serious financial problems to FAF and FASB. The new funding mechanism has solidified FASB's financial independence in the standard-setting process.

While SOx enhanced FASB's financial independence, the credit crisis repeatedly subjected the Board to interference from Congress and, at least to some extent, the SEC. As described in the previous section and discussed further in the next section and at some length in Chapter VI on pages 116 through 119, *infra*, the turmoil in the financial markets and economy generated enormous political pressure to repeal or suspend fair value accounting, especially as applied to banks and other financial institutions. On two occasions and in response to intense pressure from Congress, FASB used very abbreviated due process before issuing guidance on issues related to fair value accounting. In response, the Board's own Investors Technical Advisory Committee, a panel of thirteen members who work as security analysts or investor advocates, and other commentators expressed concerns about the perceived erosion in FASB's independence from Congressional interference and political considerations. Ironically, in seeking to preserve its independence and to respond to the credit crisis, FASB may have jeopardized exactly what it sought to maintain. *See* Steve Burkholder, *FASB Investors Technical Advisory Panel Notes 'Grave Concerns' on Board Autonomy*, 7 Corp. Accountability Rep. (BNA) 804 (June 26, 2009).

** Even before the financial crisis, FASB spent a steadily increasing portion of its time on international accounting issues and convergence projects with the International Accounting Standards Board ("IASB") in an effort to achieve a single set of high quality, global accounting standards. Dating at least back to a joint meeting with IASB on September 18, 2002 in Norwalk, Connecticut, which gave rise to the so-called "Norwalk Agreement" in October 2002, FASB has acknowledged its commitment to, and worked toward, the goal of developing a common set of high-quality, global accounting standards. In the Norwalk Agreement, the Boards agreed to work towards convergence. Two years later, in 2004, the Boards announced the ongoing joint project on a common conceptual framework. In 2006, the Boards reached a Memorandum of Understanding ("MoU"), which identified eleven major projects necessary for convergence. A year later, the Board completed their first major joint project on business combinations. In 2008, the Boards updated the MoU. Later that year and in an effort to coordinate their responses to the global economic crisis, the Boards established an eighteen-member international Financial Crisis Advisory Group ("FCAG") to advise the standard-setters on accounting issues arising from the crisis. In mid-2010, work continues on major joint projects involving fair value, revenue recognition, financial statement presentation, leases, and financial instruments.

c. CONGRESS

On pages 173 and 174, replace the carryover paragraph [the last full paragraph on page 138 of the concise] with the following:

Although the risk of legislative interference with accounting for stock options seems to have abated, Congress has already twice turned its attention to the controversy surrounding the role of fair value accounting in the credit crisis. In the so-called "bailout bill," the Emergency Economic Stabilization Act of 2008, Pub. L. No. 110-343, 122 Stat. 3765, Congress specifically authorized the SEC "to suspend, by rule, regulation, or order," FASB's controversial promulgation on fair value accounting "for any issuer . . . or with respect to any class or category of transaction" if necessary or appropriate in the public interest and consistent with the protection of investors. *Id.* § 132. The legislation also directed the SEC, in consultation with Board of Governors of the Federal Reserve System and the Secretary of the Treasury, to study mark-to-market accounting standards applicable to financial institutions and to submit a report to Congress within ninety days. At a minimum, the study needed to consider the effects of the accounting standards on a financial institution's balance sheet; the impacts of such accounting on bank failures in 2008; the impact of such standards on the quality of financial information available to investors; the process that FASB used to develop accounting standards; the advisability and feasibility of modifications to such standards; and alternative accounting standards. *Id.* § 133.

During a Congressional hearing in March 2009, bipartisan pressure from members of the House Financial Services Subcommittee on Capital Markets, Insurance, and Government Sponsored Entities essentially forced FASB to issue additional guidance on inactive markets and impairments on an accelerated basis in early April to avoid Congressional intervention. The events have caused some observers to question FASB's continued independence and credibility. *The Wall Street Journal* published a front-page article reporting that a group of thirty-one financial firms and trade groups marshalled a multimillion-dollar lobbying campaign, formed the "Fair Value Coalition" to change the accounting rules, and then directed $286,000 in campaign contributions to thirty-three legislators on the House Financial Services Committee. *See* Susan Pulliam & Tom McGinty, *Congress Helped Banks Defang Key Rule*, WALL ST. J., June 3, 2009, at A1. These developments again raise important questions about the extent to which Congress should participate in the establishment of specific accounting rules.

**   As no surprise, the financial reform bills that passed the House in December 2009 and the Senate on May 20, 2010 contain provisions on accounting and auditing issues. Whether the Senate will approve the conference agreement remains uncertain as this Supplement goes to print. The conference agreement contains a provision that would allow the proposed Financial Stability Oversight Council to review and submit comments to the SEC and any standard-setting body with respect to an existing or proposed accounting principle, standard, or procedure, but not to veto or overturn them. Earlier in the legislative process, the House Financial Services Committee approved an amendment containing that provision rather than the amendment's original draft, which would have allowed future systemic risk regulators to override FASB rules. The Senate bill did not contain a comparable provision. *See* Steven Marcy & R. Christian Bruce, *Financial Reform Bills Contain Few Differences on Accounting, Audit Issues*, 8 Corp. Accountability Rep. (BNA) 600 (June 11, 2010).

d. INTERNATIONAL ACCOUNTING STANDARDS

On pages 175 to 181, replace the discussion that begins about a quarter of the way down page 175 with the introductory clause "In 1995," and continues until the end of this section on page 181 with the following text [on pages 140 to 145 in the concise, replace the discussion that begins with the first full sentence on page 140 and continues until the end of this section on page 145]:

In 1995, the IASC and IOSCO agreed to develop and endorse international accounting standards so that businesses could raise capital across borders.

By 1999, the IASC had reviewed most of its earlier standards, and even issued some new ones in particularly troublesome areas. IOSCO endorsed IASC's standards in 2000, although IOSCO did permit each country's securities regulators to impose additional requirements, such as additional disclosure, more specific interpretations of the standards, and reconciliation of IASC-based financial statements with the country's own GAAP.

** Meanwhile, the SEC was pressing the IASC to restructure itself into a more independent body, along the lines of FASB, to earn legitimacy in the eyes of the world's capital markets. Until this point, critics often referred to the core standards as "IASC Lite" or "FASB Lite." In 2000, IASC's members, the professional accountancy bodies in more than 100 countries, adopted a new constitution that restructured IASC into an independent foundation which paralleled the FAF on an international level. Following additional constitutional amendments, governance of the IFRS Foundation ("IFRSF"), which until March 1, 2010 was known as the International Accounting Standards Committee Foundation ("IASCF"), rests with two main bodies, the Trustees and the Monitoring Board. In addition to continuing the standard setting responsibilities of IASB, which was previously known as IASC, the 2000 constitution also created both the IFRS Interpretations Committee ("IFRSIC") and the IFRS Advisory Council ("IFRSAC"), which until March 1, 2010, were known as the International Financial Reporting Interpretation Committee ("IFRIC") and the Standards Advisory Council ("IASB-SAC"). Press Release, Int'l Acct. Standards Bd., Trustees announce further governance enhancements (Feb. 15, 2010), http://www.iasb.org/News/Press+Releases/further+governance+enhancem ents.htm?m=print.

** In January 2009, amid calls to enhance the foundation's governance because IASB lacked any link to an elected body or a body linked to national authorities responsible for overseeing compliance with IFRS, the Trustees completed the first phase of their periodic review of the organization's constitution and again amended the document to create a Monitoring Board over the Trustees to enhance the foundation's public accountability. This change seeks to provide formal interaction between national authorities responsible for establishing or recognizing accounting standards for listed companies and the IFRSF. The Monitoring Board will include leaders from the Emerging Markets and Technical Committees of IOSCO, the European Commission ("EC"), the Japan Financial Services Agency, and the SEC. In addition, the Basel Committee on Banking Supervision will sit as a formal observer at Monitoring Board meetings. The Monitoring Board will meet with the Trustees at least once a year, or more often if necessary, and approve the appointment or reappointment of Trustees. Int'l Accounting Standards Bd., Monitoring Board (2009), http://www.iasb.org/About+Us/About+the+Trustees/Monitoring+Board.htm.

** The Trustees include twenty-two individuals, selected pursuant to a formula designed to ensure geographic diversity. Another formula seeks to maintain a balance of professional backgrounds, including individuals from prominent international accounting firms, organizations that prepare and use financial statements, and academia. The Trustees, who serve staggered, three-year terms, select their successors, appoint the members of IASB, raise the estimated $32 million needed each year to fund the organization's operations, and exercise general oversight over the foundation's operations. After the 2010 constitutional amendments, three-fourths of the Trustees can waive IASB's normal due process requirements, but only upon the Board's request and "in exceptional circumstances." With this governance structure, the SEC could potentially designate IASB as authorized to establish accounting principles for federal securities law purposes under SOx section 108, described on page 159 of the text [pages 134-135 of the concise].

The 2009 amendments to the organization's constitution expanded IASB from fourteen to sixteen members by 2012. Guidelines ensure a broad international basis for membership. The Trustees must appoint four members each from Asia, Europe and North America, a member from Africa, and another member from South America. The remaining two members can come from any area as long as the Trustees maintain geographic balance. The new constitution also offers additional flexibility regarding part-time membership. Previously, twelve of the Board's fourteen members had to be full-time employees of the board, who had severed all employment relationships with their former employers and who did not hold any position with economic incentives that might call into question their independence of judgment in setting accounting standards. IASB holds sole responsibility for setting accounting standards. In an effort to balance perspectives and experience, the constitution directs the Trustees to select Board members so that as a group the Board provides an appropriate mix of individuals with recent and practical experience as auditors, preparers, users, and academics. The constitution, however, designates professional competence and practical experience as the main qualifications for membership on the Board.

** For each project, the Board must publish an exposure draft for public comment and consider any comments before issuing a final International Financial Reporting Standard ("IFRS"). If the Board includes fewer than sixteen members, nine of the them must approve the publication of an exposure draft or a final Standard. When the Board contains sixteen members, ten must approve such an action.

** After the 2010 amendments, the IFRSF's constitution empowers the IFRSIC, again previously known as IFRIC, a fourteen-member panel whose members serve three-year terms, to meet as and when required to decide "contentious" accounting issues arising in the application of IFRS. In essence, IFRSIC performs the same function for IASB as the Emerging Issues Task Force does for FASB, that is, interpret IFRS, publish draft interpretations for public comment, consider timely comments before finalizing interpretations, and obtain IASB approval for final interpretations. If no more than four members of the panel vote against an interpretation, IFRSIC will ask IASB to issue the interpretation. Again depending upon the Board's size, either nine or ten members must approve the publication of a final interpretation.

IFRSAC comprises thirty or more individuals with renewable, three-year terms, having diverse geographic and functional backgrounds and an interest in international financial reporting; they assist the Board on agenda decisions and priorities for the Board's work, inform the Board of their views on major rulemaking projects, and otherwise advise the Trustees and Board, especially on any proposed changes to the constitution. The 2009 constitutional amendments sought to engage the investor community by changing the advisory council's structure, so that members would serve primarily as representatives of organizations.

** In 2002, the European Union ("EU") approved a regulation requiring all listed companies in the EU, currently about 8,000 in all, to comply with IFRS in preparing consolidated financial statements for each fiscal year beginning on or after January 1, 2005. In addition, Australia, Canada, India, Japan, and Korea have adopted similar requirements or announced plans to adopt or converge with IFRS. By mid-2010, more than 100 countries allow their use, or a variant. Observers expect that number to grow to more than 150 in the next three to five years.

** IASB has obtained a competitive advantage as to accounting standards for small- and medium-sized entities ("SMEs"). In July 2009, IASB issued the much anticipated IFRS for Small and Medium Entities ("IFRS for SMEs"). Described as "a self-contained standard of fewer than 230 pages," the rules seem likely to appeal to more than ninety-five percent of all enterprises globally that publish general purpose financial statements for external users, but need not comply with public filing or accountability requirements. Departing from its usual practice, IASB also posted the accompanying basis for conclusions, illustrative examples, and a disclosure checklist on its website, where registered users can access the materials, free of charge, via http://www.iasb.org/IFRS+for+SMEs/IFRS+for+SMEs+and+related+mater ial/IFRS+for+SMEs+and+related+material.htm. In 2008, the AICPA Council designated the IASB as "the body which is authorized to establish professional standards with respect to international financial accounting and reporting principles under Rule 202 (Compliance With Standards) and Rule 203 (Accounting Principles) of the AICPA Code of Professional Conduct." Press Release, Am. Inst. of Certified Pub. Accountants, AICPA Council Votes to Recognize the International Accounting Standards Board as a Designated Standard Setter (May 18, 2008), http://www.aicpa.org/download/news/2008/pr_20080518_iasb.pdf; *see also* 1 Am. Inst. of Certified Pub. Accountants, Professional Standards AU § 9534.06 (July 2008). As a result, private companies can potentially use IFRS, including IFRS for SMEs, and obtain audited financial statements in the United States.

Until the global credit crisis, virtually every signal indicated that the IFRS would soon become the applicable accounting principles for securities law filings in the United States. In 2005, the EU internal market commissioner and the SEC chairman reached an agreement to mutually recognize each others' accounting standards before 2009. In December 2007, the SEC issued final rules that allow foreign private issuers to use IFRS to prepare financial statements for submission to the agency without any reconciliation to U.S. GAAP. The rules, which became effective on March 4, 2008, removed a barrier that discouraged some foreign private issuers from accessing the U.S. capital markets. Acceptance From Foreign Private Issuers of Financial Statements Prepared in Accordance With International Financial Reporting Standards Without Reconciliation to U.S. GAAP, 73 Fed. Reg. 986 (Jan. 4, 2008), *available at* http://www.sec.gov/rules/final/2008/33-8879fr.pdf.

After the SEC announced its proposed roadmap for public companies to transition to IFRS for securities filings, *supra* at page 9, the financial crisis began to destroy large companies and to threaten even entire countries and economies. Ironically, while the global credit crisis has highlighted the need for international accounting standards, it has also slowed the momentum for the SEC to mandate IFRS for public companies, and threatened IASB's future as the international standard-setter.

** Unlike FASB, which enjoys financial independence via the annual support fees that SOx section 109 requires public companies to pay to the Board, IASB still relies on contributions, subscriptions to electronic databases, and sales of publications to fund its operations. Notwithstanding concerns about the international body's ability to secure stable funding, the momentum towards convergence between U.S. GAAP and IFRS seemed unstoppable in mid-2008. IASB's responses during the credit crisis, however, generated enormous political controversy in the EU and beyond. First, in October 2008, pressure from the EC persuaded IASB to suspend its normal due process and to change its rules governing financial instruments to allow banks to reclassify certain assets, thereby avoiding losses. The EC had threatened to legislate a carve-out from the relevant standard. Then, after IASB declined to amend IFRS to incorporate what the FASB had published on accounting for other-than-temporary impairments and fair value measurement in inactive markets in April 2009, the EC threatened to create its own accounting rules and to revoke the 2002 directive that mandated that public companies in the EU use IFRS. Current EU rules allow the EC to decide standard by standard whether to accept or reject new guidance. In fact, the EU enjoys a carve-out from the current international accounting standards on the recognition and measurement of financial instruments. From a practical standpoint, any change to EU-specific accounting principles would threaten the continuing global movement to IFRS. *See* Joe Kirwin, *EU Impatient With IASB, United States Over Accounting Standard Convergence*, 42 Sec. Reg. & L. Rep. (BNA) 553 (Mar. 22, 2010); Stephen Bouvier, *Political Pressure on IASB Threatens Global Standards Project, Says Crisis Adviser*, 41 Sec. Reg. & L. Rep. (BNA) 1035 (June 1, 2009); Stephen Bouvier, *IASB, FASB Financial Crisis Advisors Urge Political Restraint on Accounting Changes*, 7 Corp. Accountability Rep. (BNA) 553 (May 1, 2009); Stephen Bouvier, *IASB Bows to EU Carve-Out Threat on Financial Instruments Standard*, 40 Sec. Reg. & L. Rep. (BNA) 1716 (Oct. 20, 2008).

Under the aegis of the European Commission, a whole new support structure has emerged for screening new IASB standards on both a technical and political level. The European Financial Reporting Advisory Group ("EFRAG") was set up by private interests and supplied with an expert group from practice and academia to advise on the technical propriety of a proposed standard. The political input comes from an Accounting Regulatory Committee consisting of representatives from the fifteen EU governments. The credit crisis appears to document that multinational corporations and trade associations have subjected the Committee to the same sort of lobbying that Congress has experienced. Of particular concern, however, is the provision in the EU's accounting regulation to the effect that the EC "should take into account the importance of avoiding competitive disadvantages for European companies operating in the global marketplace," presumably an effort to preclude any IASB standard that might lead to lower net income figures than some other accounting system, such as U.S. GAAP.

In addition to independence, both financially and politically, one other significant hurdle for a single set of global accounting principles lies in the realm of enforcement of the applicable standards. On that score the U.S. has historically been well ahead of other countries, due to the strong role of the SEC with its broad administrative and regulatory powers. The U.K. and its close cousins in Canada and Australia have been moving in that direction, with the development of either public or private sector institutions which provide some oversight of company compliance with accounting standards. In the EU, the EC saw that the needed stronger regulation of financial reporting was likely to be most effectively achieved within the framework of securities regulation. The result was the promulgation in 2002 of a proposed Statement of Principles of Enforcement of Accounting Standards in Europe by a committee of European securities regulators, which was designed to assist member states in the development of their securities law regulation, including the effort to achieve conformity with accounting standards.

** After the leaders of the Group of Twenty (G-20) nations at their September 2009 meeting in Pittsburgh called upon accounting standard setters to redouble their efforts to achieve a single set of high-quality, global accounting standards and to use their independent standard-setting process to complete their convergence project by June 2011, convergence efforts regained momentum. *See* Steve Burkholder, *G-20 Call for 2011 Convergence May Signal Retreat on Financial Instruments Changes*, 7 Corp. Accountability Rep. (BNA) 1186 (Oct. 2, 2009). In November 2009, FASB and IASB issued a twenty-three page joint statement that reaffirmed their commitment to improve and converge U.S. GAAP and IFRS. The joint statement also described plans to complete, by June 30, 2011, the eleven major joint projects described in the Boards' 2006 Memorandum of Understanding ("MoU"), as updated in September 2008. Fin. Accounting Standards Bd. & Int'l Accounting Standards Bd., FASB and IASB Reaffirm Commitment to Memorandum of Understanding (Nov. 5, 2009), http://www.fasb.org/cs/ContentServer?c=Document_C&pagename=FASB% 2FDocument_C%2FDocumentPage&cid=1176156535882; *see also* Fin. Accounting Standards Bd. & Int'l Accounting Standards Bd., Completing the February 2006 Memorandum of Understanding: A progress report and t i m e t a b l e   f o r   c o m p l e t i o n   (S e p t .   2 0 0 8) , http://www.fasb.org/cs/ContentServer?c=Document_C&pagename=FASB% 2FDocument_C%2FDocumentPage&cid=1175801856967.

**   Even more recently, on June 24, 2010, the leaders of both Boards transmitted an updated work program to the G-20 leaders. The accompanying report stated that the Boards had been meeting jointly for consecutive days on a monthly basis and recognized that stakeholders have voiced concerns about their ability to provide thoughtful input on the large number of major exposure drafts planned for publication. Accordingly, the Boards developed a modified work plan that retains a June 2011 completion date for converging accounting standards deemed higher priority, including joint projects on consolidations, financial instruments, revenue recognition, fair value measurement, and leases, but allows for delays in finishing relatively lower priority projects. Press Release, Int'l Accounting Standards Bd. & Fin. Accounting Standards Bd., IASB and FASB update to G20 Leaders on modified convergence strategy (June 24, 2010), http://www.iasb.org/News/Announcements+and+Speeches/update+to+G20 +on+modified+convergence+strategy.htm.

**   Although the eventual emergence of a single set of high-quality, global accounting standards again seems inevitable, the exact timing and identity of those standards remain very uncertain. As the movement toward harmonization continues, leaders in the accounting community in the United States have speculated about FASB's decline or even demise. Most commentators predict that FASB will continue to assume an important role in standard-setting, whether nationally, internationally, or both. Even with global accounting standards, a two-tier reporting system in the United States remains a definite possibility. Under such a scenario, domestic companies could continue to apply U.S. GAAP, while multinational firms listed on certain exchanges or specialized markets within an exchange would use international accounting standards. Critics, however, complain that such a scenario would create an unlevel playing field in accounting. *See generally* James D. Cox, *Regulatory Duopoly in U.S. Securities Markets*, 99 COLUM. L.

REV. 1200, 1202, 1214 n.35 (1999) (concluding that the SEC should continue to promote convergence between international and domestic standards and describing the biggest political issue as whether to limit international standards to foreign issuers or to permit domestic firms to use international standards to satisfy SEC reporting requirements).

2.   HOW DO ACCOUNTING PRINCIPLES BECOME "GENERALLY ACCEPTED?"

On pages 182-87 [page 146 of the concise], replace the section on "The Hierarchy" with the following text:

a.   THE FASB ACCOUNTING STANDARDS CODIFICIATION

** As we have already stated, management faces the primary responsibility to prepare financial statements that conform with GAAP. Before FASB completed a landmark project in 2009 that codified all authoritative accounting principles in the United States in a single location, no one source fully supplied or detailed generally accepted accounting principles in the United States. In fact, twenty different sources and more than 2,000 promulgations set forth U.S. GAAP. For financial statements issued for interim and annual periods ending after September 15, 2009, however, the FASB Accounting Standards Codification™ (the "Codification") supersedes all nongrandfathered, non-SEC accounting and reporting standards for nongovernmental entities. Just as the United States Code organizes federal legislation, the Codification boiled about 10,000 pages in promulgations from FASB, the AICPA, and the SEC down to some 2,900 pages. Moving forward, the Codification also seems likely to assist FASB with efforts to converge accounting standards worldwide. Consequently, the Codification marks a major milestone in the development of accounting principles in the United States.

** Recall that even though the SEC has designated FASB as the standard setter, public companies must still follow SEC disclosure requirements. For this reason, the Codification also includes separate sections containing guidance from the SEC related to issues within the basic financial statements. These SEC materials carry the designation "S" before the applicable section number, so that users can distinguish between the SEC requirements and other authoritative GAAP. To date, the SEC has yet to ratify these materials. The Codification does not replace or affect how the SEC or the SEC staff issues or updates SEC content. Please also keep in mind that the SEC staff content does not constitute Commission approved rules or interpretations. Nevertheless, FASB believes the new system will simplify accounting research, improve the accessibility and usability of the entire body of literature relevant to each topic, and provide real-time updates as the FASB releases new standards.

**   When changing the content in the Codification, FASB now issues a transient document, called an Accounting Standards Update ("ASU" or "Update"), regardless of whether the Board, the Emerging Issues Task Force, the AICPA, or some other body issued the original guidance on the particular topic. In addition, the Board issues Updates both for amendments to the SEC content in the Codification and for editorial changes. Because the SEC and its staff plan to continue to use existing SEC procedures to communicate new or revised SEC content, however, users should expect delays between SEC changes and corresponding updates to the Codification. In all situations, FASB updates the Codification concurrently with an ASU's release, presents current and transitional text together to allow access to all relevant content in the same location, and identifies any new guidance as "Pending Text" until the passage of time means that the prior guidance no longer applies.

**   Each ASU summarizes the key conclusions of the project that led to the Update, details the specific amendments to the Codification, and explains the basis for the Board's decisions. The Board will not amend Updates; it will only amend the FASB Codification. Although ASUs update the Codification, FASB does not consider these Updates authoritative in their own right. Nevertheless, the Board numbers these Updates sequentially by year, beginning with 2009-01. During the second half of 2009, FASB issued seventeen ASUs. Through June 30, 2010, FASB had issued nineteen ASUs during 2010.

**   To appreciate the Codification's significance more fully, keep in mind that accounting principles sometimes offer alternative treatments and typically require judgment in their application. As a result, management occasionally must determine whether a particular rule, procedure or treatment enjoys general acceptability. In addition, auditing standards require an auditor to opine in the audit report whether the financial statements fairly present the enterprise's financial position and results of operations and cash flows in conformity with GAAP. Accordingly, an important interrelationship exists between accounting principles and auditing standards. To help management select an appropriate accounting principle or application and to assist the auditor determine whether the financial statements conform to GAAP, the Codification now establishes the rules used to prepare financial statements presented in conformity with U.S. GAAP, apart from any guidance from the SEC.

Prior to the Codification, now superseded SFAS No. 162, *The Hierarchy of Generally Accepted Accounting Principles,* set forth a GAAP hierarchy which listed four collections of sources for accounting principles and another grouping for accounting literature. The hierarchy ranked the four collections of sources for accounting principles, levels (a) through (d), respectively, with level (a) designating the highest level of authority. The grouping for accounting literature fell below level (d). Keep in mind that the Codification superseded all previously existing accounting principles, specifically including levels (a) through (d) in the previous GAAP hierarchy. In addition, FASB will no longer update and maintain the superseded standards.

Although the FASB did not expect the Codification to change existing GAAP in any material way, nevertheless the Codification now sets forth official U.S. GAAP. The current grouping for so-called "accounting literature," sometimes referred to as "level (e)," will become non-authoritative. In essence, the Codification will flatten the existing GAAP hierarchy from five levels to two camps—authoritative and non-authoritative--and the Codification contains the authoritative materials.

As you might imagine, situations will exist where the Codification does not provide any direct guidance about accounting for a particular event or transaction. For example, the business community, particularly the finance industry, constantly develops new business transactions. When no prior accounting precedent exists, the Codification encourage management in the first instance, and then any auditor, to look to the transaction's substance, to consult the accounting literature, and to select an accounting treatment that appears appropriate.

**   Although the Codification superseded all previous level (a) through level (d) standards for fiscal periods ending after September 15, 2009, accounting issues may arise in legal disputes involving fiscal periods ending on or before that date. At least for the immediate future, and especially in litigation, lawyers must pay attention to the Codification's effective date and should understand the GAAP hierarchy that previously applied. You may need to identify and evaluate the various sources of generally accepted accounting principles before the Codification's "effective date."

**   Under the now superseded GAAP hierarchy, the highest level of authority, which accountants referred to as "level (a)" or "category (a)," belonged to those principles officially promulgated by a body that the AICPA Council had designated to establish such principles under Rule 203 of the AICPA Code of Professional Conduct. As a result, this highest level included pronouncements from FASB and its predecessors, the APB and the CAP. Consequently, level (a) included FASB Statements; FASB Interpretations or implementation guidance, including FASB Staff Positions, each of which you will recall modified, extended, clarified or elaborated on previously existing FASB Statements or Interpretations; APB Opinions and their Interpretations which FASB had not superseded; and nonsuperseded ARBs. In addition, the SEC's rules and interpretative releases carried a status similar to level (a) for SEC registrants. SEC registrants also needed to follow SABs, consensus positions of the EITF, and Observer comments in EITF Issues. You will recall that SABs continue to announce practices that the SEC staff will follow in administering the disclosure and periodic reporting requirements in the federal securities laws. The SEC's Chief Accountant stated that the SEC staff would challenge any treatment that differed from an EITF consensus, because the consensus position reflected the best thinking in areas for which accounting pronouncements did not establish specific standards. Finally, the SEC staff sometimes used Observer comments to announce publicly its views on certain accounting issues for SEC registrants.

Level (b) or "category (b)," the next highest level of authority, included pronouncements from bodies of expert accountants that deliberated accounting issues in public forums to establish accounting principles or to describe existing accounting practices that qualified as generally accepted. To qualify in this level (b), however, the pronouncement needed to satisfy two additional requirements. First, the relevant body must have exposed the pronouncement for public comment. Second, a body which qualified to establish level (a) principles ("level (a) organization"),since 1973 the FASB, must have cleared the pronouncement. In other words, the level (a) organization must have indicated that it did not object to the proposed pronouncement. As a result FASB Technical Bulletins fell into level (b). In addition, if FASB did not object to their issuance, AICPA Industry Audit and Accounting Guides and AICPA Statements of Position also qualified as level (b) pronouncements.

The third highest level of authority, which accountants referred to as level (c) or "category (c)," generally included cleared pronouncements from bodies of expert accountants formed to establish or interpret accounting principles or to describe existing accounting practices that qualified as generally accepted, but which the promulgating body had not exposed for public comment. To obtain the necessary "clearance," a level (a) organization, such as the FASB needed to indicate that it did not object to the proposed pronouncement. Consequently, cleared AcSEC Practice Bulletins and EITF consensus positions fell within this level (c). In addition, this grouping included the Topics discussed in Appendix A of EITF Abstracts ("EITF D-Topics"), which the FASB staff used to announce its views on certain accounting issues. Please keep in mind that the SEC staff expected registrants to follow EITF consensus positions, EITF D-Topics announcements, and Observer comments, which effectively raised such pronouncements to level (a) status for SEC registrants.

At the fourth level, we find two different varieties of practices or pronouncements. First, the knowledgeable application of generally accepted pronouncements to specific circumstances qualified for level (d) or "category (d)." Second, this status included practices that accountants acknowledged as enjoying general acceptance. As a result, level (d) included implementation guides that FASB's staff published, often referred to as "Qs and As," AICPA accounting interpretations, AICPA Industry Audit and Accounting Guides and AICPA Statements of Position that the FASB had not cleared, and widely recognized and prevalent practices, either on a general or industry basis.

Finally, in the absence of established principles, either management or an auditor could consider other accounting literature, depending upon its relevance in the circumstances. This other accounting literature included FASB Concepts, AICPA Issues Papers, International Financial Reporting Standards, Governmental Accounting Standards Board Statements, Interpretations and Technical Bulletins, pronouncements of other professional associations or regulatory agencies, AICPA Technical Practice

Aids, and accounting textbooks, handbooks, and articles. In choosing other accounting literature in this final listing, the preparer or auditor should consider the publication's relevance to the particular circumstances, the guidance's specificity, and the reputation of the issuer or author. As an example, FASB Concepts would have qualified as more influential than other type of accounting literature in so-called "level (e)" or "category (e)."

** The chart that appears on the next page summarizes the GAAP hierarchy that applied to nongovernmental enterprises for fiscal periods ending on or before September 15, 2009:

E S T A B L I S H E D A C C O U N T I N G P R I N C I P L E S	C A T E G O R Y (a)	• FASB Statements of Financial Accounting Standards • FASB Interpretations • FASB Staff Positions • APB Opinions • Accounting Research Bulletins
	C A T E G O R Y (b)	• FASB Technical Bulletins • Cleared AICPA Industry Audit and Accounting Guides • Cleared AICPA Statements of Position
	C A T E G O R Y (c)	• Cleared AcSEC Practice Bulletins • Consensus positions of FASB's Emerging Issues Task Force • Emerging Issues Task Force Appendix D Topics
	C A T E G O R Y (d)	• FASB staff "Qs and As" • AICPA accounting interpretations • Uncleared AICPA Industry Audit and Accounting Guides • Uncleared AICPA Statements of Position • Widely recognized and prevalent industry practices
A C C O U N T I N G	L I T E R A T U R E	Other accounting literature, including FASB Concepts Statements; AICPA Issues Papers; International Financial Reporting Standards; pronouncements of other professional associations or regulatory agencies; AICPA Technical Practice Aids; and accounting textbooks, handbooks, and articles

See THE HIERARCHY OF GENERALLY ACCEPTED ACCOUNTING PRINCIPLES, Statement of Fin. Accounting Standards No. 162 (Fin. Accounting Standards Bd. 2008), superseded by the Codification.

Keep in mind that this chart does not reflect the fact that special rules often apply to SEC registrants. In addition, we should also emphasize any GAAP hierarchy only binds enterprises that seek audited financial statements. As of 2009, most of an estimated 29 million private corporations and other small businesses in the United States did not need audited financial statements for their owners or lenders; those businesses may not observe GAAP. Ignoring any opportunities to use IFRS, the chart below summarizes the accounting principles that can apply to fiscal periods after September 15, 2009 to different kinds of businesses in the United Sates, ranging from large, publicly traded corporations to small proprietorships:

Publicly traded enterprises			Closely held firms	
SEC registrants		Not traded on national securities exchange and either:	Owners or lenders require audited financial statements	Audited financial statements not required
Accelerated filers	Smaller reporting companies	(i) less than $10 million in assets or (ii) no class of equity securities with at least 500 owners		
Codification, subject to: • SEC's rules and releases and SABs • Regulations S–K and S–X apply	Codification, subject to: • SEC's rules and releases, and SABs • Scaled disclosure available under Regulation S–K	Codification	Codification	Codification optional

b. REGULATORY ACCOUNTING PRACTICES

On page 187 at the end of the first paragraph [on page 147 of the concise at the end of the carryover paragraph], insert the following text:

In the midst of the economic downturn and the debate about the role that fair value accounting has played in the global credit crisis, international bank regulators and accounting standard-setters alike correctly recognize that regulatory capital does not depend upon GAAP and financial reporting, which ultimately strive to provide useful information to investors and creditors. As a result, the primary goals of banking regulators, namely safety and soundness, may dictate different approaches and rules than the transparency that financial reporting standards seek. *See* Susan Webster, *Accounting Standards, Bank Regulation Serve Different Purposes, Officials Say*, 40 Sec. Reg. & L. Rep. (BNA) 1972 (Nov. 24, 2008).

3. WHO SELECTS AMONG GENERALLY ACCEPTED ACCOUNTING PRINCIPLES?

On page 188 [omitted from the concise], add the following example to the end of the second paragraph:

An example that appeared in *The Wall Street Journal* and arose from the credit crisis illustrates the importance of estimates to the bottom line. If an enterprise invested $100 million in GMAC LLC when General Motors Corp. sold its majority stake in 2006, what was that investment worth on December 31, 2007? The lead private-equity firm in the transaction did not mark down its investment. One Wall Street firm marked its investment down ten percent, which translated to a $90 million valuation, while two hedge funds applied twenty and twenty-five percent markdowns, which resulted in valuations of $80 million and $75 million, respectively. *See* Peter Lattman, *Valuations Still Part Art*, WALL ST. J., May 14, 2008, at C24.

On page 189 in the middle of the second paragraph [omitted from the concise], delete the references to small business issuer and Regulation S–B, which was repealed, generally effective February 5, 2008.

4. CRITIQUE

On page 195 [omitted from the concise], replace the first full paragraph with the following text:

During the implementation of Sarbanes-Oxley, the SEC approved listing standards that NYSE and Nasdaq had submitted pursuant to these requirements. Under both NYSE and Nasdaq standards, a listed company may not have employed any so-called "independent" director at any time during the previous three years. In addition, after recent amendments neither an independent director nor any immediate family member may receive more than $120,000 a year in direct non-employee compensation other than director's fees or non-contingent pensions and deferred compensation for prior service from the listed company. Self-Regulatory Organizations: New York Stock Exchange LLC; Notice of Filing and Immediate Effectiveness of Proposed Rule Change to Amend Section 303A.02(b) of the Listed Company Manual with respect to Two of its Director Independence Tests, Exchange Act Release No. 58,367 (Aug. 15, 2008),http://www.sec.gov/rules/sro/nyse/2008/34-58367.pdf; Self-Regulatory Organizations; The NASDAQ Stock Market LLC; Order Granting Approval of Proposed Rule Change to Modify the Definition of "Independent Director," Exchange Act Release No. 58,335 (Aug. 8, 2008), http://www.sec.gov/rules/sro/nasdaq/2008/34-58335.pdf.

D.   GENERALLY ACCEPTED AUDITING STANDARDS

1.   THE INDEPENDENT AUDITOR'S ROLE

On page 200 [pages 150 and 151 of the concise], please note that a new sixteen-page brochure that the Center for Audit Quality published in 2009 offers an concise and understandable overview of an independent auditor's role in providing investors with information that they need, and can rely on, in making decisions and assisting the effective functioning of capital markets. See Center for Audit Quality, Guide to Public Company Auditing (2009), http://www.thecaq.org/newsroom/pdfs/GuidetoPublicCompanyAud iting.pdf.

a.   INDEPENDENCE

On page 212 [omitted from the concise], insert the following discussion at the end of Note 6:

More recently, E&Y accepted a censure and agreed to pay almost $2.4 million in disgorgement and more than $500,000 in prejudgment interest to settle SEC administrative charges that the firm compromised its independence by engaging in business dealings that required collaboration with an individual who served as a director at three audit clients and as a member of the audit committee at one of those companies. The individual's compensation from the business relationship, which involved the production of a series of audio CDs, approximated half of his net income. At the end of each audit clients' fiscal years, E&Y expressly confirmed, in writing, that it was "independent" and qualified to serve as each client's external auditor. *In re* Ernst & Young LLP, Accounting and Auditing Enforcement Release No. 2858 (Aug. 5, 2008), http://www.sec.gov/litigation/admin/2008/34-58309.pdf.

In 2007, E&Y also paid $1.59 million to settle SEC charges that the auditor lacked independence in the 2001 audits of two clients, American International Group Inc. ("AIG") and PNC Financial Services Group Inc. ("PNC"). According to SEC findings, AIG engaged an E&Y partner to assist in the development and marketing of a new financial product, which AIG eventually sold to PNC. The partner then assisted the E&Y audit staff in advising PNC on the proper accounting treatment for the transaction. During the PNC audit, the E&Y audit staff relied mainly on the partner's conclusions, which improperly applied the relevant accounting principles, in reviewing the transaction. The SEC concluded that the partner possessed a stake, both financially and reputationally, in the success of the financial product, and therefore a conflict of interest existed in his evaluation of the accounting treatment for the product at PNC. Moreover, the audit staff violated independence principles by relying on the partner's analysis of the accounting treatment rather than performing separate audit procedures. E&Y also caused PNC to violate federal securities laws, which require the review of filings by an independent auditor. *In re* Ernst & Young LLP, Accounting and Auditing Enforcement Release No. 2580 (Mar. 26, 2007), http://www.sec.gov/litigation/admin/2007/34-55523.pdf.

** Auditor independence issues also took a prominent place in the criminal fraud charges that the Department of Justice filed against David G. Friehling, the purportedly independent auditor of Bernard L. Madoff Investment Securities LLC, for his part in the multi-billion dollar Ponzi scheme that unraveled late in 2008. Dating back to at least 1995, either Friehling, his wife, or both of them collectively held accounts showing balances exceeding $500,000, the maximum amount that Friehling could have invested with a broker-dealer and maintained his independence. In November 2009, Friehling pled guilty to fraud and other charges, admitted that he failed to conduct independent audits, and agreed to a partial judgment imposing a permanent injunction against him and his firm barring conduct that would violate certain antifraud provisions in the federal securities laws. *See* SEC v. Friehling, Litigation Release No. 21,274 (Nov. 3, 2009), http://www.sec.gov/litigation/litreleases/2009/lr21274.htm; SEC v. Friehling, Accounting and Auditing Enforcement Release No. 2992 (Mar. 18, 2009), http://www.sec.gov/litigation/litreleases/2009/lr20959.htm; *see also* Chad Bray, *Madoff Auditor Says He Was Duped, Too*, WALL ST. J., Nov. 4, 2009, at C3; Phyllis Diamond, *Madoff Accountant Sued by SEC, DOJ Over Audits of Brokerage Firm's Financials*, 41 Sec. Reg. & L. Rep. (BNA) 533 (Mar. 23, 2009).

b. THE AUDIT PROCESS

On page 216 [omitted from the concise], delete the sentence that begins "In addition, ..." from the carryover paragraph about a quarter down the page. As described *infra* at page 33, a new auditing standard no longer requires auditors to express an opinion on management's assessment of the effectiveness of internal control over financial reporting.

The auditor must, however, still express an opinion on whether the company maintained effective internal control over financial reporting.

(1) The Growing Importance of Internal Controls

a) INTERNAL CONTROL UNDER THE FEDERAL SECURITIES LAWS

(i) Management's Assessment of Internal Control and Related Audit Report

On page 218 at the beginning of this section [page 157 of the concise in the second full paragraph], note that a new auditing standard for public companies no longer requires auditors to express an opinion on management's assessment of the effectiveness of internal control over financial reporting. Instead, the auditor only expresses an opinion on whether the company maintained effective internal control over financial reporting.

On page 221 beginning with the full paragraph [page 159 of the concise beginning with the carryover paragraph starting on the page], replace the remainder of the discussion in this section with the following text:

Needless to say, from the outset the PCAOB has been actively reviewing the very contentious issue of internal control. In 2004, the PCAOB issued, and the SEC approved, Auditing Standard No. 2 ("AS 2") to provide guidance to auditors in discharging the responsibility that SOx section 404 imposes to report on a company's internal controls over financial reporting and management's assessment of their effectiveness. Unfortunately, AS 2 faced harsh and sustained criticism. Critics described the new rules as time-consuming, complicated, and expensive, asserting that much of the increased costs imposed by this new requirement came from what they saw as a mandate in AS 2 that auditors do substantial testing of a public company's internal control themselves, rather than relying to a considerable extent on the company's internal accountants. In addition, critics argued that AS 2 adopted an overly rigid approach to the responsibilities of auditors in implementing this new internal controls obligation, leading to the fear that auditors would need to check virtually every element of internal control in every case, as if pursuant to a checklist. In various forums, PCAOB representatives sought to mollify these concerns, disclaiming any notion that AS 2 contemplated a checklist, or "one size fits all," approach. Supporters pointed out that adapting to a new regimen always introduces costs and complications at the outset. Nevertheless, the consensus emerged that, because of the very serious potential consequences for a failure to comply with SOx section 404, auditors were adopting a very conservative, risk-averse approach, interpreting the requirements too strictly, spending too much time on non-critical controls, and failing to communicate with the inside accountants and thereby avoid unnecessary duplication. Various groups within the business community warned that AS 2's extensive reporting requirements would drive new public offerings to foreign stock exchanges, while the PCAOB continued to champion the benefits of audits of internal controls over financial reporting, including higher quality reporting and enhanced corporate governance. In addition, the PCAOB resisted exempting small business from the audits, emphasizing that the management of small businesses often enjoys the greatest opportunity to override internal controls.

Sustained criticism persuaded regulators of the need to issue more guidance, and both the PCAOB and the SEC responded, with separate releases in mid-May 2005. The PCAOB took the lead, with a policy statement that focused both on the scope of the internal controls audit and the level of testing required. Clarifying these requirements, seen as the primary drivers of cost, would facilitate the 2005 audit process. Both releases advocated a more flexible and individualized approach centered on the client's highest-risk controls. In May 2006, the SEC and PCAOB held a roundtable on the SOx section 404 internal control requirements. Most participants agreed that implementation in year two had gone better than year one, but requested more guidance from the SEC and PCAOB.

In December 2006, both the PCAOB and SEC proposed revised internal control auditing standards explicitly adopting a functional risk-based and scalable approach. Based on extensive review, the PCAOB acknowledged that AS 2's compliance costs had been higher than expected and that the standard at times demanded greater efforts than necessary to carry out an effective audit of internal controls. In May 2007, recognizing the need to refine AS 2, the PCAOB adopted Auditing Standard No. 5 ("AS 5"), *An Audit of Internal Control Over Financial Reporting That Is Integrated with An Audit of Financial Statements*. The SEC unanimously approved AS 5 in July 2007, replacing AS 2. The new standard takes a principles-based approach designed to provide more flexibility than the formalistic approach of the prior standard.

AS 5 adopts a top-down, risk-based approach to identifying the most important controls to test. The new standard directs auditors to focus their efforts on those controls most likely to cause a material misstatement in the financial statements, rather than spending time on low-risk controls. AS 5 features a prominent discussion of fraud risk and anti-fraud controls, high-risk areas seen as vital to investor protection. Unlike the "checklist approach" that AS 2 endorsed, AS 5 calls upon auditors to use professional judgment in identifying key transactions and processes. The auditor focuses first on "entity-level" controls and then works down to lower-level controls.

In addition, AS 5 permits "scaling" internal control auditing procedures to the client's size and complexity, thereby addressing concerns that small public companies expressed over the difficulty of implementation. The revised standard discusses "scaling" concepts throughout, with notes explaining how to tailor audits of internal controls for smaller, less complex companies and units of larger corporations. AS 5 provides relevant attributes useful in identifying these smaller businesses and units of large companies.

AS 5 also focuses on increasing audit efficiency. The standard provides that entity-level control tests may reduce the need for lower-level control tests. AS 5 gives auditors more latitude to use the work of others, even those working outside of the internal audit function. Additionally, an internal control audit no longer requires a separate opinion on management's assessment of internal control over financial reporting. The auditor now audits management's assessment, in essence, through the independent audit of the effectiveness of the entity's internal controls.

Reaction to AS 5 has been largely positive, with supporters praising its flexible standards and emphasis on the professional judgment of the auditor. While cost savings remain unquantified, advocates believe the new standard will increase audit efficiency in both scope and cost. Concerns continue to linger, however, regarding the application of the standard to smaller public companies. Critics argue that the PCAOB did not sufficiently develop the scalability concepts and that compliance still costs too much for smaller businesses. Both the PCAOB and SEC acknowledge these concerns and have pledged to continue to monitor the implementation of the new standard in smaller public companies. In January 2009, the PCAOB issued staff guidance to assist auditors in implementing AS 5 in smaller public companies.

** On October 13, 2009, the SEC yet again announced that it had decided to postpone, purportedly for the last time, the compliance date for non-accelerated filers (generally those with a public float under $75 million) to meet the auditor attestation requirement in SOx section 404(b). This sixth such deferral now gives non-accelerated filers until their annual reports for fiscal years ending on or after June 15, 2010 to file the auditor's attestation report on internal control over financial reporting. Internal Control Over Financial Reporting in Exchange Act Periodic Reports of Non-Accelerated Filers, Securities Act Release No. 9072, Exchange Act Release No. 60,813, 74 Fed. Reg. 53,628 (October 19, 2009), *available at* http://www.sec.gov/rules/final/2009/33-9072fr.pdf. These deferrals continue to generate controversy. Opponents assert that smaller businesses have had more than enough time to comply and further delays in implementation put investors at risk. The battle over this issue continues as the conference agreement on the financial reform legislation incorporated a provision from the House bill that would exempt companies with market capitalizations that do not exceed $75 million from the auditor attestation requirements. Efforts to include such a provision in the Senate bill failed. The conference agreement would also give the SEC nine months after enactment to conduct a study to determine how the SEC could reduce compliance burdens for companies between $75 million and $250 million in market capitalization. As this Supplement goes to print, Senate approval remains uncertain. *See* Steven Marcy & Mike Ferullo, *House Passes Financial Reform Bill; Would Exempt Small Issuers From SOX §404*, 8 Corp. Accountability Rep. (BNA) 707 (July 9, 2010); Steven Marcy & R. Christian Bruce, *Financial Reform Bills Contain Few Differences on Accounting, Audit Issues*, 8 Corp. Accountability Rep. (BNA) 600 (June 11, 2010).

Note that this most recent deferral applies *only* to the auditor attestation requirement; for fiscal years ending after December 15, 2007, even non-accelerated filers must evaluate their internal controls over financial reporting, disclose that management performed such evaluation, and state management's conclusions about the controls' effectiveness. Remarkably, a 2008 study found that 18.6 percent of the non-accelerated filers required to include management reports on the effectiveness of internal control over financial reporting in their securities filings failed to do so. The total market capitalization for these companies exceeded $25 billion. In addition 34.4 percent of 3,321 companies that actually filed the necessary report disclosed ineffective controls, a percentage that more than doubled the 16.9 percent of accelerated filers that admitted to ineffective controls in their initial reports four years earlier. *Small Companies Lag in Developing SOX Controls*, 23 Corp. Counsel Weekly (BNA) 292 (Sept. 24, 2008).

(iii) Foreign Corrupt Practices Act

On page 226 [omitted from the concise], insert the following below the carryover paragraph ending on the top of the page:

The number of cases brought by regulators under the FCPA has recently increased exponentially, accompanied by criminal prosecutions against involved individuals, a surge in the level of sanctions imposed, and international cooperation. According to a front-page article in *The Wall Street Journal* in May 2009, the Justice Department was investigating more than 120 companies, up from about 100 firms at the end of 2008.

In late 2008, the SEC announced that Siemens Aktiengesellschaft ("Siemens), a German-based manufacturer, had consented to an unprecedented enforcement action in U.S. federal court to resolve charges that the company violated the anti-bribery, books and records, and internal controls provisions in the FCPA. In total, Siemens agreed to pay more than $1.6 billion in disgorgement and fines, including $350 million in disgorgement to the SEC. In addition to an approximately $285 million fine that Siemens paid to the Office of the Prosecutor General in Munich, Germany, Siemens agreed to pay a $450 million criminal fine to the U.S. Department of Justice and an approximately $569 million fine to the Munich Prosecutor. Over more than a six-year period, Siemens made at least 4,283 payments to third parties in ways that obscured the purpose for, and the ultimate recipients of, approximately $1.4 billion in expenditures to bribe government officials in return for business to Siemens in Asia, Africa, Europe, the Middle East, and the Americas. Elaborate payment schemes, including slush funds, off-books accounts, and the use of business consultants, intermediaries and large amounts of cash in suitcases, concealed the corrupt payments, which Siemens recorded on its books as "management fees, consulting fees, supply contracts, room preparation fees, and commissions," and the company's inadequate internal controls allowed the illegal conduct to flourish. The conduct involved employees at all levels, including former senior management, which set a disappointing "tone at the top" that tolerated, and even rewarded, bribery. A Siemens spokesman told *The Wall Street Journal* that the cost of investigating and addressing the corruption allegations also approached the amount of the total fines. SEC v. Siemens Aktiengesellschaft, Accounting and Auditing Enforcement Release No. 2911 (Dec. 15, 2008), http://www.sec.gov/litigation/litreleases/2008/lr20829.htm; *see also* Dionne Searcey, *U.S. Cracks Down on Corporate Bribes*, WALL ST. J., May 26, 2009, at A1.

Less than two months later, the SEC announced settlements with Halliburton Co. ("Halliburton"), its former subsidiary Kellog Brown & Root LLC ("KBR-LLC"), and the subsidiary's new owner, KBR, Inc. ("KBR"). The underlying civil charges arose from bribes to governmental officials in Nigeria to obtain construction contracts worth more than $6 billion and related violations of the books and records and internal controls requirements. KBR and Halliburton agreed to pay $177 million in disgorgement to settle the SEC charges. In addition, KBR-LLC accepted a $402 million fine to settle criminal charges that the Department of Justice filed. Collectively, the sanctions easily surpassed the largest amount that U.S.-based companies ever paid for violating the FCPA, smashing the $44 million that Baker Hughes Inc. paid to resolve similar criminal and civil charges in 2007. SEC v. Halliburton Co., Accounting and Auditing Enforcement Release No. 2935 (Feb. 11, 2009), http://www.sec.gov/litigation/litreleases/2009/lr20897.htm; SEC v. Baker Hughes Inc., Accounting and Auditing Enforcement Release No. 2602 (Apr. 26, 2007), http://www.sec.gov/litigation/litreleases/2007/lr20094.htm.

**   The enforcement efforts continued in 2010. In the first quarter alone, federal agencies announced multi-million settlements to resolve FCPA corruption charges. BAE Systems PLC agreed with the Justice Department to pay more than $400 million, plus another $47 million to resolve corruption allegations with the United Kingdom's Serious Fraud Office. Daimler AG promised to pay $185 million to resolve Justice Department and SEC probes. Technip and Alcatel-Lucent also reportedly agreed to pay $400 million and $200 million, respectively, to settle investigations. *See* Yin Wilczek, *SEC's FCPA Enforcement Increasingly to Target Finance Departments, Report Says*, 8 Corp. Accountability Rep. (BNA) 325 (Apr. 2, 2010); Vanessa Fuhrmans & Thomas Catan, *Daimler to Settle with U.S. on Bribes*, WALL ST. J., Mar. 24, 2010, at B1; Daniel Michaels & Cassell Bryan-Low, *BAE to Settle Bribery Cases For More Than $400 Million*, WALL ST. J., Feb. 6, 2010, at B1.

b) OTHER INCENTIVES TO PREVENT INTERNAL CONTROL FAILURES

On page 226, replace the entire section with the following discussion [on page 157 of the concise, insert the following text below the first paragraph]:

In addition to the federal securities laws, at least two other legal considerations offer incentives for enterprises to develop strong internal controls: the enormous losses and monetary liability that can result from internal control failures, and opportunities to avoid or minimize potential criminal penalties arising from misconduct.

First, the corporate scandals in the early 2000s and the resulting losses, both personal and financial, highlight the importance of internal controls and illustrate the consequences of inadequate controls. Then, amid the credit crisis, a failure of internal controls to prevent or detect unauthorized trading in securities resulted in the world's largest-ever trading loss. In January 2008, news broke that Jérôme Kerviel, a low-level trader at the French bank Société Générale, bypassed and evaded internal controls in a two-year rogue trading scheme. As a result of his activities, the bank suffered a $7.2 billion loss. Kerviel placed risky trades on stock-index futures markets. The trader evaded detection of these unauthorized trades by covering his positions with fictitious trades in a second portfolio, resulting in a seemingly neutral trading account. At the time, the bank's internal controls only monitored the overall balance recorded in Kerviel's books. While Kerviel made the fictitious trades with actual banks or clients, he used forward transactions, which often do not involve upfront cash transfers, thereby facilitating concealment. Kerviel input computer access codes to cancel the trades before the sending of confirmations to the actual counterparties. Aware of the bank's time-table for inspections, Kerviel erased his fake trades before his books were checked and then quickly re-entered them. Internal controls failed to detect these temporary imbalances. David Gauthier-Villars & Carrick Mollenkamp, *The Loss Where No One Looked*, WALL ST. J., Jan. 28, 2008, at C1.

Société Générale's loss reveals the challenges of developing internal controls to monitor today's complex, real-time financial transactions. Weeks after the news of Société Générale's loss, a similar story surfaced involving the Memphis office of brokerage firm MF Global. In February 2008, an MF Global trader, Evan Dooley, purchased wheat futures contracts without adequate capital to support the position, resulting in a $141.5 million loss. The firm's chief executive acknowledged that existing controls, designed to protect the firm from trades potentially causing large losses, could have stopped the risky trades from being processed. The company, however, turned off the controls to allow for speedier transactions as commodities-trading volume surged. Aaron Lucchetti & Carolyn Cui, *Safety Net Breaks Again*, WALL ST. J., Feb. 29, 2008, at C1.

Second, corporate anti-corruption and legal compliance programs, prompt discovery and self-reporting, cooperation, and other appropriate responses to illegal conduct may persuade a prosecutor to exercise prosecutorial discretion and to decide not to file criminal charges against the enterprise. Although now advisory, rather than mandatory, after the decision of the Supreme Court in *United States v. Booker*, 543 U.S. 220 (2005), the United States Sentencing Commission's Organizational Sentencing Guidelines (the "Sentencing Guidelines") also provide incentives for enterprises to establish and maintain effective internal controls to foster lawful and ethical behavior. In particular, various amendments to the Sentencing Guidelines, which became effective on November 1, 2004, address important areas such as organizational culture, compliance program responsibilities of corporate directors, adequacy of program resources, authority of compliance personnel, training, evaluations of program effectiveness, and risk analysis. The Sentencing Guidelines suggest leniency for organizations that can show that they have established and maintained compliance programs that prevent, detect, and report misconduct. U.S. SENTENCING GUIDELINES MANUAL § 8C2.5(f), (g) (2008). Strong internal controls, therefore, allow an enterprise an opportunity to avoid criminal liability or to suggest reduced penalties. Judah Best, et al., *Complying With Sentencing Guidelines*, NAT'L L.J., June 8, 1992, at 19; *see also* Thomas Petzinger, Jr., *This Auditing Team Wants You to Create a Moral Organization*, WALL ST. J., Jan. 19, 1996, at B1 (discussing the efforts of one then Big Five accounting firm, KPMG Peat Marwick, to respond to clients' requests to certify that their compliance programs would satisfy the federal sentencing guidelines).

2.   THE ESTABLISHMENT OF GENERALLY ACCEPTED AUDITING STANDARDS

On pages 233 and 234, replace the text after the second sentence in the carryover paragraph at the bottom of the page with the following discussion [on page 164 of the concise, insert the following text after the third full paragraph]:

In early 2007, the American Institute of Certified Public Accountants ("AICPA") and eight public company auditing firms created the Center for Audit Quality ("CAQ"), aiming to aid investors and the capital markets by improving the audit process. Press Release, Ctr. for Audit Quality, Center for Audit Quality Formed to Foster Confidence in the Capital Markets in Time of Growing Globalization and Financial Complexity (Jan. 30, 2007), http://www.thecaq.org/newsroom/pdfs/PR_20070130_CAQFormed.pdf. Presumably, this new body will serve as a useful conduit for collaboration between practitioners, standard-setters, and users of financial statements in shaping auditing standards.

Once again, keep in mind that PCAOB's rules apply only to accounting firms that audit public companies. Consequently, the accounting profession, through the AICPA and its ASB, still establishes "generally accepted auditing standards in the United States," or "GAAS in the United States" or "U.S. GAAS," for audits involving private firms. In 2008, the ASB Chairman estimated that the body's standards applied to almost 90,000 government entities and hundreds of thousands of businesses. Stephen Joyce, *Work on AICPA 'Clarity' Project Proceeds; New Compliance Auditing Standard Expected*, Sec. L. Daily (BNA), Dec. 5, 2008. Finally, remember that the General Accounting Office ("GAO") establishes Government Auditing Standards, first published in 1972, most recently revised in July 2007, and commonly referred to as the "Yellow Book," that apply to audits involving federal entities and other organizations that receive $500,000 or more in federal funds annually. Whether by law or contract, these standards apply to more than 30,000 domestic and international entities.

a. PUBLIC COMPANIES

On page 234, insert the following text at the end of the discussion in this section [on page 164 of the concise, in the three paragraph note the distinction set forth in the discussion that follows]:

**Interestingly, because Bernard L. Madoff Investment Securities LLC, the broker-dealer at the center of the Bernard Madoff's enormous Ponzi scheme, was not a public company, its auditor legally escaped PCAOB oversight. Following discovery of the scheme, the SEC did not extend an order that since 2003 had exempted private broker-dealers from a rule that otherwise required every registered broker-dealer to obtain a qualifying audit opinion from an auditing firm registered with the PCAOB. Although auditors of private broker-dealers must now register with the PCAOB, current law does not give the Board oversight over audits of private companies. As a result, the Board can neither inspect such audits nor bring disciplinary actions based on those audits. Although Senate approval remains uncertain as this Supplement goes to print, the conference agreement on the financial reform bill would give the PCAOB inspection and disciplinary powers over auditors of securities brokers and dealers. *See* Press Release, Pub. Co. Acct. Oversight Bd., Board Statement on the PCAOB Registration Process For Auditors of Non-Public Broker-Dealers (Jan. 8, 2009), http://www.pcaob.org/News_and_Events/News/2009/01-07.aspx; *see also See* Steven Marcy & Mike Ferullo, *House Passes Financial Reform Bill; Would Exempt Small Issuers From SOX §404*, 8 Corp. Accountability Rep. (BNA) 707 (July 9, 2010); Malini Manickavasagam, *Lawmakers Anticipate More Open Dialogue With SEC Officials in Checking Madoff Probes*, 7 Corp. Accountability Rep. (BNA) 297 (Mar. 6, 2009); Crystal Tandon, *Proposed Expansion of Auditing Oversight to Private Companies Debated*, 2009 Tax Notes Today 13-5 (Jan. 23, 2009).

(1) THE SECURITIES AND EXCHANGE COMMISSION

On page 235 [omitted from the concise], delete the references to small business issuers and Regulation S–B, which was repealed, generally effective February 5, 2008.

(2) PUBLIC COMPANY ACCOUNTING OVERSIGHT BOARD

On page 237, insert the following discussion after the last paragraph [on page 166 of the concise, insert the following discussion after the second paragraph]:

In 2007, the PCAOB applied its first disciplinary actions against a Big Four accounting firm, assessing a one million dollar fine on Deloitte & Touche ("Deloitte") and barring a former Deloitte audit partner from association with a registered public accounting firm for at least two years. According to PCAOB findings, Deloitte violated professional and PCAOB standards by keeping the former partner in charge of a 2003 audit engagement, which posed "greater than normal" audit risk, despite doubts about his competence and proficiency. Deloitte also failed to apply due professional care, exercise professional skepticism, obtain sufficient competent evidential matter and evaluate subsequent events in the performance of the audit. The PCAOB faulted the former partner for failing to perform adequate audit procedures and properly supervise others. *In re* Deloitte & Touche LLP, PCAOB Release No. 105-2007-005 (Dec. 10, 2007), http://www.pcaobus.org/Enforcement/Disciplinary_Proceedings/2007/12-10_Deloitte.pdf; *In re* Fazio, PCAOB Release No. 105-2007-006 (Dec. 10, 2007), http://www.pcaobus.org/Enforcement/Disciplinary_Proceedings/2007/12-10_Fazio.pdf.

On page 238 [omitted from the concise], please add the following text after the first paragraph:

** By the end of 2007, forty-six percent of the more than 1,800 auditing firms registered with the PCAOB were based in eighty-five countries outside the United States. Earlier in that year, the PCAOB issued a proposed policy statement outlining the circumstances in which the Board would place "full reliance" on the inspection programs of qualified foreign auditor oversight entities. In assessing a foreign oversight body, the PCAOB would consider the entity's adequacy and integrity, independence from the auditing profession, sources of funding, transparency, and historical performance. At a PCAOB roundtable on the issue, panelists supported joint inspections with foreign regulators, but some questioned the wisdom of allowing foreign regulators to assume complete responsibility for inspections. In March 2010, the SEC approved a proposed PCAOB amendment that allows the Board to postpone, for up to three years, the first inspections of registered, non-U.S. firms originally required in 2009 in those jurisdictions where the Board had not conducted an inspection before 2009. This gives the PCAOB additional time to develop efficient and effective cooperative arrangements with local authorities. *See* Public Company Accounting Oversight Board; Order Approving Proposed Amendments to Board Rules Relating to Inspections, Exchange Act Release No. 61,649 (March 4, 2010), http://www.sec.gov/rules/pcaob/2010/34-61649.pdf, *see also* PCAOB Release No. 2009-003 (June 25, 2009), http://www.pcaob.org/Rules/Docket_027/

2009-06-25_Release_No_2009-003.pdf; Tina Chi, *PCAOB's 2007 Annual Report Shows Stronger Focus on Outreach and Oversight*, 6 Corp. Accountability Rep. (BNA) 1007 (Sept. 19, 2008); David Schwartz, *Roundtable Panelists Leery of Turning Over PCAOB Inspections to Non-U.S. Regulators*, 6 Corp. Accountability Rep. (BNA) 680 (June 27, 2008); Malini Manickavasagam, *PCAOB Will Seek Comment on Guidance Related to Reliance on Non-U.S. Inspections*, 5 Corp. Accountability Rep. (BNA) 1208 (Dec. 7, 2007).

** In May 2010, the PCAOB published a list containing more than 400 foreign companies whose securities trade in U.S. markets and that filed financial statements with the SEC, but for which asserted non-U.S. legal obstacles prevented the Board from inspecting the companies' PCAOB-registered auditors. At that time, the PCAOB had inspected more than 1,300 registered firms in the United States and thirty-three other countries. China, Switzerland, and eighteen EU countries, however, had denied access to PCAOB inspectors. (The Chinese refusal also affects registered auditors in Hong Kong to the extent that they audit clients that operate in China.) In addition, auditors in those jurisdictions often render assistance, often substantial, to the registered auditors for other public companies and those principal auditors rely on that audit work. In either event, the markets and the investing public should not assume that the PCAOB has reviewed the quality control practices or audit procedures at these public companies' registered auditing firm. Subject to Senate approval, language in the conference agreement on the financial reform bill would seemingly correct the situation with the EU. As more Chinese companies file financial reports in the United States, this situation raises potential, and growing, safety and soundness issues for investors. *See* Press Release, Pub. Co. Acct. Oversight Bd., PCAOB Publishes List of Issuer Audit Clients of Non-U.S. Registered Firms in Jurisdictions Where the PCAOB Is Denied Access to Conduct Inspections (May 18, 2010), http://pcaobus.org/News/Releases/Pages/05182010_ListIssuerAuditClients.aspx; *see also* Steven Marcy & Mike Ferullo, *House Passes Financial Reform Bill; Would Exempt Small Issuers From SOX §404*, 8 Corp. Accountability Rep. (BNA) 707 (July 9, 2010); Steven Marcy, *Chinese Bar Against PCAOB Inspections Is Threat to U.S. Investors, Goelzer Says*, 42 Sec. Reg. & L. Rep. (BNA) 1030 (May 24, 2010).

c. INTERNATIONAL AUDITING STANDARDS

On pages 239 and 240 [omitted from the concise], replace the text with the following discussion:

Even if some body or organization promulgates a core set of international accounting principles that gain worldwide acceptance, those principles will not achieve their purpose unless adequate auditing and enforcement ensure their application. Pursuant to its mission to protect the public interest by encouraging high quality practices by the world's accountants, the International Federation of Accountants ("IFAC"), a group of 157 national professional accountancy bodies, including the AICPA, from 123 countries and jurisdictions, representing 2.5 million accountants, formed the International Auditing and Assurance Standards Board ("IAASB"), previously known as the International Auditing Practices Committee ("IAPC"). IAASB develops and promulgates standards and statements on auditing and related services. Among other pronouncements, IAASB issues International Standards on Auditing ("ISAs") and International Auditing Practice Statements ("IAPSs") and seeks to promote their voluntary acceptance. ISAs describe basic principles and essential procedures and offer guidance through explanatory and other material. In contrast, IAPSs provide practical assistance to auditors in implementing ISAs or promoting good practice. IAPSs enjoy less authority than ISAs. In 2009, IAASB completed its so-called "clarity project," during which reviewed and revised all thirty-six of its auditing standards in an effort to advance convergence.

At this point, neither ISAs nor IAPSs establish standards which auditors in the United States must follow under either the PCAOB's rules or the AICPA's Code of Professional Conduct. Before an ISA or related IAPS will apply to audits in the United States, either the PCAOB or the ASB must specifically adopt the ISA.

So far, the PCAOB has yet to take an official position on international auditing standards. While the PCAOB has shown support for global auditing standards, the Board has not adopted or embraced any IAASB standards. At least one PCAOB board member has publicly commented that the economic crisis has drawn attention to the need for international coordination, observed that more than 100 countries have adopted ISAs and that larger auditing firms use them in their international auditing practices, and expressed the hope that standard setters can eliminate unneeded differences between the PCAOB, AICPA, and IAASB standards. In contrast, another PCAOB board member has voiced concerns that convergence to international auditing standards could harm investors in the United States, noting that Congress established the PCAOB as independent from the auditing profession and that the auditing profession funds and controls both the IAASB and ASB. *See* Tina Chi, *Adoption of Universal Auditing Standards Still Contested In and Among Audit Groups*, 7 Corp. Accountability Rep. (BNA) 75 (Jan. 16, 2009); Tina Chi, *PCAOB Founding Board Member Champions Adopting Single Auditing Standard in Speech*, Corp. Accountability & Fraud Daily (BNA), Sept. 26, 2008.

By comparison, the ASB has launched its own "clarity" project. During the process, the ASB hopes to bring the AICPA standards for audits involving nonpublic companies closer toward convergence with the IAASB Standards. *IAASB Completes Audit Standards Project, Offers Guidance on Corporate Governance*, 7 Corp. Accountability Rep. (BNA) 295 (Mar. 6, 2009).

Historically, the development of auditing standards follows closely behind the development of accounting principles. As today's global economy focuses increased attention on international accounting principles in the United States and throughout the world, we can expect international auditing standards to develop and grow in significance. Just as the financial crisis has spread globally, the accounting scandals and audit failures at Dutch grocer Ahold NV and Italian dairy and multinational food company Parmalat SpA of Italy document that accounting fraud crosses international boundaries.

5. THE EXPECTATION GAP

On page 245 [page 170 of the concise], insert the following text above subsection a.:

After the issuance of SAB No. 99, the agency became aware of diversity in how enterprises determined the materiality of financial statement errors that span multiple periods. The SEC indicated that many registrants did not consider the effect of prior year errors on current year financial statements, potentially resulting in material misstatements as the errors accumulate. In 2006, the agency issued Staff Accounting Bulletin No. 108 to improve financial reporting practices on this issue. SAB No. 108 directs registrants to consider prior year misstatements when examining misstatements in the current year. The staff explained that enterprises have largely applied two methods in practice to accumulate and quantify misstatements: the "rollover" and "iron curtain" approaches, both of which contain shortcomings. The "rollover" approach focuses on the materiality of such errors in terms of the current income statement, potentially allowing the accumulation of errors on the balance sheet. By comparison, the "iron curtain" approach analyzes the materiality of the errors accumulated on the current balance sheet, but may produce errors in the income statement.

In SAB No. 108, the SEC staff advises against exclusive reliance on either the "rollover" or "iron curtain" approach. Instead, registrants should quantify errors under both approaches and adjust the financial statements when either approach indicates a material misstatement, "considering all relevant quantitative and qualitative factors." The staff indicated that registrants need not restate prior period financial statements when applying the guidance; instead, registrants may post a cumulative effect adjustment to the opening balance of retained earnings and disclose the nature and amount of the individual errors included in the adjustment. Considering the Effects of Prior Year Misstatements when Quantifying Misstatements in Current Year Financial Statements, Staff Accounting Bulletin No. 108, 71 Fed. Reg. 54,580 (Sept. 18, 2006), *reprinted in* 7 Fed. Sec. L. Rep. (CCH) ¶ 75,701, at 64,220 (Sept. 27, 2006), *available at* http://www.sec.gov/interps/account/sab108.pdf.

6. AUDIT REPORTS

On pages 252 to 257 [pages 176-77 of the concise], please note that under AS 5, an auditor no longer needs to express an opinion on

**management's assessment of the effectiveness of the company's
internal control over financial reporting.**

The auditor only expresses an opinion on whether the company maintained
effective internal control over financial reporting. Accordingly, the "Separate
report on internal control over financial reporting" paragraph of a standard
auditor report, which appears on pages 253-54 of the unabridged fourth
edition [omitted from the concise], would no longer reference an opinion on
management's assessment; similarly, a separate report on internal control
over financial reporting, which appears on pages 256-57 of the unabridged
text only, would no longer include the opinion on management's assessment
in the opinion paragraph.

F.   PUBLISHED SOURCES OF GAAP, GAAS, & OTHER FINANCIAL INFORMATION

**On pages 265 through 267 [omitted from the concise], replace the
discussion through the first section on GAAP with the following text:**

**   No semester-long course or text can cover everything that you, or any
lawyer, will likely need to know about accounting. This text, however, can try
to offer some suggestions as to where, and how, you might find answers to
issues involving financial accounting or auditing matters and to empower you
to obtain financial information about various business enterprises.
Accordingly, this section will discuss various sources of accounting, auditing,
and financial information.

**   As a starting point, the Internet contains valuable information about
accounting principles and auditing standards and their relationship to the
practice of law. Helpful sites include:

Sponsor	Internet Address
AICPA	http://www.aicpa.org
AcSEC	http://www.aicpa.org/members/div/acctstd/index.htm
ASB	http://www.aicpa.org/members/div/auditstd/index.htm
COSO	http://www.coso.org/
FASB	http://www.fasb.org
IASB	http://www.iasb.org.
IFAC	http://www.ifac.org
Law and Accounting Committee, Business Law Section, American Bar Association	http://www.abanet.org/buslaw/lawaccount/home.html
PCAOB	http://www.pcaobus.org
SEC	http://www.sec.gov/
SECPS	http://www.aicpa.org/members/div/secps/index.htm

**   These Web sites often provide easy access to background information about various accounting and auditing standards, announce current events and meetings, provide information about ordering materials and documents, and solicit view points. We can expect these sites to provide even more information in the years ahead.

1.   GAAP

**   You will hopefully recall from the discussion on pages 21-23, *supra*, that the Codification has simplified accounting research and reorganized the accounting principles from the previous GAAP hierarchy into a unified topical arrangement, including separate sections for SEC guidance.

**   Effectively using and citing the Codification depends upon understanding its goals and organizational structure. If you plan to use the Codification, you should review the Notice to Constituents, which discusses the Codification's history, content, structure, and style.

**   The Codification simplifies user access to all authoritative GAAP by reorganizing more than two thousand GAAP pronouncements from into about ninety topics and using a consistent structure to display all topics. These topics collect related guidance in five main areas: general principles and objectives, presentation, financial statement accounts, broad transactions, and industries. Within individual topics, the Codification arranges content into subtopics, sections, and paragraphs and consistently numbers these subdivisions. For example, the Codification always labels subtopic 10 of any topic "Overall," section 00 of any subtopic "Status" to identify any updates, and section 50 of any subtopic "Disclosure."

**   Under the Codification's system, sections provide the primary working or research area. Recall that sections containing SEC content carry the prefix "S." Please note that the referencing structure does not include "subsections;" the organizational structure references "paragraphs" within "sections." As mentioned earlier, the Codification also includes separate sections containing guidance from the SEC related to issues within the basic financial statements. These SEC sections follow the same topical structure, but carry the designation "S" before the section number, so that users can distinguish between the SEC requirements and other authoritative GAAP. Each section contains at least one general subsection, but the Codification does not number subsections.

**   FASB offers three versions of the Codification--two on-line, "real time" views and a print edition that reprints the Codification as of October 31, 2009 and that FASB plans to update annually. The on-line versions include a "professional view," which normally costs $850 per user, per year, with discounts available for multiple subscriptions, and a "basic view" available at no charge. Under a program sponsored by the American Accounting Association, the leading organization for accounting educators, educational institutions offering accounting courses and their accounting students can obtain "academic access" at a greatly reduced rate.

** Anyone can register and use the barebones "basic view," which essentially allows access to content for free. That version, however, lacks many important and convenient features included in the fully functional "professional view." The professional view, for example, includes a personal annotation feature for keeping notes about relevant standards; enhanced printing options, including annotations and e-mail; search, "Go To," and glossary term quickfind and usage page capabilities; section links and the ability to join sections; and archive features for accessing previous versions of the content. Geared primarily for the "professional view," the FASB offers a free online tutorial for the Codification at <http://asc.fasb.org>.

** Because more than ninety percent of users know the general topic of interest before they begin their research, most on-line research usually begins with "browsing." To browse, a user moves the cursor over one of ten subject areas, including the Notice to Constituents, General Principles, Presentation, Assets, Liabilities, Equity, Revenue, Expenses, Broad Transactions, and Industry, or the Master Glossary. Studies show that topical browsing reduces the time otherwise spent using text searches and refining those searches. As additional navigational tools, the "professional view" allows users to search the Codification and to "Go To" a particular provision, assuming you know its citation.

** Although the Codification should reduce the time and effort required to find answers to accounting research issues, the on-line versions provide at least two additional advantages. First, the on-line version offers "real-time" update. As FASB issues ASUs, the Board concurrently updates the Codification. An individual using the Codification's print version would need to check every ASU issued since the date of the print version to avoid missing any changes to the Codification. Because FASB issued nineteen ASUs during the first half of 2010 and two ASUs during the last two months of 2009, a user of the print edition in early July 2010 would also need to consult either one of the on-line versions or twenty-one ASUs that the Board had issued in the previous eight months to ensure access to the most recent standards. Similarly, the 2009 print edition contains Notice to Constituents (v. 3.0), while the on-line versions in early July 2010 display Notice to Constituents (v. 4.1), under a system where versions containing substantive changes from the previous version end in .0, while versions ending in other than zero present editorial or clerical corrections. Please also keep in mind that the Codification presents current—at least as of the "cutoff" date for the print version—and transitional text together to allow access to all relevant content in the same location and identifies any new guidance as "Pending Text" until the passage of time means that the prior guidance no longer applies.

** Second, a cross-reference feature accompanies the on-line versions. This feature allows users to find quickly both where a particular promulgation appears in the Codification and which original promulgations supply the content within a particular topic in the Codification. Subscribers can insert information about a standard to identify the Codification sections that contain the content. Alternatively, an individual can insert information about the Codification to identify the standards that populate that portion of the Codification. The professional view also contains links that immediately navigate to the relevant section in the Codification.

**   For users that nevertheless prefer hard copy, FASB sells a four-volume, print edition, at present current through October 31, 2009, for $195. The 2009 print edition contains about 2,900 pages, again a significant simplification from the more than 10,000 pages of materials from the SEC, FASB, EITF, and AICPA that previously constituted GAAP. Anyone who prefers to use the print version will nevertheless need to check either: (i) one of the on-line versions for the "real-time" text of any provision, or (ii) the "Standards" link at the top of the FASB's website for any relevant ASUs. Once again, please remember that the Codification identifies any new guidance as "Pending Text" until the passage of time means that the prior guidance no longer applies.

**   To determine what GAAP provides or allows in a certain transaction, a lawyer need not necessarily read the Codification, although that's now the best place to start! Numerous secondary sources, including accounting textbooks and journals, usually summarize or explain GAAP and often provide excellent examples. In addition, the "Big Four" often publish or distribute materials on timely topics for clients and other interested persons. CCH Incorporated, previously known as Commerce Clearing House, Inc., sells an annual *U.S. Master™ GAAP Guide* that summarizes, explains and applies various accounting pronouncements by topic. *See, e.g.*, BRUCE POUNDER, 2010 U.S. MASTER GAAP GUIDE (2009).

**   Although not U.S. GAAP, IFRS became more accessible during 2009. In April, IASB announced that the public could obtain free, limited access to the core text of IFRS, the so-called "unaccompanied standards," via IFRS® by registering as a user with the Board. At this time, the free access does not include "additional content such as basis for conclusions." The trustees of IASCF (now known as IFRSF), IASB's parent, deferred offering free access to the full text until 2011. Int'l Accounting Standards Bd., Access to unaccompanied standards (Apr. 17, 2009), http://www.iasb.org/News/Announcements+and+Speeches/Access+to+unaccompanied+standards.htm; *see also* Stephen Bouvier, *IASB Announces Start of Free Online Access to Financial Reporting Standards' Core Text*, Sec. L. Daily (BNA), Apr. 21, 2009. In July 2009, IASB issued and posted on its website the much anticipated IFRS for SMEs. Departing from its usual practice, IASB also posted the accompanying basis for conclusions, illustrative examples, and a disclosure checklist on its website, where registered users can access the materials, free of charge, via http://www.iasb.org/IFRS+for+SMEs/IFRS+for+SMEs+and+related+material/IFRS+for+SMEs+and+related+material.htm.

**   Law students and lawyers can also access SEC materials using computer-assisted legal research. WESTLAW® allows lawyers and law students to obtain decisions and releases from the SEC in its FSEC–RELS Database. WESTLAW® also contains various trade publications about accounting and financial matters, including Accounting Horizons (ACCTHORZNS) and the Journal of Accountancy (JACCNTCY). Similarly, LEXIS®·NEXIS® offers access to SEC materials in its Federal Securities Library (FEDSEC) and to various accounting literature in the Accounting Information Library, which includes both the National Automated Accounting Research System (NAARS) Service and the Accounting, Tax & Financial Library (ACCTG).

CCH Incorporated also publishes an eight-volume looseleaf, also available to paid subscribers on-line, which contains information about the SEC and the federal securities laws. FEDERAL SECURITIES LAW REPORTER (CCH) (2010 eight vols.). The first volume contains the general guide to using the series, a topical index, and the Securities Act of 1933, as amended, and related regulations, forms, rulings and decisions. The second volume contains additional materials regarding the Securities Act of 1933. The Securities Exchange Act of 1934, as amended, and related regulations, forms, rulings and decisions appear in volumes two through five. The sixth volume contains Regulation S–X, which governs the form and content for financial statements which registrants file with the SEC, and related explanations. The seventh volume includes Regulation S–K, the standard instructions for filing forms under the federal securities laws, the Codification of FRRs, full texts of recent AAERs, full texts of SABs and related releases, various finding lists, lists of releases, and case tables. Finally, the current volume contains new SEC rulings, recent court decisions, and a topical index to new developments. In addition, transfer binders contain the ASRs, AAERs and FRRs. *See, e.g.,* [1937–1982 Transfer Binder] Fed. Sec. L. Rep. (CCH); [1982–1987 Transfer Binder] Fed. Sec. L. Rep. (CCH).

G.   ACCOUNTANTS' LEGAL LIABILITY

On page 271, replace the two full paragraphs with the following [on page 180 of the concise, replace the full paragraph with the following]:

The parade of recoveries from accounting firms and threatening lawsuits has continued unabated right up to the present. For example, in 1998 KPMG Peat Marwick agreed to pay $75 million to settle four lawsuits arising from Orange County's bankruptcy, substantially less than the $3.5 billion that the suits sought, including the county's $3 billion damage claim against its former auditor for alleged negligence in failing to warn the county about the high-risk investments that ultimately led to the nation's largest municipal bankruptcy. *KPMG Peat Marwick Settles Orange County Lawsuits for $75 Million,* 30 Sec. Reg. & L. Rep. (BNA) 801 (May 22, 1998). In 1999, Ernst & Young agreed to pay a record $335 million to settle a class action lawsuit that shareholders of Cendant Corp. brought for alleged negligence in failing to detect widespread fraud at one of Cendant's predecessors. The accounting firm later paid out nearly $300 million to settle a related lawsuit that Cendant itself brought, bringing its total settlement payments to about $635 million. *In re* Cendant Corp. Sec. Litig., 109 F. Supp. 2d 235 (D.N.J. 2000) (approving proposed settlement in a class action in which, among other things, Ernst & Young agreed to pay $335 million to the class); *In re* Cendant Corp. Sec. Litig., 109 F. Supp. 2d 285 (D.N.J. 2000) (awarding attorney fees from settlement fund and describing the Ernst & Young settlement as "the largest amount ever paid by an accounting firm in a securities class action"); David Reilly & Nathan Koppel, *Cendant Case Costs Ernst Almost $300 Million More*, WALL ST. J., Feb. 16, 2008, at B3 (discussing Ernst & Young's later settlement with Cendant). In 2008, the United States Court of Appeals for the Third Circuit upheld a $182.9 million judgment against PricewaterhouseCoopers following a jury verdict that the firm committed professional malpractice during an audit failure at Ambassador Insurance Co. *See Appeals Court Upholds $182.9 Million Award Against Auditor for Professional Malpractice*, 6 Corp. Accountability Rep. (BNA) 1003 (Sept. 19, 2008).

Audit failures related to the corporate scandals in the early 2000s leave each of the Big Four facing potentially enormous legal liability. Industry sources estimate that the Big Four spend more than ten percent of their auditing and accounting revenues each year to defend and settle lawsuits. For one recent example, Deloitte reportedly paid about $250 million during 2005 to settle litigation related to the collapse of Fortress Re, once the largest aviation reinsurer in the world. Interestingly, Deloitte never received more than $100,000 in any year from that engagement. Mark Maremont & Miho Inada, *Deloitte Pays Insurers More Than $200 Million*, WALL ST. J., Jan. 6, 2006, at C3; Mark Maremont, *Deloitte Reaches Deal With Japanese Insurers*, WALL ST. J., Sept. 21, 2005, at C3. In 2007, PricewaterhouseCoopers paid $225 million, the firm's largest settlement to date, to resolve malpractice claims arising from audits at Tyco International Ltd. David Reilly & Jennifer Levitz, *PwC Sets Accord in Tyco Case*, WALL ST. J., July 7, 2007, at A3. The following year, the firm agreed to pay $97.5 million to settle a securities-fraud class action arising from the audits of American International Group Inc. The settlement ranked as one of the ten highest amounts that an accounting firm had agreed to pay to resolve a securities-fraud class action. Bebe Raupe, *PwC Will Pay Ohio Pension Plans $97 Million to Settle Claims Over AIG Audits*, 6 Corp. Accountability Rep. (BNA) 1105 (Oct. 10, 2008). In 2009, Ernst & Young agreed to the reportedly eighth highest amount, $109 million, to settle a similar suit arising from the financial fraud at HealthSouth Corp. Yin Wilczek, *Court Approves $109M Settlement Against Auditor Over HealthSouth Fraud*, 41 Sec. Reg. & L. Rep. (BNA) 640 (Apr. 6, 2009).

** Lawsuits and court decisions continue to worry accounting firms. In 2007, a Florida jury found BDO Seidman, LLP ("BDO"), a second-tier accounting firm, grossly negligent in failing to detect a loan-fraud scheme during its audit of E.S. Bankest, LLC, a Miami-based financial services company. The jury awarded a staggering $521 million, including $351 million in punitive damages. Although a Florida appellate court reversed the award in June 2010, the judgment remands the case to the trial court for a new trial. Nevertheless, a cloud still remains over BDO's future financial viability. *See* Drew Douglas, *Florida Appeals Court Reverses, Remands $521 Million Verdict Against BDO Seidman*, 42 Sec. Reg & Law. Rep. (BNA) 1268 (June 28, 2010); David Reilly, *BDO Seidman Damages Rise to $521 Million*, WALL ST. J., Aug. 15, 2007, at C3. In another case, the United States District Court for the Southern District of New York denied the motions for summary judgment that the international firm Deloitte Touche Tohmatsu and its U.S. affiliate, Deloitte & Touche LLP, filed to dismiss claims seeking to hold the firms liable for alleged fraud at an Italian affiliate, Deloitte & Touche, S.p.A, during audits of Parmalat S.p.A., and related companies. *In re* Parmalat Sec. Litig., 594 F. Supp. 2d 444, *reconsideration denied*, 598 F. Supp. 2d 537, *motion for order certifying interlocutory appeal denied*, 599 F. Supp. 2d 535 (S.D.N.Y. 2009). Because both the Big Four and the second-tier accounting firms market themselves as world-wide, seamless organizations the decision marks an important development. For the first time, an influential court recognized that plaintiffs can potentially hold a global accounting firm and its U.S. affiliate responsible for an audit failure at a foreign affiliate. See Steven Marcy, *Parmalat Ruling Will Cause Audit Firms to Rethink Liability Threat, Lawyers Say*, 41 Sec. Reg. & L. Rep. (BNA) 381 (Mar. 2, 2009); Nathan Koppel, *A Parmalat Ruling May Broaden Liability*, WALL ST.J., Jan. 29, 2009, at C4.

Members of the accounting community have called for liability caps on accounting firm malpractice judgments on the grounds that enormous litigation judgments, as illustrated in the BDO case described in the previous paragraph, could drive major accounting firms out of business. Supporters of these caps point out that such a demise of a Big Four accounting firm would devastate competition and drive audit fees higher. Critics worry that liability caps could hamper audit quality. In 2008, the European Commission recommended liability limits for large audit firms. U.S. regulators have resisted that idea, and the final report from the Treasury Department's Advisory Committee on the Auditing Profession addressing the issue did not recommend imposing limits on auditor liability. Instead, the Advisory Committee favored an approach where the SEC could appoint a court-approved trustee to preserve or rehabilitate a large accounting firm facing catastrophic legal liability. *European Commission Calls for Limits on Auditor Liability Awards in Civil Lawsuits*, 6 Corp. Accountability Rep. (BNA) 636 (June 13, 2008); David Schwartz, *Panelists Recall That Treasury Committee Could Not Agree on Auditor Liability Limits*, 6 Corp. Accountability Rep. (BNA) 1336 (Dec. 12, 2008).

On page 273 [omitted from the concise], add the following to the paragraph ending on top of the page:

The government dismissed the criminal charges in 2007 after KPMG satisfied its obligations under the deferred prosecution agreement. Alison Bennett, *Government Drops Felony Charge Document After KPMG Meets Deferred Prosecution Pact*, 39 Sec. Reg. & L. Rep. (BNA) 28 (Jan. 8, 2007).

On page 296, insert the following paragraph after the carryover paragraph ending on the top of the page [on page 202 of the concise, insert the following paragraph at the end of Note 1]:

In 2008, the Supreme Court of the United States narrowed statutory liability under the federal securities laws by rejecting so-called "scheme liability." The Court refused to allow a private action by investors against a third-party that did not violate the antifraud provisions in the federal securities laws but that may have aided or abetted another entity's fraudulent scheme. Stoneridge Inv. Partners, LLC v. Scientific-Atlanta, Inc., 128 S. Ct. 761 (2008). Accounting and law firms closely followed the case, fearing the Court could expand their liability for their clients' frauds. In *Stoneridge*, investors sued Charter Communications, Inc. ("Charter") for fraudulent securities violations, along with Scientific-Atlanta, Inc. and Motorola, Inc. ("respondents"), who supplied set-top cable boxes to Charter. As described more fully in this Supplement on page 105 in the materials for Chapter VI, Charter devised a fraudulent revenue recognition scheme to increase reported revenue and operating cash flow. In the 5-3 decision, the Court upheld an earlier precedent that investors cannot pursue a private right of action against third-party aiders and abettors. *Id.* at 767-69 (citing Cent. Bank of Denver v. First Interstate Bank of Denver, 511 U.S. 164, 191 (1994)). Because the respondents did not commit a primary violation of the securities law, the investors could not maintain their claims against the respondents. *Id.* at 774. The Court, however, noted that secondary actors remain subject to criminal penalties, civil enforcement actions by the SEC, and state securities laws. *Id.* at 773-74.

CHAPTER III

THE TIME VALUE OF MONEY

N.B. for the unabridged fourth edition: as a result of various errors, for which I apologize, you will find a corrected Appendix B on pages 201-206, *infra*. When we retyped the time value of money tables to enlarge them, we inadvertently introduced errors into Table I in Appendix B on page 1103 of the text. In the 6% column, the correct factors for n=8, 9, and 10, respectively, are 1.59385, 1.68948, and 1.79085. For the first printing, we also inadvertently switched the order of Tables II and III in Appendix B in the text. Each table contained the correct heading, formula, and factors, but the wrong label. If your copy of the unabridged fourth edition contains stickers on pages 1101, 1104, and 1105, Foundation Press has already remedied that glitch. In addition, the second printing also corrected the error. When the text directs you to Table II, it refers to the Future Value of $1.00 in Arrears, which in the first printing appears as Table III on page 1105. Similarly, when the text directs you to Table III, it refers to the Present Value of $1.00, which may appear on Table II on page 1104. Given these errors, I decided to reprint all the tables in this Supplement and to assign new page numbers! Please accept my apologies.

A. IMPORTANCE TO LAWYERS

On the bottom of page 298 and before the sentence that carries over to the next page [before the penultimate sentence in the last paragraph in this section on page 206 of the concise], insert the following sentence:

As credit and financial markets froze during the credit crisis, enterprises frequently switched to discounted, expected cash flows to calculate fair values for various financial assets and financial liabilities.

B. INTEREST

1. FACTORS DETERMINING INTEREST RATES

On page 300, insert the following text after the carryover paragraph at the top of page [on page 207 of the concise, insert the following text after the second full paragraph]:

In today's global economy, Libor, the London interbank offered rate, often serves as a benchmark to fix the cost of borrowing for trillions of dollars in mortgages, corporate debt, and financial contracts worldwide. Using information provided by sixteen large, mostly European, international banks, the British Bankers' Association calculates average interest rates at which banks extend unsecured, short-term loans in dollars, for periods ranging from one month to one year, to one another. As the credit crisis in the United States both deepened and widened, critics complained that the use of Libor renders global markets especially susceptible to financial troubles in Europe. Other observers noted that after the sudden collapse of Bear Stearns Companies, banks avoided loans to one another for even three-month periods. *The Wall Street Journal* further heightened scrutiny regarding Libor's use, as well as its accuracy, by publishing a front-page story detailing an analysis that suggested that several participating banks had understated their borrowing rates in an effort to mask their own financial difficulties. Such understatements would translate to an estimated $45 billion reduction in interest payments by borrowers during the first four months in 2008. In response, the British Bankers' Association announced several reforms to expand and to better police the published rates. Carrick Mollenkamp, *U.K. Bankers to Alter Libor to Address Rate Doubts*, WALL ST. J., June 11, 2008, at C1; Carrick Mollenkamp & Laurence Norman, *British Group Largely Maintains Libor Procedures*, WALL ST. J., May 31, 2008, at B6; Carrick Mollenkamp & Mark Whitehouse, *Study Casts Doubt on Key Rate*, WALL ST. J., May 29, 2008, at A1. Alternative benchmarks to Libor include the Federal Reserve's federal funds target rate–the rate at which the Federal Reserve suggests that banks lend to each other overnight–or its discount rate, the rate at which member banks may borrow from the Federal Reserve.

C.   FUTURE VALUE

1.   SINGLE AMOUNTS

c.   PRACTICAL ADVICE PART I: WHY YOU SHOULD START SAVING FOR YOUR RETIREMENT AS SOON AS POSSIBLE

On page 306 [omitted from the concise], replace the last full paragraph with the following:

**   Skeptics will respond that this illustration assumes an unrealistically high interest rate and ignores income taxes and inflation. From 1926 through 2009, according to Morningstar, Inc., a Chicago-based investment advisory firm, stocks in Standard & Poor's 500, an index which tracks the stock market performance of 500 large companies, have gained an average of 9.8 percent each year. Stocks in smaller companies have done even better, posting gains averaging 11.9 percent per year. During the same period, long-term government bonds posted a 5.4 percent average annual return, short-term U.S. Treasury bills earned a 3.7 percent average annual return, and inflation averaged 3.0 percent per year. MORNINGSTAR, INC., 2010 IBBOTSON® STOCKS, BONDS, BILLS, AND INFLATION® (SBBI®) CLASSIC YEARBOOK 26-27 (2010).

CHAPTER IV

INTRODUCTION TO FINANCIAL STATEMENT ANALYSIS AND FINANCIAL RATIOS

B. ANALYTICAL TOOLS AND TECHNIQUES

1. GENERAL COMMENTS ABOUT READING FINANCIAL STATEMENTS

On pages 334 and 335 [page 232 of the concise], please note in the carryover paragraph [item (9) in the carryover paragraph ending on the top of the page in the concise] that after AS 5, an auditor will not report on management's assessment of internal control over financial reporting. The auditor, however, will continue to express an opinion as to whether the company maintained effective internal control over financial reporting.

C. THE BALANCE SHEET

2. ANALYTICAL TERMS AND RATIOS

b. FINANCIAL RATIOS

(2) Leverage Ratios

On page 348 at the end of the carryover paragraph at the top of the page [on page 244 of the concise at the end of the first full paragraph], insert the following text:

Among the biggest casualties in the ongoing credit crisis, the inability to repay short-term obligations led to the demise of both Bear Stearns Companies and Lehman Brothers Holdings Inc., both highly leveraged investment banks. Bear Stearns ultimately merged with J.P. Morgan Chase & Co., while Lehman Brothers filed for bankruptcy. The credit crisis accelerated as concerns about excessive leverage caused investors and firms to sell assets at steadily declining prices and repay debts in an effort to reduce leverage. *See* Peter Eavis & David Reilly, *Losing Leverage: Some Firms Cut Debt in This Uncertain Era*, WALL ST. J., Apr. 7, 2008, at C1 (noting that Merrill Lynch's assets had increased from 17.9 times its equity at the end of 2003 to 27.8 times equity in mid-2007 and that Morgan Stanley and Lehman Brothers had asset to shareholders' equity ratios that exceeded thirty-to-one in early 2008).

D.   THE MEASUREMENT OF INCOME

1.   RESULTS OF OPERATIONS

a. THE INCOME STATEMENT

(3) Extraordinary Items

On page 365 [omitted from the concise], please delete the first full paragraph. Under FASB ASC Topic 805, *Business Combinations*, which codified a pronouncement by that same name– SFAS No. 141(R), an acquirer simply includes any gain arising from a bargain purchase in operating income. The Codification defines a bargain purchase as a business combination in which the fair value of net assets acquired exceeds the consideration transferred plus the fair value of any noncontrolling interest in the acquiree. FASB ASC ¶ 805-30-25-2 (a codification of SFAS No. 141(R), ¶¶ 36–38).

On page 370 [page 257 of the concise] immediately before the Problems, please insert the following new section:

(6) [(2) in the concise] Noncontrolling Interests

According to ASC Topic 810, *Consolidation*, which codified SFAS No. 160, *Noncontrolling Interests in Consolidated Financial Statements*, for-profit enterprises must now separately show the amount of consolidated net income attributable (i) to the parent and (ii) to the noncontrolling interest in the parent's less-than-wholly owned subsidiaries on the face of a consolidated statement of income. As a result, you may soon see amounts labeled "net income before income from noncontrolling interests," "net income attributable to noncontrolling interests," and "net income attributable to the company" on future income statements. The change, however, does not effect the so-called "bottom line" because enterprises have never included income attributable to minority ownership interests in subsidiaries in net income, typically treating any such income as an expense in "Other expense." In contrast, the minority's share of a subsidiary's loss has effectively increased net income historically and would likewise mean that the "net income attributable to the company" would exceed "net income before losses related to noncontrolling interests." Because the pronouncement applies to fiscal years, and interim periods within those fiscal years, beginning on or after December 15, 2008, SFAS No. 160 did not apply to Starbucks, for example, until the first quarter in its 2010 fiscal year. *See* FASB ASC ¶ 810-10-50-1A (a codification of ARB

No. 51, ¶ 38, as amended by SFAS No. 160); *see also* Michael Rapoport, *New FASB Rule Aims to Clarify 'Net Income,'* WALL ST. J., May 1, 2009, at B5.

b. PRO FORMA METRICS

On page 375, replace the last fourteen lines of the first full paragraph [on page 266 of the concise, replace the second full paragraph] with the following text:

**   Regulation G also expressly prohibits the use of non-GAAP measures to smooth earnings and bans companies from designating items as "special," "nonrecurring," or "unusual" in certain public filings, specifically 10-Ks and 10-Qs, if similar items have occurred in the previous two years or if the enterprise expects such events or transactions to occur again within two years. Public companies, however, may still use such designations to define pro forma metrics in earnings or other releases, and post that information on the corporate website, as long as the enterprise explains where the pro forma metric comes from and includes the necessary reconciliation to GAAP. As a result, a two-tiered reporting system has developed, where enterprises use press releases and the corporate website to disseminate information about such items, but then omit such information from SEC annual or quarterly reports.

**   In January 2010, the Division of Corporation Finance updated its Compliance and Disclosure Interpretations on non-GAAP measures and opined that the prohibition against designations as "non-recurring, infrequent or unusual" arises from the description and not from the item's nature. The staff continued: "The fact that a registrant cannot describe a charge or gain as non-recurring, infrequent or unusual, however, does not mean that the registrant cannot adjust for that charge or gain. Registrants can make adjustments they believe are appropriate, subject to Regulation G and [Regulation S-K]." Staff of the Sec. & Exch. Comm'n, Non-GAAP Financial Measures, Q. 102.03 (Jan. 15, 2010), *available at* http://www.sec.gov/divisions/corpfin/guidance/nongaapinterp.htm. In essence, such disclosures cannot mislead, must provide a reconciliation to the most directly comparable GAAP number, and should explain why the presentation provides information useful to investors.

**   Although the SEC staff seemingly seeks a better balance between permissible non-GAAP presentations and unlawful disclosures, late in 1999 the SEC brought its first enforcement action under Regulation G against SafeNet, Inc. ("SafeNet"), its former CEO, its former CFO, and three former accountants. All the defendants agreed to settle the civil injunctive action, which alleged that at the CFO's direction, SafeNet: (i) recorded improper accounting adjustments to various expenses, (ii) incorrectly classified ordinary operating expenses as non-recurring expenses to integrate acquired businesses into current operations, and (iii) represented to investors that the company's non-GAAP earnings excluded certain non-recurring expenses, when, in fact, the company had missclassified and excluded a significant amount of ordinary operating expenses from its non-GAAP earnings in an effort to meet or exceed quarterly targets. In addition to a permanent injunction, SafeNet agreed to pay a $1 million civil penalty. The former officers and accountants consented to disgorgement, civil penalties, officer and director bars, and administrative orders suspending them from appearing or practicing before the SEC as accountants. SEC v. SafeNet, Inc., Accounting and Auditing Enforcement Release No. 3068 (Nov. 12, 2009), http://www.sec.gov/litigation/litreleases/2009/lr21290.htm; *see also* Yin Wilczek & Steven Marcy, *SEC's Cross Seeks Staff Review of Non-GAAP Accounting Measures,* 7 Corp. Accountability Rep. (BNA) 1450 (Dec. 11, 2009).

**   Because enterprises have historically used pro formas to show what an enterprise's financial statements would look like after a merger or other business acquisition, the SEC rules contain an important exception for such disclosures. Any such disclosures, however, remain subject to SEC regulations regarding mergers and business combinations that predate SOx.

c. COMPREHENSIVE INCOME AND THE FUTURE

On page 380 [page 269 of the concise], replace the carryover paragraph starting on the bottom of the page with the following:

**   In 2005, the FASB and IASB completed deliberations on the first phase of the project, addressing what constitutes a complete set of financial statements and the requirements to present comparative information. As a result, the IASB revised international accounting standards to align with U.S. GAAP that now appears in FASB ASC Topic 220, *Comprehensive Income,* which codified SFAS No. 130, *Reporting Comprehensive Income.* As described more fully in our discussion regarding the on-going joint project on financial statement presentation in the next paragraph, FASB decided to wait until the second phase to publish an exposure draft. The Board, however, has tentatively decided that a business enterprise should report all items of revenue, expense, gain, and loss in a revised, single "statement of comprehensive income." This redesigned statement would supplant both the current income statement and the existing statement of comprehensive income. Ultimately, a complete set of financial statements may include the statements of financial position, comprehensive income, cash flows, and changes in equity.

**   In July 2009, while working on the second phase of their joint project on financial instruments, FASB and IASB reached a preliminary decision that an enterprise should present a single statement of comprehensive income. Currently, both U.S. GAAP and IFRS allow enterprises to display the components of net income and the components of other comprehensive income in separate financial statements. In fact, most enterprises report comprehensive income and the components of other comprehensive income on the statement of changes in owners' equity, however labeled. On May 26, 2010, FASB issued a proposed Accounting Standards Update, *Statement of*

Comprehensive Income, that would require enterprises to report all components of comprehensive income in a continuous financial statement that displays the components of both net income and other comprehensive income within comprehensive income. The comment period ends on September 30, 2010. COMPREHENSIVE INCOME (TOPIC 220), STATEMENT OF COMPREHENSIVE INCOME, Proposed Accounting Standards Update (Fin. Accounting Standards Bd. May 26, 2010), *available via* http://www.fasb.org/cs/ContentServer?c=Page&pagename=FASB%2FPage %2FSectionPage&cid=1175801893139; Fin. Accounting Standards Bd., Project Updates, Statement of—Joint Project of the IASB and FASB (June 1, 2010). Interested readers can access project updates via <http://www.fasb.org/jsp/FASB/Page/SectionPage&cid=1218220137074>.

On page 274 of the concise [no adjustment needed in the unabridged version], in the first line under the heading for "Activity Ratio," please note that we only discuss two (and not three) activity ratios, receivables turnover and inventory turnover. The discussion of the third, asset turnover, appears only in the unabridged version.

F.   MANAGEMENT'S DISCUSSION AND ANALYSIS

2.   COMPLIANCE WITH GAAP ALONE DOES NOT SATISFY MD&A REQUIREMENTS

On page 421, insert the following discussion after the first full paragraph [on page 286 of the concise, insert the following discussion after the third paragraph]:

In 2007, Tenet Healthcare Corporation ("Tenet") agreed to pay a $10 million civil penalty to settle SEC charges that, among other things, the company's MD&As misled the investing public. In particular, Tenet failed to disclose that the company had exploited a loophole in the Medicare reimbursement system related to so-called "outlier payments," designed to compensate hospitals for caring for extraordinarily sick Medicare patients. This unsustainable strategy allowed Tenet to report strong growth in revenues and earnings from 1999 to 2002. Once Tenet admitted that it could not sustain this strategy, its shares lost more than $11 billion in market value. Civil fraud charges remain pending against two former company executives, including Christi R. Sulzbach, the former general counsel and chief compliance officer. SEC v. Tenet Healthcare Corp., Accounting and Auditing Enforcement Release No. 2591 (Apr. 2, 2007), http://www.sec.gov/litigation/litreleases/2007/lr20067.htm.

3.   ENFORCEMENT ISSUES ARISING FROM LIQUIDITY PROBLEMS

On page 426, replace note 3 with the following new notes [on page 288 of the concise, replace the last paragraph in the section with the following discussion regarding SEC developments related to MD&A]:

**3. Even before the credit crisis, which has only highlighted the importance of discussions about liquidity in MD&A, SEC officials publicly stated that MD&A disclosure failures remained a top enforcement priority. In 2009, a jury returned a verdict in the SEC's favor on civil charges the agency filed against Kmart's former CEO for material misrepresentations and omissions about the company's liquidity in the MD&A section of Kmart's Form 10-Q for the third quarter and nine months ended October 31, 2001. The SEC's complaint alleged the company's former CEO and former CFO failed to disclose the reasons for a massive inventory overbuy in the summer of 2001 and the impact it had on the company's liquidity. In 2010, the district court ordered the former CEO to pay more than $10 million in disgorgement, prejudgment interest, and civil penalties. Kmart filed for bankruptcy in early 2002. The former CFO agreed to settle shortly before trial. SEC v. Conaway, Litigation Release No. 21438 (Mar. 5, 2010), http://www.sec.gov/litigation/litreleases/2010/lr21438.htm; SEC v. Conaway, Litigation Release No. 21065 (June 1, 2009), http://www.sec.gov/litigation/litreleases/2009/lr21065.htm; *see also* Michael Bologna, *Firms Getting Disclosure Message, But MD&A Still Enforcement Priority*, 38 Sec. Reg. & L. Rep. (BNA) 867 (May 15, 2006).

4. In March 2008, relatively early in the credit crisis, the SEC sent a letter to those public companies reporting significant amounts of asset-backed securities, loans carried at fair value, and derivative assets and liabilities. The letter, which highlighted the importance of describing liquidity issues in MD&A, outlined appropriate disclosures that now appear in FASB ASC Topic 820, *Fair Value Measurements and Disclosures,* and that SFAS No. 157, *Fair Value Measurements*, originally set forth. As described in detail in Chapter VI of this Supplement on pages 113 to 114, *infra*, FASB ASC Topic 820 provides a framework for companies to use in measuring assets and liabilities at fair value. The SEC letter encouraged public companies to include, in the MD&A section, disclosures on valuation techniques employed and how changes in the fair values of assets and liabilities could impact liquidity and capital resources. If a company uses material unobservable inputs to measure fair value, so-called "Level 3" inputs, the company should disclose how it determined those inputs. Other recommended disclosures include: the percentage of assets and liabilities measured at fair value using Level 3 inputs; the amount and reason for any material change in assets and liabilities measured with Level 3 inputs; and the nature and type of assets underlying any asset-backed securities. Sec. & Exch. Comm'n, Sample Letter Sent to Public Companies on MD&A Disclosure Regarding the Application of SFAS 157 (Mar. 2008), http://www.sec.gov/divisions/corpfin/guidance/fairvalueltr0308.htm.

In September 2008, at about the time that Lehman Brothers Holdings Inc. filed its bankruptcy petition, the Federal government bailed out American International Group, and Bank of America purchased Merrill Lynch & Co., the SEC sent a second reminder letter to the chief financial officers at certain public companies highlighting various disclosure issues related to fair value measurements that companies should consider in preparing their MD&As. The letter encouraged "clearer and more transparent disclosure regarding . . . fair value measurements, particularly with regard to financial instruments that are not currently actively traded and whose effects have had, or are reasonably likely to have, a material effect on your financial condition or results of operations." Sec. & Exch. Comm'n, Sample Letter Sent to Public Companies on MD&A Disclosure Regarding the Application of SFAS 157 (Fair Value Measurements) (Sept. 2008), http://www.sec.gov/divisions/corpfin/guidance/fairvalueltr0908.htm.

**   More recently, in August 2009, the SEC sent letters to the chief financial officers at certain public banks identifying disclosure issues financial institutions may wish to consider in preparing MD&A. The letter opines that while GAAP has not changed as to how to account for loan losses, "the current economic environment may require you to reassess whether the information upon which you base your accounting decisions remains accurate, reconfirm or reevaluate your accounting for these items, and reevaluate your [MD&A] disclosure." In particular, the letter offered disclosure suggestions regarding higher- risk loans, changes in practices to determine the allowance for loan losses, and declines in collateral value. Sec. & Exch. Comm'n, Sample Letter Sent to Public Companies on MD&A Disclosure Regarding Provisions and Allowances for Loan Losses (Aug. 2009), http://www.sec.gov/divisions/corpfin/guidance/loanlossesltr0809.htm.

G.   THE FUTURE OF FINANCIAL AND NON-FINANCIAL REPORTING

On page 427 [page 288 of the concise], replace the carryover sentence at the bottom of the page with the following text:

**In addition, and as described earlier in this chapter, *supra* at 60, the FASB and IASB continue their efforts on a joint project on financial statement presentation. As their objective, the rulemakers want to establish a standard to guide the way management organizes and presents information in the financial statements to users, such as present and potential equity investors, lenders, and other creditors. As core principles, the financial statements should convey information that (1) disaggregates information by activity into categories that enable users to predict the enterprise's future cash flows and (2) portrays a cohesive financial picture of the enterprise's activities, such that an obvious relationship exists between items across financial statements and that the enterprise's financial statements compliment each other as much as possible.

** In deliberations on the comments that the Boards received in response to discussion papers issued in October 2008 on the project, the Boards have tentatively concluded that enterprises should use separate sections to present business and financing activities, discontinued operations, and income taxes, separately, but cohesively, on the statements of financial position, comprehensive income, and cash flows. The concept of extraordinary items would no longer exist. The business sections should include separate categories for operating, investing, and financing arising from operating activities. The financing section should include debt and equity categories. Notably, the statement of cash flows would use the direct method, rather than the almost completely dominate indirect method, to present all cash flows, including operating cash flows. Finally, enterprises must analyze changes in all significant asset and liability line items, disaggregating changes arising from six different components. Cash inflows and outflows, repetitive and routine noncash--or accrual--transactions, and nonroutine or nonrepetitive noncash transactions or events comprise the first three components. In addition, enterprises must distinguish changes resulting from accounting allocations, such as depreciation; accounting provisions or reserves, such as bad debts or obsolete inventory; and remeasurements, such as changes in fair value. The Boards hope the redesigned statements will better reflect how businesses actually operate and prevent undue fixation on any one measure, such as net income. Critics to the proposal have complained about the potential increase in the number of line items in the proposed financial statements and have questioned the costs arising from a transition to a new system of financial reporting, especially those related to the direct method for presenting operating cash flows. *See* Fin. Accounting Standards Bd., Project Updates, Financial Statement Presentation--Joint Project of the IASB and FASB (July 1, 2010), including Appendix--Summary of tentative decisions to date (as of Apr. 22, 2010); *see also* Stephen Bouvier, *Accounting Preparers Voice Concerns About Statement Presentation Proposals*, Sec. L. Daily (BNA), Apr. 2, 2009. Interested readers can access project updates via <http://www.fasb.org/jsp/FASB/Page/SectionPage&cid= 1218220137074>.

On page 428 [omitted from the concise], in the carryover paragraph starting on the bottom of the page, "mid-2206" should read "mid-2006."

On page 429, insert the following new text after the carryover paragraph ending on the top of the page [on page 289 of the concise, note these developments related to XBRL in the discussion of the future of financial reporting]:

Based on the success of the SEC's pilot program, in which more than 100 companies ultimately participated, the Commission issued a final rule in early 2009 that obligates public companies to provide their financial statements to the Commission and on their corporate web sites in interactive data format using XBRL. After the SEC announced the completion of the

XBRL "taxonomy," or the standardized collection of more than 13,000 "tags" used to identify pieces of data, for U.S. GAAP in late 2007, the SEC proposed the mandatory use of XBRL in May 2008.

**   The new rules required domestic and foreign companies with more than $5 billion in market capitalization and that use U.S. GAAP, or approximately the 500 largest public companies in the United States, to begin using XBRL for financial statements for quarterly or annual fiscal periods ending on or after June 15, 2009, with delayed phase-in rules for other companies. Other large accelerated filers, whose market capitalizations equal or exceed $700 million, which did not exceed the $5 billion threshold, must comply with the new rule for their financial reports for periods ending on or after June 15, 2010. Companies with market capitalizations below $700 million, the so-called "non-accelerated filers," need not use XBRL until their reporting periods ending on or after June 15, 2011. In each case, the new rule gradually phases-in the required level of detail in the tags and allows a thirty-day grace period during the first two years. Companies can "block tag" the notes to the financial statements and any schedules for the first year that an enterprise uses XBRL. In later years, companies must tag the detailed quantitative disclosures in the notes and any schedules.

The SEC believes that XBRL will make financial data more useful to investors because the technology allows them to download the information from the financial statements directly into spreadsheets, analyze it using commercial off-the-shelf software, or use the information within investment models in other software formats. As additional benefits, XBRL reporting may help public companies automate regulatory filings and business information processing. Such automation could increase the speed and accuracy of financial disclosure, reduce compliance costs, and provide new information to management to analyze operations. *See* Interactive Data To Improve Financial Reporting, 74 Fed. Reg. 6776 (Feb. 10, 2009) (to be codified at 17 C.F.R. §§ 229, 230, 232, 239, 240, 249), *available at* http://www.sec.gov/rules/final/2009/33-9002fr.pdf.

In addition to formalizing arrangements to modernize the online EDGAR filing database to accommodate the XBRL format, the SEC has announced plans to replace the EDGAR system with the Interactive Data Electronic Application ("IDEA") system. The SEC expects that IDEA will facilitate the use and analysis of information submitted to the agency in interactive data format and allow quick comparisons of different companies or various fiscal periods. *See* Malini Manickavasagam, *Cox Unveils SEC's Plan to Replace EDGAR with New, Interactive, XBRL-Based System*, 6 Corp. Accountability Rep. (BNA) 882 (Aug. 22, 2008).

**   FASB's decision to approve the Codification as the single source of authoritative GAAP beginning on July 1, 2009, meant that most non-SEC references in the *XBRL US GAAP Taxonomy 2009* no longer apply. After that decision, three developments merit mention. First, the publisher, XBRL US, Inc., promptly provided an additional taxonomy database that supplements the 2009 taxonomy and allows users to access the Codification references. Second, the Codification itself now provides a list of all XBRL elements that contain an electronic link to each paragraph in a Codification. Finally, the FAF has announced that the 2011 release will include the latest Codification references. For additional developments regarding FASB efforts to link XBRL to the Codification, interested readers can access project updates, listed under the heading "Other technical activities," via <http://www.fasb.org/jsp/FASB/Page/SectionPage&cid=1218220137074>.

** On the international front, the IASCF has released *IFRS Taxonomy 2010*, which for the first time translates both IFRS and IRFS for small and medium-sized entities, as issued at January 1, 2010, into XBRL and replaces *IFRS Taxonomy 2009*. Press Release, Int'l Acct. Standards Bd, IASC Foundation releases IFRS Taxonomy 2010 (April 30, 2010), http://www.iasb.org/News/XBRL/IASC+Foundation+releases+IFRS+Taxonomy+2010.htm?m=print.

CHAPTER V

LEGAL ISSUES INVOLVING SHAREHOLDERS' EQUITY AND THE BALANCE SHEET

A. IMPORTANCE TO LAWYERS

On page 432 [page 292 of the concise] at the end of first full paragraph, insert the following text:

Similarly, and especially during the credit crisis, lawyers should recognize that regulators may apply completely different rules when assessing whether the decision of a financial institution's board of directors to declare a dividend leaves the regulated institution in an unsafe and unsound condition to transact business.

C. DISTRIBUTIONS AND LEGAL RESTRICTIONS

1. DIVIDENDS AND REDEMPTIONS

On page 440 [omitted from the concise], replace the last three sentences of text in the first paragraph, along with the related citations, with the following text:

**In 2006, Microsoft enlarged its buyback plans, launching a $20 billion tender offer to repurchase its shares and announcing a program to spend another $20 billion to redeem shares by 2011. Robert A. Guth, *Microsoft Buyback Falls Short of Goal But May Bode Well*, WALL ST. J., Aug. 19, 2006, at B1. Companies in the S&P 500, again a listing which tracks 500 large public companies, paid out $196.2 billion in dividends during 2009, a record $52 billion decrease from the all-time peak $247.9 billion in dividends during 2008. Standard & Poor's Index Services expects companies in the S&P 500 to pay $210.8 billion in dividends in 2010. Peter A. McKay, *Dividends Take to the Comeback Trail*, WALL ST. J., Mar. 22, 2010, at C1; Paul Vigna & John Shipman, *Dividends Lag Behind Upturn*, WALL ST. J., Feb. 10, 2010, at B7. These same companies paid a record $597.8 billion more to repurchase their own shares during 2007, but such buybacks dropped 42 percent in 2008 to about $342 billion and then plunged another almost 74 percent to just $89.7 billion in 2009. Liam Denning, *New American Cash Conundrum: Too Much*, WALL ST. J., Jan. 21, 2010, at C16; Kerry E. Grace & Rob Curran, *Stock*

Buybacks Plummet, Wall St. J., Mar. 27, 2009, at C9. Unless Congress passes additional legislation, the statutory tax rates on dividends will increase to a maximum 39.6 percent in 2011, while the maximum statutory rate on long term capital gains rises to a more modest 20 percent.

**   In March 2010, Starbucks announced that its board of directors had approved a $0.10 per share quarterly cash dividend. The company paid its first dividend on April 23, 2010 to shareholders on record at the close of business on April 7. In addition, the board also authorized Starbucks to repurchase 15 million shares of common stock, which added to the 6.3 million shares that the company could repurchase under previous authorizations. Press Release, Starbucks Corp., Starbucks Announces First Ever Cash Dividend; Authorizes Additional Share Buyback (Mar. 24, 2010), http://news.starbucks.com/article_display.cfm?article_id=341.

2.   Stock Dividends and Stock Splits

On page 442 [omitted from the concise], insert the following text at the end of the second full paragraph:

**More recently, Berkshire Hathaway split those new Class B shares fifty-to-one in 2010 in connection with the company's plan to purchase the railroad company Burlington Northern Santa Fe Corp. The stock split, which significantly reduced the market price per share, also enabled Standard & Poor's to include the shares in the S&P 500, coincidentally replacing the railroad's shares in the index and creating increased demand for the Class B shares. Scott Patterson, *Berkshire Hathaway Shares Added to the S&P 500 Index*, Wall St. J., Jan. 26, 2010, at C4.

3.   Restrictions on Corporate Distributions

a.   STATUTORY RESTRICTIONS

(2) Creditors' Rights Statutes

On page 460 [omitted from the concise], add the following citation at the end of the second paragraph:

For a recent article discussing the "balance sheet," "unreasonably small capital," and "ability to pay debts" tests and offering practical suggestions for counsel seeking to prove solvency and defending against litigation asserting a fraudulent conveyance, see Robert J. Stearn, Jr., *Proving Solvency: Defending Preference and Fraudulent Transfer Litigation*, 62 Bus. Law. 359 (2007).

b. CONTRACTUAL RESTRICTIONS

On page 473 [omitted from the concise], replace the last sentence in the first paragraph in this section with the following discussion:

Indeed, every once in a while, a corporation's articles will contain a clause regarding distributions. These provisions can specifically prohibit, or require, distributions in certain situations. In one recent case, the Ninth Circuit cited the unabridged fourth edition on several occasions in an opinion that interpreted a corporation's articles of organization. Affirming the district court's decision granting summary judgment for a preferred shareholder, the appellate court concluded that because the corporation's net worth exceeded $5 million, determined in accordance with GAAP and as shown on the relevant balance sheet, the articles required the corporation to redeem certain preferred shares. Bolt v. Merrimack Pharm., Inc., 503 F.3d 913, 915-17 (9th Cir. 2007).

On page 476 [on page 306 of the concise], at the end of the carryover paragraph, insert the following new paragraphs:

In connection with the recent scandals involving backdated stock options, numerous companies delayed filing financial statements with the SEC until they could complete internal investigations. In response, bondholders declared technical defaults and either demanded immediate repayment or charged additional fees, sometimes in the millions of dollars, to extend the default deadlines. In 2006, for example, Mercury Interactive Corp., one of the first companies implicated in the stock options scandals, agreed to pay $7.1 million to creditors and granted an option, which could have potentially cost the company an additional $40.2 million, to redeem certain notes at a premium to avoid default on certain bonds. Peter Lattman & Karen Richardson, *Hedge Funds Play Hardball With Firms Filing Late Financials*, WALL ST. J., Aug. 29, 2006, at A1 (also describing other recent examples involving companies that missed SEC deadlines after accounting woes).

Before the recent credit crisis began in 2007, the financial markets witnessed a steady erosion in covenants in debt agreements, a trend that accelerated in early 2006. *The Wall Street Journal* has reported that in the late 1990s, the traditional secured loan contained between three and six so-called "maintenance tests," which required the borrower to meet certain performance targets. By 2006, however, the safest secured loans typically contained fewer than three covenants. At least in partial response to the trend toward so-called "covenant-lite" loan agreements, the credit crisis and concerns about voluntary issuer actions that erode bondholder value, such as debt-financed distributions, more than fifty large lenders banded together to form the Credit Roundtable. In late-2007 that organization issued a white paper setting forth certain model covenants that the group would like borrowers to include in bond indentures. Credit Roundtable, Improving Covenant Protections in the Investment Grade Bond Market (Dec. 17, 2007), http://www.creditroundtable.org/Article.aspx?EID=40037; *see also* Cynthia

Koons, *Risky Business: Growth of 'Covenant-Lite' Debt*, WALL ST. J., June 18, 2007, at C2. As the credit crisis has deepened, lenders have toughened loan terms, including restrictive covenants.

D. DRAFTING & NEGOTIATING AGREEMENTS & OTHER LEGAL DOCUMENTS CONTAINING ACCOUNTING TERMINOLOGY AND CONCEPTS

On pages 500 to 506, replace Note 4 with the following [on pages 313-16 of the concise, replace Note 3 with the following new notes, numbered for the unabridged edition]:

4. Some covenants require borrowers to supply lenders or indenture trustees with financial statements and related information within a certain period, typically fifteen days, after filing periodic reports with the SEC. Disagreements have arisen in at least two different circumstances.

First, does the failure to submit timely filings to the SEC breach the loan agreement? Trial courts have reached opposite conclusions on this question. *Compare* Bank of N.Y. v. BearingPoint, Inc., No. 600169/06, 824 N.Y.S.2d 752 (unpublished table decision), 2006 WL 2670143 (N.Y. Sup. Ct. Sept. 18, 2006), *appeal withdrawn*, No. M-6818X, 2007 N.Y. App. Div. LEXIS 524 (N.Y. App. Div. Jan. 16, 2007) (granting the indenture bank trustee's motion for summary judgment, holding the agreement "unambiguously obligates BearingPoint to make the required SEC filings," finding the company liable for breach of contract, and ruling that trial would determine the amount of damages arising from the breach), *with* Cyberonics, Inc. v. Wells Fargo Bank, N.A., No. H-07-121, 2007 WL 1729977 (S.D. Tex. June 13, 2007) (granting borrower Cyberonics' motion for summary judgment because the indenture agreement only required delivery of copies of documents that the borrower had actually filed with the SEC and setting a timetable for Cyberonics to file an affidavit in support of its request for attorneys' fees and for the bank to respond to that affidavit). To date, the federal appellate courts have uniformly affirmed decisions granting summary judgments to the issuer. *See, e.g.*, Affiliated Computer Servs., Inc. v. Wilmington Trust Co., 565 F.3d 924 (5th Cir. 2009) (affirming district court order granting summary judgment for borrower because neither the indenture nor the Trust Indenture Act required the borrower to file timely reports with the SEC); UnitedHealth Group Inc. v. Wilmington Trust Co., 548 F.3d 1124 (8th Cir. 2008) (similarly affirming district court's grant to summary judgment for the issuer).

In *Cyberonics*, the district court observed that if "the parties desired to impose a filing obligation rather than a delivery obligation, they could have easily done so." Cyberonics, Inc. v. Wells Fargo Bank, N.A., No. H-07-121, 2007 WL 1729977, at *4 (S.D. Tex. June 13, 2007). Prudent lawyers for lenders and indenture trustees will follow that advice. Interestingly, BearingPoint ultimately reached an agreement with its bondholders that waived the requirement that the company file reports with the SEC, but increased the interest rate on the obligations "by an amount ranging from 0.1 to 0.85 percentage points." *BearingPoint Reaches Deal With Bondholders*, WASH. POST, Nov. 4, 2006, at D01. Thanks in part to the recent stock option scandals and during an eighteen-month period in 2006 and 2007, missed deadlines for filing periodic reports forced at least twenty-five companies to redeem bonds on an accelerated basis or to pay multimillion dollar fees for waivers. Peter Lattman & Karen Richardson, *Hedge Funds Play Hardball With Firms Filing Late Financials*, WALL ST. J., Aug. 29, 2006, at A1.

Second, what happens if the SEC's filing requirements no longer apply to the borrower? In its recent white paper on improving covenant protections, the Credit Roundtable observed that "[o]n more than a few occasions in recent years, issuers of investment grade bonds have withdrawn from the periodic reporting requirements" in the federal securities laws. Credit Roundtable, Improving Covenant Protections in the Investment Grade Bond Market 6 (Dec. 17, 2007), http://www.creditroundtable.org/Article.aspx?EID=40037. In an effort to ensure that bondholders can obtain reasonable access to financial information about an issuer for as long as its bonds remain outstanding, the Roundtable has proposed a model covenant. *Id.* at 6, 21-23 (rider 4).

**5. The Codification changes the way knowledgeable lawyers reference accounting principles and promulgations in legal documents. References to now superseded accounting pronouncements indicate that person who prepared the document qualifies as either careless or "accounting-challenged."

6. Given the devastating effects that changes in accounting principles can cause in restrictive covenants and other legal documents, lawyers should try to stay abreast of the movement toward IFRS in the United States, as well as pay attention to the agendas at both the FASB and the IASB. In that regard, we highlight several recent developments and areas to watch that potentially affect topics covered in the first five chapters.

(a) *International accounting principles.* Imagine a restrictive covenant based on financial results under an accounting system that suddenly converts to new rules. On January 1, 2005, many lawyers representing public companies in the European Union faced that exact scenario, when an EU regulation took effect that required all listed companies to use IFRS to prepare consolidated financial statements for fiscal years beginning on or after January 1, 2005. As a result, lawyers in the United States already need to consider IFRS in transactions with EU companies and their subsidiaries.

**   As discussed earlier on page 9, *supra*, in early 2010 the SEC issued a statement reaffirming the agency's belief that a single set of high-quality globally accepted accounting standards would benefit U.S. investors. In addition, the statement expressed the SEC's continued support for efforts to converge U.S. GAAP and IFRS and announced that before the end of 2011, the SEC expects to decide whether to incorporate IFRS into the financial reporting system in the United States. In the meantime, U.S. lawyers will also need to monitor FASB developments as convergence continues to cause changes in U.S. GAAP. As mentioned earlier on page 13, *supra*, FASB and IASB have been meeting together each month to work on various projects intended to converge accounting principles world-wide.

**   Notwithstanding lingering doubts about whether the SEC will require, or allow, public companies in the United States to file financial statements using IFRS, the almost certain likelihood remains that the industrialized world will soon embrace some system of global accounting standards. This likelihood deserves serious consideration, especially when drafting or negotiating agreements involving enterprises interested in cross-border securities listings. In this regard, note that the audit report that appears on page 76 of the Starbuck's 2005 Form 10-K in Appendix A of the text, refers to "accounting principles generally accepted in the United States of America." As a result, GAAP in this country could potentially become APGAUS. In addition, please observe that the same audit report also refers to "the standards of the Public Company Accounting Oversight Board (United States)." *Id.*

(b) *Fair value and related accounting issues related to the credit crisis.* In recent years, FASB has been gradually moving away from the so-called mixed-attribute accounting model that generally uses historical cost to an across-the-board, fair value-based alternative that IASB has espoused, which would require enterprises to report all financial assets and liabilities at fair value. As described on page 298 of the unabridged fourth edition [page 206 of the concise], FASB recently issued a new concepts statement that sets forth discounted future cash flows and present value as the basis for various accounting measurements. The concepts statement, plus FASB ASC Topic 820, *Fair Value Measurements and Disclosures*, which codified SFAS No. 157 on fair value measurements, and the on-going joint effort between FASB and IASB to develop a conceptual framework and to converge global accounting principles, will presumably eventually lead to new or revised accounting standards that would modify the amounts at which various assets and liabilities appear on the balance sheet and establish rules for how changes in those amounts would affect the financial statements. Accordingly, fair value accounting could over the next several years significantly affect many financial ratios and, indeed, the entire framework for financial accounting. While the fair value rules have attracted considerable attention during the credit crisis, proposed changes related to off-balance sheet reporting and loan losses could potentially prove even more significant to balance sheets.

(c) *Derivatives, Hedge Accounting, and the Fair Value Option.* FASB ASC Topic 815, *Derivatives and Hedging*, which codified SFAS No. 133, *Accounting for Derivative Instruments and Hedging Activities*, generally requires enterprises to show derivatives–a term which you may recall describes financial contracts that derive their value from some underlying asset–as either assets or liabilities on the balance sheet, to measure those instruments at fair value, and to include the changes in those fair values during a period in earnings as either gains or losses. Before this pronouncement, literally trillions of dollars of derivatives contracts and changes in the value of those contracts did not appear in financial statements. In public statements about the 1998 financial crisis involving Long-Term Capital Management L.P. ("LTCM"), then-chairperson of the Commodity Futures Trading Commission Brooksley Born noted that at the time of its near collapse, LTCM held derivative positions with a notional value of $1.25 trillion, more than 1,000 times the firm's capital and significantly greater than its debt-equity ratio of 100-to-1. Michael Bologna, *LTCM Crisis Shows Need for Better Controls Over OTC Derivatives Markets, Born Says*, 30 Sec. Reg. & L. Rep. (BNA) 1514 (Oct. 16, 1998). In a May 2009 article, *The Wall Street Journal* sized the total derivatives market at $684 trillion. Serena Ng, *Banks Seek Role in Bid to Overhaul Derivatives*, WALL ST. J., May 29, 2009, at C1. Derivatives, specifically credit default swaps, led to AIG's collapse and governmental bailout in 2008.

Even before AIG's collapse, users of financial statements complained that despite the recent increase in the use and complexity of derivative instruments and hedging activities, the financial accounting rules set forth in SFAS No. 133, and now codified in FASB ASC Topic 815, *Derivatives and Hedging*, did not provide adequate information about how such instruments and activities affect an enterprise's financial position, financial performance, and cash flows. In March 2008, the FASB issued a new pronouncement, effective for financial statements issued for fiscal years and interim periods beginning after November 15, 2008, with early application encouraged, that requires an enterprise to provide enhanced disclosures about derivative instruments and hedging activities. FASB ASC Topic 815 now requires an enterprise to disclose how and why the enterprise uses derivative instruments, how the enterprise accounts for derivative instruments and hedged items, and how those instruments and items affect an enterprise's financial position, financial performance, and cash flows. FASB ASC § 815-10-50 (a codification of DISCLOSURES ABOUT DERIVATIVE INSTRUMENTS AND HEDGING ACTIVITIES (AN AMENDMENT OF FASB STATEMENT NO. 133), Statement of Fin. Accounting Standards No. 161 (Fin. Accounting Standards Bd. 2008)).

FASB ASC Topic 815 authorizes an exception to the general rules for so-called "hedges," or derivatives designed to avoid exposure to various risks, such as changes in interest rates or fluctuation in foreign currency exchange rates. Under the complex hedge accounting rules, an enterprise need not report any changes in value in certain hedges on the income statement, a treatment which translates to more predictable earnings. To qualify for hedge accounting, however, enterprises must meet stringent rules, including various documentation requirements. *The Wall Street Journal* has reported that at least forty companies, including General Electric Co., restated their financial statements during 2005 to correct problems with hedge accounting.

Under current accounting rules, a company that cannot or does not use hedge accounting and wants to protect itself against a change in the value of a financial instrument, such as a fixed-rate loan to a third-party, must carry the loan on its books at the historical cost, while those same rules require the company to use fair value to account for any derivative that hedges the fixed-rate loan against changes in interest rates. A decline in interest rates could drop the derivative's value, while at the same time increasing the fair value of the fixed-rate loan. Because the company must reduce earnings for the decline in the derivative's value, but cannot recognize any income for the offsetting increase in the loan's fair value, which remains on the company's books at historical cost, such swings in value affect reported net income.

As described in the materials related to page 76 in Chapter I of the unabridged fourth edition [page 56 of the concise], *supra* at 3, FASB recently adopted a rule that allows companies to elect to use "fair value" accounting for various financial assets. As a result, FASB ASC Topic 815, described in more detail in this Supplement in the materials for Chapter VI at pages 116-122, *infra*, grants enterprises an option to record many financial assets at fair value. The FASB expects the option to help companies avoid the complex compliance requirements necessary to qualify for fair value hedge accounting. Rather than designating and documenting a hedging relationship, enterprises can now apply the fair value option at the inception of the hedging relationship. In the example above, the Codification allows companies to record both the fixed-rate loan and the hedging derivative at their fair values. Once again, reporting such financial assets at their fair values and including their changes in earnings obviously affects numerous financial ratios and can cause, or cure, defaults in many contracts and lending agreements. James R. Hagerty & David Reilly, *Simply Put: Accounting-Rule Makers May Change How to Book Derivatives*, WALL ST. J., Feb. 23, 2006, at C1; Michael Rapoport, *Hedge Accounting Gets on Regulators' Radar*, WALL ST. J., Jan. 27, 2006, at C3.

(d) *Uncertain tax positions.* Under a new interpretation, described in more detail in materials for Chapter VI in this supplement, enterprises must record a liability for "unrecognized tax benefits," tax benefits claimed on tax returns which may not withstand scrutiny by taxing authorities. Most enterprises will record more tax liabilities than under previous practice. Analysts note that debt ratios may artificially increase as the liabilities recorded will likely exceed the cash ultimately paid to taxing authorities. The new approach may also overstate tax liabilities because a newly assessed tax can result in offsetting deductions or credits in other jurisdictions.

(e) *Noncontrolling interests.* In December 2007, FASB concluded a joint project with the IASB and issued a new standard that requires enterprises to present noncontrolling interests, including the minority interests described in Chapter I on page 144 of the unabridged fourth edition [page 117 of the concise] and earlier in this Supplement on page 6, *supra*, as equity, but separate from the parent shareholders' equity. As Note 11 on page 63 of Starbucks' 2005 Form 10-K in Appendix A of the text sets forth, Starbucks included $11,153,000 as "[m]inority interest liabilities" in "Other long-term liabilities" on the company's October 2, 2005 consolidated balance sheet.

Other companies currently report these amounts in the "mezzanine," or in a section between liabilities and equity on the balance sheet. The new rules, which apply to fiscal years, and interim periods within those fiscal years, beginning after December 14, 2008, will require Starbucks and these other companies to reclassify these minority interests as equity. FASB ASC ¶¶ 810-10-45-15 to -16 (codifications of SFAS No. 160). Yet again, the reclassifications that the new rules require could affect leverage and coverage ratios in loan agreements and other contracts.

(f) *Pensions.* In the early 2000s, the sharp decline in the stock market, which dropped three years in a row for the first time since before World War II, left many companies facing significant unfunded pension liabilities related to defined benefit plans, which entitle participants to a precisely determinable payment each period after retirement. If the investments in a defined benefit plan do not perform as expected, the employer must absorb any losses. (By comparison, a defined contribution plan requires the employer to pay a certain amount, typically a percentage of compensation up to certain limits, to an account established for the participant's benefit, but does not guarantee any specific benefits after an employee's retirement. As a result, the employee bears all investment losses.)

In the *Report and Recommendations Pursuant to Section 401(c) of the Sarbanes-Oxley Act of 2003 on Arrangements with Off-Balance Sheet Implications, Special Purpose Entities, and Transparency of Filings by Issuers*, the SEC staff identified accounting for defined pension plans as a topic that the FASB should add to its technical agenda, preferably in collaboration with the IASB. At the time, then-existing accounting rules enabled enterprises to report important information about pensions in the notes to the financial statements, rather than on their balance sheets. The SEC staff concluded that improved pension accounting could improve the quality and transparency of financial statements and eliminate inconsistent accounting treatment for pensions. After various industrial firms and airlines defaulted on their pension obligations and following requests from advisory groups and other constituencies to address the topic, FASB added a project to reconsider the accounting for postretirement benefit obligations, including pensions, to its agenda. Jonathan Weil, *FASB Votes to Revise Pension Rules*, WALL ST. J., Nov. 11, 2005, at C3; Jonathan Weil, *FASB to Evaluate Possible Overhaul Of Pension Rules*, WALL ST. J., Nov. 10, 2005, at C4.

During the project's first phase, FASB issued a pronouncement, SFAS No. 158, now codified in FASB ASC Topic 715, *Compensation--Retirement Benefits*, that requires enterprises to recognize the overfunded or underfunded status of their defined benefit postretirement plans as an asset or a liability on the balance sheet, rather than simply disclosing that amount in a note to the financial statements. These new accounting rules, along with recent tax law changes, have led numerous businesses to terminate, or close to new employees, their defined benefit plans. Generally effective to public companies with fiscal years ending after December 15, 2006 and to all other entities for their fiscal years ending after June 15, 2007, the new rules require an enterprise to measure the asset or liability as the difference between the fair value of plan assets and the projected benefit obligations, which include assumptions about inflation, employment longevity, and employee mortality. The promulgation also directed enterprises to record as an adjustment to the ending balance of accumulated other comprehensive income any previously unrecognized gains and losses and requires enterprises to report any changes in the net asset or liability in other comprehensive income. FASB ASC §§ 715-20-55, 715-30-55, 715-60-55 (codifications of EMPLOYERS' ACCOUNTING FOR DEFINED BENEFIT PENSION AND OTHER POSTRETIREMENT PLANS–AN AMENDMENT OF FASB STATEMENTS NO. 87, 88, 106, AND 132(R), Statement of Fin. Accounting Standards No. 158 (Fin. Accounting Standards Bd. 2006) & CONFORMING AMENDMENTS TO THE ILLUSTRATIONS IN FASB STATEMENTS NO. 87, NO. 88, AND NO. 106 AND TO THE RELATED STAFF IMPLEMENTATION GUIDES, FASB Staff Position No. FAS 158-1 (Fin. Accounting Standards Bd. 2007)).

As of January 1, 2006, *The Wall Street Journal* reported that companies in the Standard & Poor's 500-stock index faced $461 billion in underfunded postretirement liabilities, $140 billion in pensions and $321 billion in health-care obligations. As a result, the new rules increased liabilities and adversely affected debt-to-equity ratios for numerous companies, including some which needed to renegotiate lending agreements. Denise Lugo, *Practitioners Say New FASB Pension Rules Produce More Prominent Tax Implications*, 5 Corp. Accountability Rep. (BNA) 19 (Jan. 5, 2007); Ian McDonald, *Health Benefits Ail as Pensions Heal*, WALL ST. J., June 6, 2006, at C3; David Reilly, *FASB to Move Pension Accounting From Footnotes to Balance Sheets*, WALL ST. J., Mar. 31, 2006, at C3 (referencing a Standard & Poor's study).

In an effort to leverage FASB and IASB resources during the second phase, which will reconsider comprehensively the accounting for pensions and other postretirement benefits, FASB decided to start that phase separate from a parallel IASB project and to assess opportunities for convergence later. To enhance transparency as to the types and values of assets and associated risks in defined benefit pension plans and other postretirement plans, FASB ASC § 715-20-50, which codified FSP No. 132(R)-1, *Employers' Disclosures About Postretirement Benefit Plan Assets*, requires additional disclosures for fiscal years ending after December 15, 2009, with earlier application permitted. Although FASB's current technical plan lists this second phase as "not active," the project update states that FASB continues to monitor IASB's work to determine the next steps on this phase, which seeks to improve the quality of information provided to investors, creditors, employees, retirees, donors, and other users of financial statements. Fin. Accounting Standards Bd., Project Updates, Phase II: Postretirement Benefit Obligations, Including Pensions (Jan. 21, 2009). Interested readers can access and monitor project updates via <http://www.fasb.org/jsp/FASB/Page/SectionPage&cid=1218220137074>. Lawyers should keep these recent and potential changes in mind when drafting and negotiating legal agreements and remind clients to assess how pension assets and obligations could hinder distributions and affect loan covenants and other legal agreements.

(g) *Distinguishing liabilities and equity*. Some financial instruments, commonly referred to as *hybrid instruments*, contain both debt and equity characteristics. For example, *mandatorily redeemable preferred shares* obligate the issuer to repurchase the shares at particular times or under certain conditions. Just as different rules may apply for preparing financial statements or for determining the legality of distributions to owners, still other rules may apply for tax purposes. In that regard, *trust preferred stock* has historically qualified as equity for financial accounting purposes, but as debt for federal income tax purposes. Under the Internal Revenue Code, a corporate issuer can deduct interest on debt, but not amounts paid as dividends, in calculating taxable income. *See generally* Ellen Engel et al., *Debt-Equity Hybrid Securities*, J. ACCT. RES., Autumn 1999, at 249 (describing the structure, tax treatment and financial reporting treatment of trust preferred stock).

**   In 2003, FASB issued a new standard governing mandatorily redeemable preferred shares and certain other financial instruments, including put options that give a shareholder the right to sell shares back to the issuer for a fixed price. Whenever an issuer may need to repurchase its own shares in exchange for cash or other assets, FASB ASC Topic 480, *Distinguishing Liabilities from Equity*, which codified SFAS No. 150, *Accounting for Certain Financial Instruments with Characteristics of both Liabilities and Equity*, now requires the issuer to treat the financial instruments as liabilities, rather than as equity—the more typical result under previous accounting principles. Similarly, enterprises must treat payments or accruals of "dividends" on mandatorily redeemable preferred shares as interest on the income statement and statement of cash flows. FASB ASC ¶¶ 480-10-25-4, -8 (recognition), 480-10-45-1 (presentation), & 480-10-55-8 to -9 (trust preferred stock illustration) (codifications of SFAS No. 150, ¶¶ 9, 11, 18, A5). The new rules became effective at the start of the first interim period beginning after June 15, 2003, or in the case of private companies, at the start of the first interim period beginning after December 15, 2004. The FASB, however, deferred the effective date for certain mandatorily redeemable noncontrolling interests for both public and private companies. FASB ASC § 480-10-65 (a codification of EFFECTIVE DATE, DISCLOSURES, AND TRANSITION FOR MANDATORILY REDEEMABLE FINANCIAL INSTRUMENTS OF CERTAIN NONPUBLIC ENTITIES AND CERTAIN MANDATORILY REDEEMABLE NONCONTROLLING INTERESTS UNDER FASB STATEMENT NO. 150, FASB Staff Position No. FAS 150-3 (Fin. Accounting Standards Bd. 2003)).

**   In the second phase of this project, which FASB now describes as "Financial Instruments with Characteristics of Equity" and which also seeks to converge international accounting standards, FASB has decided to reconsider the rules for numerous financial instruments. Ultimately, FASB hopes to supersede the rules in FASB ASC Topic 480, which codified more than sixty pieces of literature that inconsistently address various aspects of accounting for financial instruments, with new standards that provide a single, comprehensive model for classifying all financial instruments. In

November 2007, FASB issued a preliminary views document on distinguishing between equity and liabilities or assets. The document proposed a basic ownership approach that would classify only the lowest residual interest in the entity, such as common stock in a corporation, as equity. PRELIMINARY VIEWS ON FINANCIAL INSTRUMENTS WITH CHARACTERISTICS OF EQUITY (Fin. Accounting Standards Bd. 2007), *available via* http://www.fasb.org/draft/index.shtml. Since the comment period ended on May 30, 2008, the Boards have been deliberating the draft principles that enterprises could use to distinguish between equity and liabilities and a related set of decision rules to apply those principles. The project encountered unexpected difficulties, however, when seven external reviewers offered about 600 comments on a draft accounting standards update. Denise Lugo, *FASB Project on Financial Instruments With Characteristics of Equity Hits Snag*, 42 Sec. Reg. & L. Rep. (BNA) 983 (May 17, 2010). In mid-2010, FASB's technical plan envisioned issuing an exposure draft with the IASB during the first quarter in 2011, potentially leading to a final document late in 2011. Interested readers can access and monitor project updates via < h t t p : / / w w w . f a s b . o r g / j s p / F A S B / P a g e / SectionPage&cid=1218220137074>. At this point, the project seems likely to cause enterprises to treat more financial instruments as liabilities than under the current rules. Recall that any required reclassifications could affect the ratios commonly contained in loan agreements and other contracts. *See* Michael Rapoport & Jonathan Weil, *More Truth-in-Labeling for Accounting Carries Liabilities*, WALL ST. J., Aug. 28, 2003, at C1.

To further illustrate the importance of both the accounting rules for financial instruments and this ongoing project, GAAP forced the Treasury Department to revise its $250 billion Capital Purchase Program under the EESA so that participating banks could treat the preferred shares and warrants sold to the government as equity for financial accounting purposes. The original "term sheet" stated that the Treasury could exchange the warrants purchased for senior debt if the selling bank lost its listing on a securities exchange. Under GAAP, such a conversion feature would have required the banks to treat the warrants as liabilities, rather than as equity, as the program intended. After altering the offer sheet, the Treasury Department obtained a letter from senior staff accountants at the SEC and the FASB stating that the staffs would not object if the participating banks treated the warrants as permanent equity. *See* Letter from James Kroeker, Deputy Chief Accountant, Sec. & Exch. Comm'n, & Russell Golden, Technical Dir., Fin. Accounting Standards Bd., to David G. Nason, Assistant Sec'y for Fin. Inst., U.S. Dep't of Treasury (Oct. 24, 2008), http://www.ustreas.gov/ press/releases/reports/secfasbletter.pdf; *see also* Steve Marcy, *Government Mulls Action to Resolve Accounting Issues Clouding Bank Bailout*, 6 Corp. Accountability Rep. (BNA) 1159 (Oct. 24, 2008).

We will identify other recent and potential developments potentially affecting contractual agreements and other legal documents in later chapters.

On page 512 [omitted from the concise], insert the following new problem:

Problem 5.6. The following excerpts come from a Credit Agreement dated as of August 12, 2005 among Starbucks Corporation and, among others, Bank of America, N.A. The entire agreement can be found at: http://www.sec.gov/Archives/edgar/data/829224/000095012405005008/v117 82exv10w1.txt

[Page 1]
CREDIT AGREEMENT

This CREDIT AGREEMENT ("Agreement") is entered into as of August 12, 2005, among STARBUCKS CORPORATION, a Washington corporation (the "Company"), each lender from time to time party hereto (collectively, the "Lenders" and individually, a "Lender"), and BANK OF AMERICA, N.A., as Administrative Agent, Swing Line Lender and L/C Issuer.

* * *

ARTICLE I.
DEFINITIONS AND ACCOUNTING TERMS

1.01 DEFINED TERMS. As used in this Agreement, the following terms will have the meanings set forth below:

* * *

[Page 3]
"Audited Financial Statements" means the audited consolidated balance sheet of the Company and its Subsidiaries for the fiscal year ended October 3, 2004, and the related consolidated statements of income or operations, shareholders' equity and cash flows for such fiscal year of the Company and its Subsidiaries, including the notes thereto.

* * *

[Page 7]
"Consolidated EBITDA" means, for any period, for the Company and its Subsidiaries on a consolidated basis, an amount equal to Consolidated Net Income for such period plus (a) the following to the extent deducted in calculating such Consolidated Net Income: (i) Consolidated Interest Charges for such period, (ii) the provision for Federal, state, local and foreign income taxes payable by the Company and its Subsidiaries for such period, (iii) depreciation and amortization expense and (iv) other expenses of the Company and its Subsidiaries reducing such Consolidated Net Income which do not represent a cash item in such period or any future period and minus (b) the following to the extent included in calculating such Consolidated Net Income: (i) Federal, state, local and foreign income tax credits of the Company and its Subsidiaries for such period and (ii) non-recurring gains

increasing Consolidated Net Income (or reducing net loss) which do not represent cash items for such period or any future period.

"Consolidated Fixed Charge Coverage Ratio" means, as of the end of any fiscal quarter, for the four fiscal quarters ending on such date, for the Company and its Subsidiaries on a consolidated basis, the ratio of (a) (i) Consolidated EBITDA during such period plus (iii) Operating Lease and Rental Expense during such period to (b) the sum of (x) Consolidated Interest Charges during such period plus, without duplication, (y) Operating Lease and Rental Expense during such period.

"Consolidated Interest Charges" means, for any period, for the Company and its Subsidiaries on a consolidated basis, the sum of (a) all interest, premium payments, debt discount, fees, charges and related expenses of the Company and its Subsidiaries in connection with borrowed money (including capitalized interest) or in connection with the deferred purchase price of assets, in each case to the extent treated as interest in accordance with GAAP, and (b) [page 8] the portion of rent expense of the Company and its Subsidiaries with respect to such period under capital leases that is treated as interest in accordance with GAAP.

"Consolidated Net Income" means, for any period, for the Company and its Subsidiaries on a consolidated basis, the net income of the Company and its Subsidiaries (excluding extraordinary gains but including extraordinary losses) for that period.

"Consolidated Total Assets" means, as of the date of determination, the total assets of the Company and its Subsidiaries which would be shown as assets on a consolidated balance sheet of the Company as of such time prepared in accordance with GAAP.

* * *

[page 12]
"GAAP" means generally accepted accounting principles in the United States set forth in the opinions and pronouncements of the Accounting Principles Board and the American Institute of Certified Public Accountants and statements and pronouncements of the Financial Accounting Standards Board or such other principles as may be approved by a significant segment of the accounting profession in the United States, that are applicable to the circumstances as of the date of determination, consistently applied.

* * *

[page 13]
"Indebtedness" means, as to any Person at a particular time, without duplication, all of the following, whether or not included as indebtedness or liabilities in accordance with GAAP:

(a) all obligations of such Person for borrowed money and all obligations of such Person evidenced by bonds, debentures, notes, loan agreements or other similar instruments;

(b) all direct or contingent obligations of such Person arising under letters of credit (including standby and commercial), bankers' acceptances, bank guaranties, surety bonds and similar instruments;

(c) net obligations of such Person under any Swap Contract;

[page 14]

(d) all obligations of such Person to pay the deferred purchase price of property or services (other than trade accounts payable in the ordinary course of business and, in each case, not past due for more than 90 days after the date on which such trade account payable was created);

(e) indebtedness (excluding prepaid interest thereon) secured by a Lien on property owned or being purchased by such Person (including indebtedness arising under conditional sales or other title retention agreements), whether or not such indebtedness will have been assumed by such Person or is limited in recourse;

(f) capital leases and Synthetic Lease Obligations;

(g) all obligations of such Person to purchase, redeem, retire, defease or otherwise make any payment in respect of any Equity Interest in such Person or any other Person, valued, in the case of a redeemable preferred interest, at the greater of its voluntary or involuntary liquidation preference plus accrued and unpaid dividends; and

(h) all Guarantees of such Person in respect of any of the foregoing.

For all purposes hereof, the Indebtedness of any Person will include the Indebtedness of any partnership or joint venture (other than a joint venture that is itself a corporation or limited liability company) in which such Person is a general partner or a joint venturer, unless such Indebtedness is expressly made non-recourse to such Person. The amount of any net obligation under any Swap Contract on any date will be deemed to be the Swap Termination Value thereof as of such date. The amount of any capital lease or Synthetic Lease Obligation as of any date will be deemed to be the amount of Attributable Indebtedness in respect thereof as of such date.

* * *

[page 15]
"Internal Control Event" means a material weakness in, or fraud that involves management or other employees who have a significant role in, the Company's internal controls over financial reporting, in each case as described in the Securities Laws.

* * *

[page 17]

"Operating Lease and Rental Expense" means, for any period, all operating lease expense and all other rental expense incurred by the Company and its Subsidiaries during such period.

* * *

[page 24]

1.03 ACCOUNTING TERMS. (a) Generally. All accounting terms not specifically or completely defined herein will be construed in conformity with, and all financial data (including financial ratios and other financial calculations) required to be submitted pursuant to this Agreement will be prepared in conformity with, GAAP applied on a consistent basis, as in effect from time to time, applied in a manner consistent with that used in preparing the Audited Financial Statements, except as otherwise specifically prescribed herein.

(b) Changes in GAAP. If at any time any change in GAAP would affect the computation of any financial ratio or requirement set forth in any Loan Document, and either the Company or the Required Lenders will so request, the Administrative Agent, the Lenders and the Company will negotiate in good faith to amend such ratio or requirement to preserve the original intent thereof in light of such change in GAAP (subject to the approval of the Required Lenders); provided that, until so amended, (i) such ratio or requirement will continue to be computed in accordance with GAAP prior to such change therein and (ii) the Company will provide to the Administrative Agent and the Lenders financial statements and other documents required under this Agreement or as reasonably requested hereunder setting forth a reconciliation between calculations of such ratio or requirement made before and after giving effect to such change in GAAP.

* * *

[page 60]
ARTICLE V.
REPRESENTATIONS AND WARRANTIES

* * *

[page 61]

5.05 FINANCIAL STATEMENTS; NO MATERIAL ADVERSE EFFECT; NO INTERNAL CONTROL EVENT.

(a) The Audited Financial Statements (i) were prepared in accordance with GAAP consistently applied throughout the period covered thereby, except as otherwise expressly noted therein; (ii) fairly present the financial condition of the Company and its Subsidiaries as of the date thereof and their results of operations for the period covered thereby in accordance with GAAP consistently applied throughout the period covered thereby, except as otherwise expressly noted therein; and (iii) show all material indebtedness and other material liabilities, direct or contingent, of the Company and its Subsidiaries as of the date thereof.

(b) The unaudited consolidated balance sheet of the Company and its Subsidiaries dated April 3, 2005, and the related consolidated statements of income or operations, shareholders' equity and cash flows for the fiscal quarter ended on that date (i) were prepared in accordance with GAAP consistently applied throughout the period covered thereby, except as otherwise expressly noted therein, and (ii) fairly present the financial condition of the Company and its Subsidiaries as of the date thereof and their results of operations for the period covered thereby, subject, in the case of clauses (i) and (ii), to the absence of footnotes and to normal year-end audit adjustments. Schedule 5.05 sets forth all material indebtedness and other material liabilities, direct or contingent, of the Company and its consolidated Subsidiaries as of the date of such financial statements.

[page 62]
(c) Since the date of the Audited Financial Statements, there has been no event or circumstance, either individually or in the aggregate, that has had or could reasonably be expected to have a Material Adverse Effect.

* * *

[page 65]
ARTICLE VI.
AFFIRMATIVE COVENANTS

So long as any Lender will have any Commitment hereunder, any Loan or other Obligation hereunder will remain unpaid or unsatisfied, or any Letter of Credit will remain outstanding, the Company will, and will (except in the case of the covenants set forth in Sections 6.01, 6.02, and 6.03) cause each Subsidiary to:

6.01 FINANCIAL STATEMENTS. Deliver to the Administrative Agent and each Lender, in form and detail satisfactory to the Administrative Agent and the Required Lenders:

(a) as soon as available, but in any event within 90 days after the end of each fiscal year of the Company (commencing with the fiscal year ending October 2, 2005), a consolidated balance sheet of the Company and its Subsidiaries as of the end of such fiscal year, and the related consolidated statements of income or operations, shareholders' equity and cash flows for such fiscal year, setting forth in each case in comparative form the figures for the previous fiscal year, all in reasonable detail and prepared in accordance with GAAP, audited and accompanied by a report and opinion of a Registered Public Accounting Firm of nationally recognized standing as to whether such financial statements are free of material misstatement, which report and opinion will be prepared in accordance with audit standards of the Public Company Accounting Oversight Board and will not be subject to any "going concern" or like qualification or exception or any qualification or exception as to the scope of such audit or with respect to the absence of material misstatement; and

(b) as soon as available, but in any event within 45 days after the end of each of the first three fiscal quarters of each fiscal year of the Company (commencing with the fiscal quarter ending January 1, 2006), a consolidated balance sheet of the Company and its Subsidiaries as of the end of such fiscal quarter, and the related consolidated statements of income or operations, shareholders' equity and cash flows for such fiscal quarter and for the portion of the Company's fiscal year then ended, setting forth in each case in comparative form the figures for the corresponding fiscal quarter of the previous fiscal year and the corresponding portion of the previous fiscal year, all in reasonable detail, certified by a Responsible Officer of the Company as fairly presenting the financial condition, results of operations, shareholders' equity and cash flows of the Company and its Subsidiaries in accordance with GAAP, subject only to normal year-end audit adjustments and the absence of footnotes.

As to any information contained in materials furnished pursuant to Section 6.02(c), the Company will not be separately required to furnish such information under clause (a) or (b) above, but the [page 66]foregoing will not be in derogation of the obligation of the Company to furnish the information and materials described in clauses (a) and (b) above at the times specified therein.

6.02 CERTIFICATES; OTHER INFORMATION. Deliver to the Administrative Agent and each Lender, in form and detail satisfactory to the Administrative Agent and the Required Lenders:

(a) (A) management's assessment of the effectiveness of the Company's internal control over financial reporting as of the end of the Company's most recent fiscal year for which such assessment was required in accordance with Item 308 of SEC Regulation S-K expressing a conclusion as to which the Required Lenders reasonably do not object, and (B) with respect to the most recent fiscal year of the Company for which such assessment was required, an attestation report (or reports) of a Registered Public Accounting Firm on management's assessment and the opinion of the Registered Public Accounting Firm independently assessing the effectiveness of the Company's internal control over financial reporting in accordance with Item 308 of SEC Regulation S-K, PCAOB Auditing Standard No. 2, and Section 404 of Sarbanes-Oxley expressing a conclusion as to which the Required Lenders reasonably do not object;

* * *

[page 67]

6.03 NOTICES. Promptly notify the Administrative Agent and each Lender:

* * *

[page 68]

(d) of any material change in accounting policies or financial reporting practices by the Company or any Subsidiary;

(e) of the occurrence of any Internal Control Event;

* * *

[page 69]

6.09 BOOKS AND RECORDS. Maintain proper books of record and account, in which full, true and correct entries in conformity with GAAP consistently applied will be made of all financial transactions and matters involving the assets and business of the Company or such Subsidiary, as the case may be.

* * *

ARTICLE VII.
NEGATIVE COVENANTS

So long as any Lender will have any Commitment hereunder, any Loan or other Obligation hereunder will remain unpaid or unsatisfied, or any Letter of Credit will remain outstanding, the Company in Section 7.01 and Sections 7.03 through 7.06 will not, nor will it permit or allow any Subsidiary in any section of this Article VII to, directly or indirectly:

* * *

[page 72]

7.06 CONSOLIDATED FIXED CHARGE COVERAGE RATIO. Permit the Consolidated Fixed Charge Coverage Ratio as of the last day of any period of four consecutive fiscal quarters of the Company to be less than 2.50 to 1.00.

* * *

[page S-14]

[The Schedules references in the table of contents have been omitted for purposes of this filing, but will be furnished supplementally to the Securities and Exchange Commission upon request.]

* * *

[page E-3]
SCHEDULE 2
TO THE COMPLIANCE CERTIFICATE
($ IN 000'S)

I. SECTION 7.06 - CONSOLIDATED FIXED CHARGE COVERAGE RATIO.

A. Consolidated EBITDA for four consecutive fiscal quarters ending on above date ("Subject Period"):

1. Consolidated Net Income for Subject Period:

    $_____

2. Consolidated Interest Charges for Subject Period:

    $_____

3. Provision for income taxes for Subject Period:

    $_____

4. Depreciation expenses for Subject Period:

    $_____

5. Amortization expenses for Subject Period:

    $_____

6. Non-cash reductions of Consolidated Net Income for Subject Period:

    $_____

7. Income tax credits for Subject Period:

    $_____

8. Non-recurring gains increasing Consolidated Net Income (or reducing net loss) which do not represent cash items for Subject Period or any future period:

    $_____

9. Consolidated EBITDA (Lines I.A.1 + 2 + 3 + 4 + 5 + 6 - 7 - 8): $_____

B. Operating Lease and Rental Expense

    $_____

C. Consolidated Interest Charges for Subject Period:

    $_____

D. Consolidated Fixed Charge Coverage Ratio ((Lines I.A.9 + I.B) / (Lines I.B + I.C)):   ____to 1

Questions:

(1) Do the accounting-related provisions in this agreement favor Starbucks or the Lenders? Explain and support your answer.

(2) If you represented Starbucks, what advice would you give your client regarding the accounting terminology and concepts used in the Credit Agreement?

(3) If you represented the Lenders, what advice would you give your clients regarding the accounting terminology and concepts used in the Credit Agreement?

CHAPTER VI

REVENUE RECOGNITION AND ISSUES INVOLVING THE INCOME STATEMENT

A. IMPORTANCE TO LAWYERS

On page 515 [omitted from the concise], replace the last two sentences and the related citation in the carryover paragraph at the top of the page with the following:

**In 2002, FASB added a project to develop a comprehensive accounting standard on revenue recognition to its technical agenda. Later that year, and in an effort to promote convergent international accounting standards, FASB and IASB reached a formal agreement to undertake a joint project on the subject to simplify the rules and to improve comparability across companies, industries and capital markets. Although the Boards try to coordinate their deliberations on the issues, each Board discusses and votes on each issue individually. In June 2010, the Boards issued an exposure draft proposing new rules that would supersede most of the guidance in FASB ASC Topic 605, *Revenue Recognition*, and IFRS. As a core principle, an enterprise should recognize revenue when it transfers goods or services to a customer in the amount of the consideration that the enterprise expects to receive from the customer. To apply that principle, an enterprise would: (i) identify the contract or contracts with a customer; (ii) identify the separate performance obligations in each contract; (iii) determine the transaction price; (iv) allocate the transaction price to the separate performance obligations; and (v) recognize revenue when the enterprise satisfies each performance obligation. The comment period on the exposure draft closes on October 22, 2010. According to their memorandum of understanding, the Boards plan to issue a final standard before June 30, 2011. REVENUE RECOGNITION (TOPIC 605), REVENUE FROM CONTRACTS WITH CUSTOMERS, Proposed Accounting Standards Update (Fin. Accounting Standards Bd. June 24, 2010), *available via* http://www.fasb.org/cs/ContentServer?c=Page&pagename= FASB%2FPage%2FSectionPage&cid=1175801893139; Fin. Accounting Standards Bd., Project Updates, Revenue Recognition—Joint Project of the IASB and FASB (June 24, 2010). Interested readers can access project updates via <http://www.fasb.org/jsp/FASB/Page/SectionPage&cid =1218220137074>.

On page 515, add the following discussion before the last sentence and related citations at the bottom of the page [on page 320 of the concise, add the following discussion before the last sentence and related citation in the carryover paragraph ending on the top of the page]:

More than a year later, Bristol-Myers terminated both its chief executive and general counsel after the federal monitor recommended their dismissal. After the agreed two-year oversight period ended, the U.S. Attorney in New Jersey dismissed the criminal charges. Sarah Rubenstein, *Bristol-Myers Pact on Oversight Expires, Buyers May Crop Up*, WALL ST. J., June 15, 2007, at A13; John Carreyrou & Barbara Martinez, *Board Members at Bristol-Myers Told to Fire CEO*, WALL ST. J., Sept. 12, 2006, at A1; Paul Davies et al., *Bristol-Myers Ex-Officials Are Indicted*, WALL ST. J., June 16, 2005, at A3; Jonathan Weil, *Win Lawsuit—and Pay $300 Million*, WALL ST. J., Aug. 2, 2004, at C3. Both deferred prosecution agreements ("DPAs") and non-prosecution agreements ("NPAs") have become popular because they allow the government to punish or reform an enterprise without causing the excessive losses and often irreparable harm to the employees and owners that typically flow from an indictment, a la Arthur Andersen. In a DPA, the prosecutor files criminal charges, but agrees to drop them after a specified period if the company fulfills certain conditions. By comparison, a NPA allows the enterprise to obtain the prosecutor's agreement not to prosecute the firm in exchange for sanctions, such as a fine, cooperation, improvements to the enterprise's compliance or education programs, or some combination. Rachel McTague, *Lawyer Says Variability in DOJ Agreements To Defer Prosecution Makes for Uncertainty*, 39 Sec. Reg. & L. Rep. (BNA) 1570 (Oct. 15, 2007).

On page 516, replace the last two sentences in the first paragraph and the related citations with the following text [on page 320 of the concise, replace the last two sentences in the second full paragraph and the related citations with the following text]:

Federal regulators brought criminal as well as civil charges against those now-former executives, which eventually led to three guilty pleas and one conviction. In addition, more than a dozen employees or agents of USF suppliers who signed those false confirmations in an effort to retain a profitable business relationship pleaded guilty to criminal charges. In September 2006, federal prosecutors in New York reached a non-prosecution agreement with the company, shortly after a federal district court approved a $1.1 billion settlement in a class action arising from the scheme. *Former USF Exec Sentenced to 7 Years for Role in Accounting Fraud*, 5 Corp. Accountability Rep. (BNA) 540 (May 25, 2007); John Herzfeld, *U.S. Attorney in New York Reaches Non-Prosecution Deal With Royal Ahold*, 38 Sec. Reg. & L. Rep. (BNA) 1670 (Oct. 2, 2006).

On page 517, replace the last sentence and the related citations in the carryover paragraph at the top of the page with the following [on page 321 of the concise, add the following to the first full paragraph]:

In September 2007, Saks's parent corporation settled civil charges that it violated financial reporting, books-and records, and internal control provisions under the federal securities laws. SEC v. Saks Inc., Accounting and Auditing Enforcement Release No. 2674 (Sept. 5, 2007), http://www.sec.gov/litigation/litreleases/2007/lr20266.htm.

Beginning on page 517 with the carryover paragraph that starts near the middle of the page and ending with the carryover paragraph that concludes near the middle of page 519, please replace the text on financial statement abuses involving insurance with the following discussion [replace the section beginning on page 321 of the concise with the carryover paragraph on the bottom of the page and ending with the first full paragraph on page 323 with the following discussion]:

Regulators investigating possible financial statement abuses have focused on insurance companies, after learning that buyers had used certain novel insurance products to manage, or smooth, their earnings. The spotlight has shone especially brightly on American International Group Inc. ("AIG"), perhaps the largest insurance company in the world, and once a favorite of Wall Street because of its history of continuous, steady earnings growth over many years. In addition, the company's apparent ability to keep the ratio of its underwriting losses (payments on insurance claims) to its premium revenues at the lowest levels in the industry impressed investors. While we could accurately describe the financial accounting rules for the insurance business as especially complex, particularly with respect to reinsurance transactions, some of the efforts to manage earnings were fairly straight-forward. The most controversial scenario involved so-called "finite insurance," developed in the 1980s and designed to limit an insurance company's maximum risk if a covered loss did occur, while also providing both an accounting and a tax advantage for the insured. In its simplest form, finite insurance consists of a multi-year contract calling for total premiums almost equaling the amount of the potential losses being covered, but with the further proviso that at the end of the contract the insurance company would refund most of the total amount of premiums paid in excess of any reimbursed losses. Thus, such policies limited the insurance company's risk to the difference between the maximum of losses that the policy covered and the total premiums paid by the insured. Buyers, on the other hand, could avoid paying significantly more in premiums than their actual loss experience, as often happened to insureds with favorable loss experiences. Of course, self-insurance could provide these same advantages, but at a cost of much greater earnings volatility, which investors have frowned upon. In other words, with finite insurance the buyer could provide for its losses over a period of years in a stable, budgeted manner, while also securing an annual deduction for tax purposes.

When an insurance company assumes little, if any, risk, however, the question arises as to whether the arrangement really constitutes insurance, or whether the parties should instead treat the agreement as akin to loan from the customer to the insurance company, which the latter will repay, except to the extent of losses incurred. In 1992, after intense debate, the FASB ruled that to qualify for being treated as insurance for accounting purposes the arrangement had to include a "reasonable possibility" that the insurer might "realize a significant loss." While the FASB never formally defined these terms, industry practices developed an informal guideline of at least a ten percent chance of a ten percent loss. Because management determined the chance and possible amount of loss, the informal guideline offered ample opportunity to stretch to find compliance.

** So-called "income smoothing," or "earnings management," seeks to reduce variability in net income over accounting periods by shifting revenues or expenses from good quarters or years to bad reporting periods. Depending upon its desires, management shifts future income or deductions to the present or vice versa. The technique results in financial statements that reflect economic results not as they are, but rather as management wants them to look. Finite insurance became a particularly tempting vehicle for abuse because it could help to hide losses and thereby avoid full disclosure in financial statements. In one notable case involving AIG, another company, Brightpoint, Inc., had suffered a $29 million trading loss. Brightpoint's management wanted to avoid disclosing the full amount because the company had earlier indicated that the loss would fall between $13 million and $18 million. Brightpoint arranged to purchase a policy from AIG under which in exchange for $15 million in future premiums Brightpoint immediately received $11.9 million in "insurance" proceeds, which the company set off against its trading loss and hence avoided showing the full amount of the loss. Because AIG never incurred any risk of loss, however, the arrangement did not qualify as an insurance transaction, so no basis existed for such a set-off. In 2007, a federal jury found the Brightpoint official who helped to devise and execute the scheme civilly liable for aiding and abetting the fraud. The Second Circuit affirmed the ruling in 2009. Both AIG and Brightpoint had previously settled SEC charges arising from the transaction, with AIG paying a $10 million civil penalty. SEC v. Brightpoint, Inc., Accounting and Auditing Enforcement Release No. 2632 (July 9, 2007), http://www.sec.gov/litigation/litreleases/2007/lr20185.htm.

Although not involving AIG, one other recent case illustrates the abuse of a purported reinsurance transaction, only this time to defer earnings from a good quarter to an accounting period in the future, creating a so-called "cookie jar" reserve that management could save for a "rainy day" to boost earnings at some point in the future. In this case, the "round-trip" transaction enabled RenaissanceRe Holdings Ltd. ("RenRe") to "bank" excess revenue from a good year for a future accounting period. To accomplish this desired result, RenRe used two seemingly unrelated contracts with another reinsurance company. In the first contract, RenRe purported to assign $50 million in receivables to the other company for $30 million, which resulted in a $20 million net transfer to the other company. The second contract, disguised as a reinsurance contract even though the arrangement did not transfer any risk, allowed the other company to refund the $20 million, plus investment income earned on that amount in the interim, less transactional fees and costs, to RenRe. Among other things, RenRe agreed to pay a $15 million civil penalty and to retain an independent consultant to resolve securities fraud charges. SEC v. RenaissanceRe Holdings Ltd., Accounting and Auditing Enforcement Release No. 2550 (Feb. 6, 2007), http://www.sec.gov/litigation/litreleases/2007/lr19989.htm.

** The AIG transaction that has received by far the most attention (and criticism) arose at a time when investors were expressing some concern that AIG's loss reserves, the amount that AIG estimated as necessary to pay for losses that its policyholders had incurred, might not in fact prove sufficient to cover the total of those losses. As an obvious cure for this problem, AIG could have charged additional expense against income to increase the reserve, but the insurer did not want to incur the resulting reduction in net income. Instead, AIG entered into a putative reinsurance deal—an arrangement in which an insurance company itself in effect buys insurance from another company to obtain protection against the possibility of incurring a particularly large loss claim on an existing policy—with an insurance company called General Reinsurance Corp. ("General Re"), a subsidiary of Berkshire Hathaway Inc., the company run by fabled investor Warren Buffet, which only added to the media attention this transaction ultimately received. In exchange for a $5 million fee, General Re purportedly helped AIG boost its loss reserves by $500 million. In two transactions, AIG received $500 million in premiums in exchange for providing reinsurance to General Re for $500 million of possible losses on which General Re had issued insurance policies. Although AIG did not undertake any risk in the transactions, AIG treated the $500 million received from General Re as income from reinsurance premiums. When coupled with a $500 million charge against income for additional potential losses, AGI raised its loss reserve by that amount while its net income remained the same as it would have been without these transactions. General Re treated the transactions not as the purchase of reinsurance, but rather as loans, which AIG would repay, presumably with interest for the use of the money, or some other compensation to General Re for entering into the deal. By mid-2005, the new top management at AIG acknowledged that the company had improperly accounted for these transactions, along with a number of others. AIG restated its financial statements through 2004 to correct these accounting improprieties, which reduced the company's shareholders' equity by several billion dollars, or about three percent. After two former senior General Re executives pled guilty to criminal conspiracy to commit fraud in 2005, a federal grand jury indicted three other former senior General Re executives, including an assistant general counsel, and one former senior executive of AIG for their alleged involvement in the financial fraud at AIG. Shortly thereafter in 2006, AIG agreed, without admitting or denying wrongdoing, to pay more than $1.6 billion to resolve SEC, New York state, and Justice Department charges arising from the accounting fraud and other alleged misconduct. In February 2008, a federal jury convicted the four indicted individuals, plus another former General Re executive, on all the charges arising from their roles in the scheme. In 2009, former AIG CEO Maurice "Hank" Greenberg, without admitting or denying wrongdoing, agreed to settle SEC charges that alleged his involvement in material misstatements that enabled AIG to create the false impression that the company consistently met or exceeded key earnings and growth targets. In so doing, Greenberg consented to a judgment directing him to pay $7.5 million in disgorgement and a $7.5 million penalty. In 2010, General Re agreed to pay about $92 million and to implement certain corporate-governance changes to enter into a nonprosecution agreement with the federal government. *See* SEC v. Greenberg, Accounting and Auditing Enforcement Release No. 3032 (Aug. 6, 2009), http://www.sec.gov/litigation/litreleases/2009/lr21170.htm; SEC v. Ferguson, Accounting and Auditing Enforcement Release No. 2369 (Feb. 2, 2006), http://www.sec.gov/litigation/litreleases/lr19552.htm; *see also* Amir Efrati, *GenRe, U.S. Reach Accord in AIG Case*, WALL ST. J., January 21, 2010; Karen Richardson et al., *Jury Convicts Five of Fraud in Gen Re, AIG Case*, WALL ST. J., Feb. 26, 2008, at A1; Kip Betz et al., *AIG to Pay $1.6B to Resolve NY, SEC, DOJ Charges Over Accounting*, 38 Sec. Reg. & L. Rep. (BNA) 263 (Feb. 13, 2006); Karen Richardson et al., *AIG Legal Thicket Grows Thornier*, WALL ST. J., Feb. 3, 2006, at A3; *Second General Re Official Pleads Guilty in Stock Fraud Case Over AIG Financials*, 37 Sec. Reg. & L. Rep. (BNA) 1081 (June 20, 2005).

In addition to the joint project between the FASB and IASB to develop a comprehensive accounting standard on revenue recognition described earlier in this section on page 85, *supra*, in October 2008, the FASB Chairman announced the Board's decision to join in the IASB's project to develop common standards addressing recognition, measurement, presentation and disclosure requirements for insurance contracts and to improve and simplify the financial reporting requirements for insurance contracts. Fin. Accounting Standards Bd., Project Updates, Insurance Contracts–Joint Project of the IASB and FASB (June 1, 2010). Interested readers can access project updates via <http://www.fasb.org/jsp/FASB/Page/SectionPage&cid=1218220137074>.

On page 521, replace the last paragraph with the following updated discussion on restatements [on page 325 of the concise, replace the first full paragraph with the following discussion]:

**   After disturbing increases in the number of public companies restating prior financial statements beginning in the late 1990s, statistics from Audit Analytics show that restatements have fallen the last three years in a row.

In 2006, 1,564 SEC registrants filed 1,795 restatements. Those numbers dropped to 1,095 companies reporting 1,217 restatements in 2007, 830 companies submitting 923 restatements in 2008, and 630 registrants filing 674 restatements in 2009, a twenty-seven percent decline from 2008. Steve Burkholder, *SEC's Chief Accountants Advise Caution on Disclosure, Including Non-GAAP Items*, 8 Corp. Accountability Report (BNA) 472 (May 7, 2010). Although various methodologies generate different numbers, and companies that file periodic reports with the SEC but whose shares do not trade on the major stock exchanges accounted for sixty-two percent of the restatements in 2006, a recent U.S. Treasury-commissioned study found that restatements by public companies exploded from ninety in 1997 to 1,577 in 2006. Susan Scholz, The Changing Nature and Consequences of Public Company Financial Restatements 1997-2006 (2008), http://www.treas.gov/press/releases/reports/FinancialRestatements_1997_2006.pdf. Interestingly, when announcing the Department of the Treasury's Advisory Committee on the Auditing Profession in May 2007, Treasury Secretary Paulson noted that financial restatements soared to 1,876 in 2006, a number that translates to more than ten percent of public companies. Press Release, U.S. Dep't of Treasury, Paulson: Financial Reporting Vital to US Market Integrity, Strong Economy (May 17, 2007), http://www.treas.gov/press/releases/hp407.htm. In any event, most observers attribute the growing number of restatements to increased management and auditor focus on accurate financial reporting after Sarbanes-Oxley, arising from (1) the requirement that executives certify that the financial statements fairly present, in all material respects, the entity's financial condition and operating results; (2) the internal controls provisions in section 404; and (3) greater financial reporting review and enforcement by financial regulators. On the plus side, the Treasury-commissioned study reports the percentage of restatements related to revenues decreased from forty-one percent in 1997 to eleven percent in 2006. Similarly, although a 2007 AuditAnalytics study found that revenue recognition questions appeared in twenty-seven percent of the comment letters that the SEC staff sent to 5,105 public companies regarding their Form 10-K filings from 2004 through October 2007 and after the SEC began publicly releasing the correspondence between the staff and the companies in 2005, a higher percentage than for any other topic, the firm found that revenue recognition issues ranked only number six among the top reasons companies restated their earnings during 2008. *See Financial Restatements Continued Decline in 2008, Data Research Service Reports*, 7 Corp. Accountability Rep. (BNA) 323 (Mar. 13, 2009); Steven Marcy, *Revenue Recognition Is Top Concern in SEC Comment Letters to Companies*, 6 Corp. Accountability Rep. (BNA) 16 (Jan. 4, 2008).

On page 523, after the first full paragraph insert the following discussion [on page 326 of the concise, after the carryover paragraph ending on the top of the page insert the following]:

**   Since the publication of the fourth edition, involvement in financial frauds has continued to cost various lawyers their jobs, their ability to practice law, and their professional reputations. In addition to the firing of Bristol-Myers' general counsel mentioned above, the recent stock option backdating scandals cost lawyers similar positions at Apple Inc., Comverse Technology Inc., Juniper Networks Inc., McAfee Inc., Monster Worldwide Inc, and UnitedHealth Group Inc. Not surprisingly, the SEC and the Justice Department have continued to bring enforcement actions and criminal charges against lawyers, including at least eight general counsels of public companies. In early 2009, for example, United Health's former general counsel David Lubben agreed to a final judgment that ordered him to pay more than $1.4 million in disgorgement,$350,000 in prejudgment interest, and a $575,000 civil penalty. He also consented to an antifraud injunction, a five-year bar from serving as an officer or director for a public company, and a three-year suspension from appearing or practicing as an attorney before the SEC. *In re* Lubben, Accounting and Auditing Enforcement Release No. 2939 (Feb. 19, 2009), http://www.sec.gov/litigation/admin/2009/34-59423.pdf; SEC v. UnitedHealth Group Inc., Litigation Release No. 20,836 (Dec. 22, 2008), http://www:sec.gov/litigation/litreleases/2008/lr20836.htm. In 2009, a jury convicted Joseph P. Collins, a former partner at Mayer Brown LLP and the longtime, primary outside counsel for Refco Group Ltd. and its successor, Refco Inc., on conspiracy, securities fraud, and other charges for his participation in the scheme that failed to disclose hundreds of millions of dollars in related party transactions and ultimately led to the commodity broker's bankruptcy. After the district court sentenced Collins to seven years in prison in early 2010, he appealed his conviction to the Second Circuit. Based on the conviction, the SEC has issued an administrative order suspending Collins from appearing or practicing before the agency as an attorney. Although Collins and the SEC reached a proposed settlement on related civil charges, the district court has deferred action on the settlement until the judge presiding over the criminal charges issues a decision on restitution. Refco investors have also named Collins as a defendant in a class action, currently on appeal before the Second Circuit. *See* Yin Wilczek, *Former Refco Attorney Appeals Conviction on Charges Related to Collapse of Company*, 42 Sec. Reg. & L. Rep. (BNA) 604 (Mar. 29, 2010); *see also* SEC v. Collins, Litigation Release No. 20402 (Dec. 18, 2007), http://www.sec.gov/litigation/litreleases/2007/lr20402.htm.

The SEC and several state courts have also finally completed disciplinary actions against lawyers involved in earlier financial frauds. In 2009, Jordan H. Mintz, a former Enron Vice President and general counsel of Enron's Global Finance Group, and Rex R. Rogers, a former Enron Vice President and Associate General Counsel, who served as Enron's top securities lawyer, consented to judgments that ordered them each to pay one dollar in disgorgement and $25,000 in civil penalties and suspended them from appearing or practicing before the SEC as an attorney for two years. The charges arose from the lawyers' participation in a fraudulent transaction involving a Brazilian power plant intended to inflate Enron's earnings. *In re* Mintz, Accounting and Auditing Enforcement Release No. 2926 (Jan. 26, 2009), http://sec.gov/litigation/admin/2009/34-59296.pdf; *In re* Rogers,

Accounting and Auditing Enforcement Release No. 2927 (Jan. 26, 2009), http://sec.gov/litigation/admin/2009/34-59297.pdf. Even more recently, the Appellate Division, Second Department, of the New York Supreme Court disbarred Steven Woghin, the former general counsel of Computer Associates, a company that used so-called "thirty-five day months" to recognize revenue prematurely and to meet revenue and earnings expectations. In 2004, Woghin pled guilty to conspiracy to commit federal securities fraud and obstruction of justice, admitting that he not only supervised attorneys who routinely backdated agreements or reported them as having been signed within the earlier quarter, but also that he personally participated in such activities and sought to conceal such practices from the authorities. *In re* Woghin, 880 N.Y.S.2d 74 (N.Y. App. Div. 2009). Previously, Woghin agreed to a suspension from appearing or practicing before the SEC as an attorney. *In re* Woghin, Accounting and Auditing Enforcement Release No. 2133 (Nov. 10, 2004), *available at* http://www.sec.gov/litigation/admin/34-50653.htm. In 2009, the SEC issued an administrative order suspending Christi R. Sulzbach, formerly the chief compliance officer, executive vice president and general counsel at Tenet Healthcare Corporation from 1999-2003, from appearing or practicing before the Commission as an attorney. Earlier in the year, a federal district court ordered Sulzbach to pay one dollar in disgorgement and a $120,000 civil penalty for either knowing or recklessless failing to know about Tenet's unsustainable strategy to inflate its Medicare revenues and failing to disclose that unsustainable strategy. *In re* Sulzbach, Accounting and Auditing Enforcement Release No. 3000 (June 25, 2009). Finally, in 2007 the Supreme Court of Oregon ordered a 120-day suspension from the practice of law for an in-house lawyer who violated a disciplinary rule prohibiting dishonesty, fraud, deceit and misrepresentation. The lawyer signed a management representation letter to his company's independent auditor when he knew that the letter contained false statements. Based on the letter, the auditor allowed the company to recognize a $4.1 million sale even though the purported purchaser never entered into a fixed contract. *In re* Fitzhenry, 162 P.3d 260 (Or. 2007); *see also In re* FLIR Systems, Inc., Accounting and Enforcement Release No. 1637, [2001-2003 Transfer Binder] Fed. Sec. L. Rep. (CCH) ¶ 75,152 (Sept. 30, 2002), *available at* http://www.sec.gov/litigation/admin/33-8135.htm; *In re* Fitzhenry, Accounting and Enforcement Release No. 1670, [2001-2003 Transfer Binder] Fed. Sec. L. Rep. (CCH) ¶ 75,185 (Nov. 21, 2002), *available at* http://www.sec.gov/litigation/admin/34-46870.htm (barring the accused from practice before the SEC for five years).

On page 523 [page 326 of the concise], please note in the second full paragraph [first full paragraph in the concise] that Tyco International Ltd. agreed in 2007 to pay approximately $3 billion to resolve a class action arising from the financial fraud at that company, displacing the Cendant amount as the largest settlement by a corporate defendant in a securities fraud class action. *Tyco Shareholder Suit Ends in Record $3 Billion Settlement*, 5 Corp.

Accountability Rep. (BNA) 508 (May 18, 2007). In 2008, UnitedHealth Group Inc. tentatively agreed to pay $895 million to settle a class action arising from its stock-option backdating scandal. Laura Mahoney & Mark Wolski, *United Health Group Agrees to Pay $895M, Reform Governance in CalPERS Settlement*, 6 Corp. Accountability Rep. (BNA) 720 (July 11, 2008).

On page 524, replace the penultimate sentence and related citation in the first full paragraph with the following [on page 327 of the concise, replace the last sentence in the first full paragraph with the following]:

The Wall Street Journal reported that Enron's bankruptcy has generated a record-breaking and "eye-popping" almost $1 billion in fees to lawyers, financial advisors, and turnaround experts. Other recent bankruptcy cases involving financial frauds at two different auto-parts manufacturers each have generated more than $100 million in professional fees. Bernard Wysocki Jr., *Rising Fees Charged in Bankruptcy Cases Elicit a Backlash*, WALL ST. J., Aug. 4, 2007, at B1.

On page 524 [omitted from the concise], insert the following text and citation before the last sentence in the second full paragraph:

A recent study examining all 585 companies that the SEC brought enforcement actions against from 1978 to 2002 for financial misrepresentation found that the largest financial losses from the misconduct arose from damaged reputations rather than penalties paid to regulators. For each dollar that a company misleadingly inflated its market value, on average the company lost that dollar, plus an additional $3.08, when the misbehavior came to light. Moreover, the study estimated the reputational damage amounted to more than 7.5 times any penalties that the legal and regulatory system imposed. Steve Burkholder, *Money Loss from Cooking the Books Stems from Hurt Reputation, Study Says*, 4 Corp. Accountability Rep. (BNA) 1160 (Nov. 17, 2006). An even more recent study found that the companies that the SEC cited for fraud in accounting and auditing enforcement releases ("AAERs") between 2000 and 2007 show higher incidences of significant drops in stock prices, investor lawsuits, and bankruptcy. *Deloitte Group Finds Companies Take Major Hits for Fraud Involvement*, Sec. L. Daily (BNA), Dec. 17, 2008.

B.   ESSENTIAL REQUIREMENTS FOR REVENUE RECOGNITION

On page 532 [omitted from the concise], insert the following text after the first paragraph in Note 1:

After jury convictions arising from the corporate scandals in the early 2000s, judges have imposed the following prison sentences on prominent corporate executives: Bernard Ebbers, former WorldCom CEO (twenty-five years); Dennis Kozlowski, former Tyco CEO, and Mark Swartz, former Tyco CFO (both up to twenty-five years); Walter A. Forbes, former Cendant Corp. chairman (twelve years and seven months); and Sanjay Kumar, former Computer Associates International CEO (twelve years). In 2009, the United States Court of Appeals for the Fifth Circuit affirmed the convictions of Jeffrey Skilling, Enron's former CEO, but vacated his sentence of more than twenty-four years because the district court improperly applied federal sentencing guidelines. In 2010, the Supreme Court, in turn, vacated the Fifth Circuit's decision, ruling that "honest-services" fraud applies only to bribery and kickback schemes, and remanded the case to the lower courts to determine how the ruling affects the jury verdict convicting Skilling on nineteen felony counts, leaving the length of his remaining sentence very much in doubt.

On page 533 [omitted from the concise], insert the following discussion at the end of Note 1:

**More recently, Richard M. Scrushy, the former chairman and CEO of HealthSouth Corporation, consented to a final judgment that, among other things, ordered him to pay $77.5 million in disgorgement, subject to an offset for any amounts paid in certain other lawsuits. SEC v. Scrushy, Accounting and Auditing Enforcement Release No. 2599 (Apr. 23, 2007), http://www.sec.gov/litigation/litreleases/2007/lr20084.htm. In 2005, a federal jury acquitted Scrushy on thirty-six criminal fraud charges after he became the first CEO indicted under SOx. The final judgment in the SEC action, which also permanently bars Scrushy from serving as an officer or director of a public company, further imposed $3.5 million in civil penalties, illustrating some important differences between civil and criminal liability. Earlier, the Alabama Supreme Court affirmed a partial summary judgment ordering Scrushy to repay almost $48 million, including more than $46 million in bonuses he received from HealthSouth and prejudgment interest. Scrushy v. Tucker, 955 So. 2d 988 (Ala. 2006). Multiplying Scrushy's financial woes exponentially, an Alabama state court entered a $2.88 billion judgment against him in a shareholders' derivative action for HealthSouth in 2009, reportedly the largest judgment against a single executive. *See* Tucker v. Scrushy, No. CV 02-5215 (Ala. Cir. Ct. Jefferson County June 19, 2009) (final judgment); *see also* Valerie Bauerlein & Mike Esterl, *Judge Orders Scrushy to Pay $2.88 Billion in Civil Suit*, Wall St. J., June 19, 2009, at B1.

In late 2007, the SEC announced a record $468 million settlement in an enforcement action in a stock options backdating case against Dr. William W. McGuire, the former CEO and chairman of UnitedHealth Group Inc. The SEC's release described the settlement as "the first with an individual under the 'clawback' provision (Section 304) of the Sarbanes-Oxley Act to deprive corporate executives of their stock sale profits and bonuses earned while their companies were misleading investors." McGuire agreed to "reimburse UnitedHealth for all incentive- and equity-based compensation he received from 2003 through 2006, totaling approximately $448 million in cash bonuses, profits from the exercise and sale of UnitedHealth stock, and unexercised UnitedHealth options." He also agreed to disgorge other ill-gotten gains, plus prejudgment interest, and to pay a $7 million civil penalty. In addition, the order bars McGuire from serving as an officer or director of a public company for ten years. SEC v. McGuire, Accounting and Auditing Enforcement Release No. 2754 (Dec. 6, 2007), http://www.sec.gov/litigation/litreleases/2007/lr20387.

**   SOx section 304, which requires a CEO or CFO to return incentive-based or equity-based compensation to an issuer when an accounting restatement occurs "as a result of misconduct," suffers from important limitations. First, the provision applies only to CEOs and CFOs. Second, the disgorgement only applies to compensation received during the twelve-month period following the misstated financials. Third, section 304 requires an accounting restatement. At least one federal district court has held that the SEC cannot invoke the statute without the actual filing of a restatement, potentially after the SEC compels or orders the company to restate its financial statements. SEC v. Shanahan, No. 4:07CV270 JCH, 2008 WL 5211909, at *5 (E.D. Mo. Dec. 12, 2008). Fourth, to date the federal courts have rejected the argument that the provision creates a private right of action to address violations. In a case of first impression in the federal appellate courts, the Ninth Circuit agreed with dicta in an earlier Third Circuit decision and the decisions of at least eight different district courts and held that no private remedy exists under section 304. *See In re* Digimarc Corp. Deriv. Litig., 549 F.3d 1223, 1230-33 (9th Cir. 2008); *see also* Pirelli Armstrong Tire Corp. Retiree Med. Benefits Trust ex rel. Fed. Nat. Mortg. Ass'n v. Raines, 534 F.3d 779, 793 (3rd Cir. 2008).

**   The statute also does not clearly set forth what misconduct can trigger a so-called "clawback." Does misconduct encompass negligence? Must the CEO or CFO engage in wrongdoing? In 2009, the SEC brought the first action under section 304 that sought only reimbursement and that did not allege that the defendant engaged in fraudulent conduct. The SEC filed suit to recover more than $4 million in bonuses and profits from the stock sales that the former CEO of CSK Auto Corporation received while the company was committing accounting fraud. *See* SEC v. Jenkins, Accounting and Auditing Enforcement Release No. 3025 (July 23, 2009), http://www.sec.gov/litigation/litreleases/2009/lr21149a.htm. As a result, any accounting restatement now creates worries for any CEO or CFO who received incentive-based or equity-based compensation during the twelve-month period that begins when the issuer issued or filed the misstated financial document. *See* Tina Chi, *SEC's Latest Use of SOX 'Clawback' Statute Seen Shifting Calculus About Restatements*, 7 Corp. Accountability Rep. (BNA) 1050 (Aug. 28, 2009.

**   Recognizing these limitations, various institutional investors have encouraged public companies to adopt broader "clawback" or executive compensation recoupment policies than federal law authorizes and to disclose such policies. In particular, these investors want, first, policies that apply to all senior executives, for longer periods of time, and in situations beyond misconduct and, then, actual enforcement of the policies. Increasingly, such corporate policies also apply to excessive risk-taking or detrimental conduct, which can include failing to "blow the whistle" when someone else violates a corporate policy. *See* Tina Chi, *Companies Assessing Risk Should Review Pay Programs, Implement Clawback Policies*, 8 Corp. Accountability Rep. (BNA) 162 (Feb. 19, 2010); *see also* Robin Sidel, *Wall Street Toughens Its Rules on Clawbacks*, WALL ST. J., Jan. 27, 2010, at C1. According to the executive compensation research firm Equilar Inc., by the end of 2008 almost seventy-two percent of *Fortune 100* companies had adopted clawback policies that allow those firms to recoup executive compensation following a financial restatement or misconduct. *See* Mary Hughes, *Firm Clawback Polices Go Beyond SOX to Recoup Ill-Gained Profits, Study Finds*, 7 Corp. Accountability Rep. (BNA) 1364 (Nov. 20, 2009).

Responding first to concerns about excessive compensation and risk-taking as major contributing factors to the credit crisis and then to public outrage over staggering bonuses for 2008 at firms that received investments under the federal government's Capital Purchase Program, both the Emergency Economic Stabilization Act of 2008 ("EESA") and the American Recovery and Reinvestment Tax Act of 2009 ("ARRA") contained provisions mandating so-called "clawbacks." As amended in the ARRA, section 111 of the EESA requires the Secretary of the Treasury to establish standards for executive compensation and corporate governance, including provisions allowing any entity that has received federal assistance to recover any bonus, retention award, or incentive compensation paid to a senior executive officer or to certain highly compensated employees based upon materially inaccurate financial statements or other performance metrics. *See* Pub. L. No. 111-5, § 7001, 123 Stat. 115, 516-520.

**   The conference agreement on the financial reform bill would require the SEC to issue rules directing the national securities exchanges to prohibit from listing any issuer that does not develop, implement, and disclose a clawback policy. Under the bill, these policies must apply to any current or former executive officer who received incentive-based compensation, including stock options, based on erroneous financial information required under the federal securities laws in the three-year period before an accounting restatement. These policies must also require the executive to repay the excess over what the issuer would have paid under the restatement. Senate approval remains uncertain as this Supplement goes to print. *See* Steven Marcy & Mike Ferullo, *House Passes Financial Reform Bill; Would Exempt Small Issuers From SOX §404*, 8 Corp. Accountability Rep. (BNA) 707 (July 9, 2010).

On page 545 at the end of Note 5 [page 349 of the concise at the end of Note 4], insert the following discussion:

**   In addition to the finite insurance and purported reinsurance schemes described earlier on pages 87 to 90, *supra*, the SEC has continued to bring enforcement actions against companies that improperly manage earnings, whether via "cookie jar" reserves or so-called "top-side adjustments." With "top-side adjustments" or "top-side journal entries," senior executives, such as the CFO, or upper-level accountants use special (and sometimes manual) entries at the end of a fiscal period to change the books, avoiding the normal accounting process, usually to attain or avoid significantly exceeding a financial target. *See, e.g.*, SEC v. Diebold, Inc., Accounting and Auditing Enforcement Release No. 3137 (June 2, 2010), http://www.sec.gov/litigation/litreleases/2010/lr21543.htm (announcing a $25 million civil penalty to settle charges that the company engaged in fraudulent accounting practices to inflate the company's earnings to meet forecasts, including manipulating reserves and accruals); SEC v. VeriFone Holdings, Inc., Accounting and Auditing Enforcement Release No. 3044 (Sept. 1, 2009), http://www.sec.gov/litigation/litreleases/2009/lr21194.htm (announcing permanent injunctions against the company and a former finance department employee and a $25,000 civil penalty against the individual for recording large manual adjustments to inventory balances during the first three quarters in 2007 to meet internal forecasts and guidance to investors); SEC v. Gen. Elec. Co., Accounting and Auditing Enforcement Release No. 3029 (Aug. 4, 2009), http://www.sec.gov/litigation/litreleases/2009/lr21166.htm (announcing a $50 million penalty to settle civil charges that the company used improper accounting methods to increase its reported earnings or revenues and avoid reporting negative financial results on four separate occasions in 2002 and 2003); *In re* Beazer Homes USA, Inc., Accounting and Auditing Enforcement Release No. 2884 (Sept. 24, 2008), http://www.sec.gov/litigation/admin/2008/33-8960.pdf (imposing an administrative cease-and-desist order on the homebuilder for intentionally and improperly managing its quarterly and annual earnings between 2000 and 2007); SEC v. ConAgra Foods, Inc., Litigation Release No. 20206 (July 25, 2007), http://www.sec.gov/litigation/litreleases/2007/lr20206.htm (announcing a $45 million penalty to settle civil charges that, among other allegations, ConAgra misused "excess reserves to offset, dollar-for-dollar, unrelated, unplanned-for and unreserved-for losses" or current period operating expenses); *In re* OM Group, Inc., Accounting and Auditing Enforcement Release No. 2643 (July 18, 2007), http://www.sec.gov/litigation/admin/2007/33-8826.pdf (consenting to a cease-and-desist order arising from more than 700 improper and unsupported "top-side" adjustments during the consolidation process directed and recorded by three former executives to manage earnings).

**   In the credit crisis, senior executives sometimes failed to recognize expenses and create reserves or understated expenses and established inadequate reserves for impaired assets or known liabilities arising from credit or investment losses. *See, e.g.*, SEC v. Strauss, Accounting and Auditing Enforcement Release No. 2967 (Apr. 28, 2009), http://www.sec.gov/litigation/litreleases/2009/lr21014.htm (senior executive at American Home Mortgage Investment Corp. agreed to permanent injunction, approximately $2.2 million in disgorgement and rejudgment interest, and a $250,000 penalty for allegedly under stating loan loss reserves); *see also* Yin Wilczek, *New Type of Reserve Accounting Case Emerging from Crisis, SEC Official Says*, 41 Sec. Reg. & L. Rep. (BNA) 1968 (Oct. 26, 2009).

1.   A BONA FIDE EXCHANGE TRANSACTION

On page 546 [page 350 of the concise], add the following text to the end of this introductory discussion:

A recent and important exception to the exchange transaction requirement arises from "fair value accounting." With a new accounting standard establishing a unified approach to measuring fair values and a second standard granting enterprises the option to record more assets and liabilities at fair value, businesses will increasingly report unrealized holding gains and losses in the income statement without a corresponding exchange transaction. While fair value accounting involves a potential sacrifice of reliability for relevance and has generated significant controversy during the global credit crisis, both the FASB and the IASB remain committed to developing rules that will require enterprises to report additional assets and liabilities at fair value.

a.   THE NATURE OF THE EXCHANGE TRANSACTION

(1) In General

b) SHAMS

On page 547 [page 350 of the concise], replace the text at the bottom of the page with the following introduction and new principal case:

Although some transactions facially appear to qualify as market transactions, a closer examination into the underlying circumstances may reveal that the exchange lacks economic substance or that the parties have not transferred the risks that usually accompany ownership. In other words, while "form" satisfies the exchange transaction requirement, the "substance" or economic realities do not.

In re Motorola, Inc.
Securities and Exchange Commission, 2007.
Accounting and Auditing Enforcement Release No. 2607 (May 8, 2007),
http://www.sec.gov/litigation/admin/2007/34-55725.pdf.

[The SEC instituted public administrative proceedings against Motorola, Inc. ("Motorola" or "Respondent."). In anticipation of the proceedings, Motorola submitted an Offer of Settlement, which the Commission accepted. Solely for the purpose of these proceedings, and any other proceedings brought by or on behalf of the Commission, or to which the Commission is a party, and without admitting or denying the findings set forth, Motorola consented to the following:]

[III.]A. Summary

1. This case involves a round-trip of cash between Motorola and Adelphia Communications Corporation ("Adelphia"). Pursuant to a purported marketing support agreement entered into in 2001, Adelphia paid money to Motorola which was immediately returned to Adelphia in the form of marketing support payments. No marketing was specified in the agreement and no marketing was done pursuant to the agreement. Adelphia used Motorola's marketing support payments to falsify its earnings in 2000 and 2001.

2. In the Fall of 2000, Adelphia, a cable television system owner and operator, asked Motorola, a vendor that provided digital cable television set-top boxes used by Adelphia, to enter into a marketing support agreement for the stated purpose of helping Adelphia fund its roll-out of digital cable television service. Adelphia proposed to pre-fund Motorola's marketing support payment obligation through a retroactive and offsetting price increase applied to digital cable television set-top boxes Motorola had supplied Adelphia in the past and was to supply Adelphia in the future pursuant to a pre-existing purchase contract.

3. The marketing support agreement, which was not finalized until March 2001, was backdated to the prior fiscal year and applied retroactively to set-top boxes that had already been sold to Adelphia. The agreement also contained a false reason for the retroactive price increase.

4. The transaction had no economic substance, amounting to a round-trip of cash, and was designed by Adelphia to increase artificially its Earnings Before Interest, Taxes, Depreciation, and Amortization ("EBITDA") by reducing operating costs by the amount of the marketing support payments from Motorola. In this manner, Adelphia was able to use the transaction to reduce improperly its operating costs and increase its earnings by approximately $18.3 million in 2000 and $28 million in 2001.

5. Motorola knew or should have known that Adelphia was misusing the marketing support agreement. The marketing support agreement was backdated to a prior fiscal year, it applied retroactively to set-top boxes that

had already been sold to Adelphia, and it contained a false reason for the price increase. Motorola executives also knew that (i) the marketing support agreement did not identify any marketing to be done by Adelphia and Motorola did not require that any marketing be done pursuant to the agreement; (ii) the transaction was a round-trip transfer of cash; and (iii) Motorola accounted for the transaction as economically neutral to Motorola.

B. Respondent

6. * * * Motorola is a global manufacturer and seller of wireless, broadband, and automotive communications technologies. At all relevant times, Motorola's common stock was * * * publicly traded on the New York Stock Exchange.

C. Relevant Entity

7. * * * Adelphia owns, operates, and manages cable television systems and other related telecommunications businesses. * * *

D. Facts

Background

* * *

9. In May 2000, Adelphia and Motorola entered into a purchase agreement that governed the pricing of digital cable television set-top boxes through December 2001 based upon the contemplated purchase by Adelphia of 1.6 million set-top boxes over the life of the contract. The purchase agreement did not require Adelphia to purchase any set-top boxes and it did not provide for a penalty if Adelphia purchased less than the 1.6 million set-top boxes contemplated by the agreement.

10. In June 2000, Adelphia realized that its second quarter reported EBITDA would fall below analysts' expectations. Adelphia executives devised a plan to inflate artificially EBITDA by reducing operating costs through the purported marketing support agreement with Motorola.

11. In late August 2000, Adelphia approached Motorola with the idea of entering into the marketing support agreement.

Key Factors That Should Have Put Motorola On Notice That Adelphia Was Not Using The Marketing Support Agreement For Its Intended Purpose

12. Between August 2000 and March 2001, when the marketing support agreement documents were signed, the executives who reviewed, or were told the substance of, the proposed transaction, were confronted with the following unusual facts unique to this transaction:

• Adelphia's request was the first time any customer had asked the Motorola executives to increase the price of Motorola's products;

• The marketing support agreement, which Adelphia provided to Motorola, contained a false reason for the price increase;

• Motorola executives insisted as a condition to entering into the transaction that Adelphia provide a letter from its counsel that Adelphia would not use the transaction in contravention of federal regulations governing cable television rates. Instead, an Adelphia finance executive who was later implicated in Adelphia's fraud sent a short confirmatory letter to Motorola without advising Motorola whether its counsel had been consulted;

• The marketing support agreement did not contain any details of marketing to be done by Adelphia and required no input from Motorola's marketing department;

• The marketing support agreement was backdated and the price increase and marketing support payment obligation were made retroactive to the beginning of the prior fiscal year and applied to products that had already been sold to and paid for by Adelphia;

• The transaction was a "wash" transaction with no economic impact on Motorola; and

• Motorola did not treat the transaction as a marketing transaction for accounting purposes.

Motorola Asked Adelphia To Purchase More Set-Top Boxes Than Adelphia Needed In Exchange For Signing The Marketing Support Agreement

13. Shortly before the marketing support agreement was due to be signed in March 2001, Adelphia's orders for set-top boxes declined below the number called for under the May 2000 purchase agreement. Motorola knew that Adelphia did not need any additional set-top boxes at that time, but told Adelphia that it wanted Adelphia to purchase 100,000 additional set-top boxes. Adelphia agreed to make the purchase before the marketing support agreement was signed and before the close of Motorola's first quarter for fiscal year 2001.

Motorola Signed The Backdated Marketing Support Agreement And Made A Retroactive Marketing Support Payment

14. On or about March 21, 2001, Motorola signed the marketing support agreement documents that were backdated to the prior fiscal year. The marketing support agreement did not specify any marketing to be done by Adelphia and it contained a false reason for the price increase. In the document memorializing the price increase, Motorola stated falsely that the purpose of the price increase was to secure "incremental component volumes and factory capacity" to meet Adelphia's needs. In fact, Motorola executives

knew that the true purpose of the price increase was to pre-fund Motorola's marketing support payment obligation to Adelphia.

15. In May 2001, Motorola made the first $18.3 million marketing support payment for marketing purportedly done in 2000. The payment was funded by Adelphia three days earlier when it paid Motorola the retroactive price increase on set-top boxes previously purchased by Adelphia in 2000.

Motorola Again Asked Adelphia To Purchase More Set-Top Boxes Than It Needed And Defrayed The Costs Of Warehousing The Boxes In A Third-Party Warehouse In Exchange For Maintaining The Marketing Support Agreement

16. In early June 2001, Adelphia told Motorola that it would be reducing its orders of set-top boxes due to decreased demand. Motorola knew that Adelphia had excess inventory that would carry it to the middle of the following year. Nevertheless, Motorola insisted that Adelphia purchase an additional 150,000 set-top boxes. Motorola proposed to finance the purchase through Motorola Credit Corporation, so that Adelphia would be able to pay for the additional set-top boxes in two installments over a period of one year and Motorola would be able to record the sales before the close of its second fiscal quarter.

17. * * * Motorola knew or should have known that Adelphia did not actually need any additional set-top boxes, so it offered Adelphia credits that could be used for other Motorola services, including marketing, to offset the cost of warehousing the 150,000 set-top boxes in a third-party warehouse. Adelphia agreed to purchase the additional set-top boxes before the close of Motorola's second quarter for fiscal year 2001.

* * *

Adelphia Used The Marketing Support Agreement To Artificially Decrease Marketing Expenses And Increase EBITDA

19. Adelphia recorded the marketing support payments as a contra-expense to marketing costs. This accounting treatment lowered the amount of recorded marketing expenses and, in turn, artificially inflated Adelphia's EBITDA. Adelphia recorded the price increases paid to Motorola as capital expenditures, which are depreciated over time and, therefore, have no impact on EBITDA and a minimal impact on earnings.

20. In total, from April 2000 through December 2001, Adelphia recorded improperly approximately $46.3 million in marketing support payments as reductions in current operating expenses, with the intended effect of inflating its reported EBITDA by $46.3 million over that period. Adelphia's accounting treatment violated Generally Accepted Accounting Principles ("GAAP") because it reflected the round-trip transaction as decreasing its reported expenses and increasing its reported earnings when it did not have that effect.

[Based on the above, the SEC found that Adelphia violated various securities laws and regulations by filing periodic reports containing materially false and misleading financial statements and improperly accounting for the marketing support and artificial price increases on the set-top boxes. In addition, Motorola served as "a cause of" Adelphia's violations. The SEC ordered Motorola to cease and desist from committing or causing any further violations and to pay $25 million in disgorgement and prejudgment interest.]

NOTES

1. The enforcement action against Motorola illustrates both "round-trip" arrangements and "channel stuffing." As one type of "sham" transaction, "round-trips" involve two or more parties exchanging the same amount of consideration, usually money, in transactions lacking economic substance. In the arrangement underlying this SEC enforcement action, Adelphia paid Motorola for retroactive "price increases" on set-top cable boxes, only after Motorola agreed to pay the same amount back to Adelphia for "marketing support." The transactions lacked economic substance because Motorola had already sold the set-top boxes to Adelphia, and the latter did not undertake any actual marketing pursuant to the agreement.

Adelphia applied improper accounting principles to record the transactions, thereby artificially increasing its profits. First, Adelphia recorded the "marketing support" payments as an offset to decrease other marketing expenses. Second, Adelphia treated the "price increases" on the set-top boxes as a capital expenditure, depreciable over time, rather than treating the costs as an immediate expense, which overstated net income and operating cash flow. To illustrate the financial accounting consequences, suppose that Adelphia and Motorola consummate the agreement at the start of the year. Adelphia pays $1,000,000 in cash to Motorola for "price increases" on cable boxes, and Motorola then pays Adelphia $1,000,000 for "marketing support." Adelphia improperly records the $1 million cable-box payment as an asset and applies company accounting policy to depreciate the expenditure over five years, the estimated useful life of the cable boxes. During the first year, Adelphia will record a $200,000 depreciation expense, but will decrease total marketing expenditures by $1,000,000, thereby fraudulently increasing net income by $800,000. This treatment would also overstate operating cash flow by $1,000,000 because Adelphia could add back the $200,000 in depreciation to $800,000 in additional net income when computing operating cash flows. *See also* SEC v. Scientific-Atlanta, Inc., Accounting and Auditing Enforcement Release No. 2443 (June 22, 2006), http://www.sec.gov/litigation/litreleases/2006/lr19735.htm(describing a similar arrangement with Scientific-Atlanta that Adelphia used to inflate its earnings by approximately $43 million and for which Scientific-Atlanta agreed to pay $20 million in disgorgement to resolve civil SEC charges that the vendor aided and abetted Adelphia's violations).

As discussed in the unabridged fourth edition on page 135 [page 111 of the concise], Tyco used a similar sham transaction involving an identical "growth bonus" and "dealer connection fee" to boost its earnings and operating cash flows. William Bulkeley, *SEC Charges Former Tyco Officials With Fraud*, WALL ST. J., Dec. 22, 2006, at C3.

The *Stoneridge* case, discussed in this Supplement in the materials for Chapter II on page 50 in the context of accountants' legal liability, involves the alleged participation by both Motorola and Scientific-Atlanta in other "round-trip" schemes involving the sale of their cable boxes. In that case, Charter Communications, Inc. ("Charter"), a cable operator like Adelphia, used a "round-trip" scheme to boost net income and operating cash flow. Charter would overpay Motorola or Scientific-Atlanta $20 for each set-top box purchased, with the equipment vendor returning the overpayment by purchasing advertising from Charter. Charter capitalized and depreciated the cost of the boxes over time while recording the advertising revenue upfront. Stoneridge Inv. Partners, LLC v. Scientific-Atlanta, Inc., 128 S. Ct. 761, 766-67 (2008) (describing the fraudulent scheme and attempts to disguise the transactions as alleged in the complaint). Adelphia utilized novel accounting to record the sham payments as contra-expenses, which actually reduced the company's overall marketing expenses. As Charter's improper accounting in *Stoneridge* exhibits, most "round-trip" perpetrators record the sham payment directly as additional revenue. In any event, this case and the SEC enforcement actions against Motorola and Scientific-Atlanta illustrate the need for public companies to maintain appropriate policies and internal controls, to train personnel adequately, and to foster a culture that will not allow participation in financial frauds either within the corporation itself or that third parties might commit. This responsibility falls upon top management and the board of directors, both of whom often rely on lawyers for assistance.

By comparison, "channel stuffing" more fundamentally involves disclosure issues because an enterprise's sales practices in the current period adversely affect the likely prospects for sales in future accounting periods by forcing sales into the current accounting period. At several points during the Adelphia "round-trip" scheme, Motorola engaged in "channel stuffing" by pressuring Adelphia to buy more set-top boxes than it actually required in return for Motorola's cooperation in the "marketing support" scheme. As mentioned in the opening section of this chapter, "channel stuffing" occurs when a manufacturer or distributor uses bargaining power or financial incentives, such as cash payments, price discounts, reimbursements or other arrangements, to persuade customers to order and to keep—and not return—more goods than currently needed so that the manufacturer or distributor can record additional income for the accounting period. In the principal case, Motorola conditioned its initial participation in the "round-trip" scheme on Adelphia purchasing 100,000 more set-top boxes than necessary before the close of Motorola's first quarter in 2001. Motorola later insisted that Adelphia purchase an additional 150,000 set-top boxes in exchange for Motorola maintaining the "marketing support" agreement.

Motorola offered to defray Adelphia's warehousing costs for the units to facilitate the sale before the end of the second quarter. Adelphia fraudulently increased its net income through the scheme, but Motorola's revenues and net income also benefitted from the forced sale of more cable boxes than Adelphia likely would have otherwise purchased.

The SEC has also brought enforcement actions against public companies that participate in their suppliers' channel-stuffing schemes by engaging in highly irregular transactions. *See, e.g., In re* Ingram Micro Inc., Accounting and Auditing Enforcement Release No. 2968 (May 12, 2009), http://www.sec.gov/litigation/admin/2009/34-59903.pdf (respondent Ingram Micro, McAfee, Inc.'s largest customer, agreed to disgorge $15 million to settle administrative charges that Ingram violated books and records and internal control provisions by disregarding its own inventory goals and participating in McAffee's channel-stuffing scheme by purchasing large amounts of excessive inventory in exchange for excess inventory fees, nonrefundable discounts, and other secret, cash payments that Ingram misrecorded and mischaracterized).

2. Enterprises sometimes employ "round-trip" transactions only to inflate revenue or transaction volumes, but not net income. In these "round-trip" transactions, the entity records both the revenue and the equivalent expense upfront, resulting in no effect on net income. During the Internet bubble, when the markets typically valued enterprises based upon their revenues or revenue growth, rather than on net income, nascent "dot-com" companies found this manipulative accounting practice particularly attractive. During the boom, devising "round-trip" schemes would increase revenues for both parties involved, a seemingly "win-win" situation.

Perhaps the most publicized cases of "round-tripping" during the Internet boom occurred at America Online, Inc. ("AOL"). Investors and analysts closely followed AOL's advertising revenue as a key measure of the company's success. Between mid-2000 and 2002, as sales of online advertising declined, AOL used fraudulent "round-trip" arrangements to bolster online advertising revenue. AOL, in essence, funded its own revenue by giving customers the money to pay for advertising they would not otherwise have purchased from AOL. While AOL attempted to portray the "round-trip" schemes as separate, legitimate transactions, the purported "purchasers" of the advertising often had little or no control over the advertising received. Time Warner, Inc., the parent of AOL, eventually paid $300 million to settle SEC charges and $2.65 billion to settle a shareholder class action suit related to the sham revenue scheme and other fraudulent practices. SEC v. Time Warner Inc., Accounting and Auditing Enforcement Release No. 2216, [2003-2006 Transfer Binder] Fed. Sec. L. Rep. (CCH) ¶ 75,878 (Mar. 21, 2005), *available at* http://www.sec.gov/litigation/litreleases/lr19147.htm; *In re* AOL TimeWarner, Inc., No. MDL 1500, 02 Civ. 5575(SWK), 2006 WL 903236 (S.D.N.Y. Apr. 6, 2006). The SEC now estimates that AOL overstated revenue by more than $1 billion and has continued to bring new enforcement actions stemming from the schemes. *See, e.g.*, SEC v. Kelly, Accounting and Auditing Enforcement Release No. 2829 (May 19, 2008), http://www.sec.gov/litigation/litreleases/2008/lr20586.htm (discussing new fraud charges brought against eight former AOL Time Warner executives); SEC v. Veritas Software Corp., Accounting and Auditing Enforcement Release No. 2562 (Feb. 21, 2007), http://www.sec.gov/litigation/litreleases/2007/lr20008.htm (settling charges related to a fraudulent earnings scheme in which Veritas agreed to buy online advertising from AOL in exchange for AOL paying inflated prices for Veritas software).

3. "Round-trip" transactions may involve more than two parties when entities use intermediaries to try to conceal the fraudulent arrangement. For example, Homestore, Inc. ("Homestore"), an Internet provider of real estate and related services, used multi-party "round-trips" in an effort to prevent auditors or regulators from detecting the scheme. In Homestore's "triangular" arrangements, it first purchased products and services from vendors; the vendors then used the funds to buy online advertising from media companies; finally, the media companies bought advertising from Homestore. This circular flow resulted in Homestore recognizing its own cash as revenue. In some transactions, Homestore employed two intermediaries in an attempt to further conceal the arrangement. *See, e.g., In re* Wiegand, Accounting and Auditing Enforcement Release No. 1866, [2003-2006 Transfer Binder] Fed. Sec. L. Rep. (CCH) ¶ 75,527 (Sept. 22, 2003), *available at* http://www.sec.gov/litigation/admin/33-8291.htm (imposing a cease-and-desist order on the CEO of entities involved in four-party "round-trip" transactions with Homestore).

4. Boosting revenues through "round-tripping" has also occurred at some non-Internet companies, even though the arrangements did not seek to increase net income. For instance, Suprema Specialties, Inc. ("Suprema"), a producer and distributor of Italian cheeses, filed for bankruptcy in 2002 as details of a fraudulent "round-trip" revenue scheme surfaced. Suprema sold cheese products to enterprises posing as "customers," which then sold the fictitious products to entities masquerading as "suppliers." The "suppliers" would then sell the products back to Suprema. In most of the transactions, the "customer" and "supplier" shared a common owner who earned commissions on the fictitious transactions. On paper, Suprema appeared to grow at a spectacular pace, with revenues increasing by 400% over a two-year period. In reality, the growth resulted from the fraudulent sales scheme. *In re* Suprema Specialties, Inc. Sec. Litig., 438 F.3d 256 (3d Cir. 2006) (reversing the dismissal of several claims in a complaint by shareholders for securities fraud violations against Suprema).

Another notable "round-trip" scheme occurred at Reliant Resources, Inc. ("Reliant") and CMS Energy Corp. ("CMS"). The companies engaged in "round-trip" energy swaps with each other and other companies to boost transaction volume and improve their standings in the industry trading rankings. The companies expected increases in the rankings to lead to more business. The trades involved simultaneous energy purchases and sales for the same volume at the same price on the same terms with no actual delivery contemplated. The companies improperly accounted for the trades on a gross basis, recording both the revenues and offsetting expenses associated with the "round-trip" trades. While the "round-trip" trades did not increase profitability, they did provide an illusory boost in the companies' rankings. Reliant's "power ranking" improved from tenth in 1999 to third in 2001; CMS moved up from number 287 on the Fortune 500 list in 1999 to number 156 in 2001. Both Reliant and CMS later settled antifraud charges with the SEC, restating their financial reports as part of the settlement. *In re* Reliant Res., Inc., Accounting and Auditing Enforcement Release No. 1780, [2003-2006 Transfer Binder] Fed. Sec. L. Rep. (CCH) ¶ 75,440 (May 12, 2003), *available at* http://www.sec.gov/litigation/admin/33-8232.htm; *In re* CMS Energy Corp., Accounting and Auditing Enforcement Release No. 1978, [2003-2006 Transfer Binder] Fed. Sec. L. Rep. (CCH) ¶ 75,639 (Mar. 17, 2004), *available at* http://www.sec.gov/litigation/admin/33-8403.htm.

** As a final example, a jury in the U.S. District Court for the District of South Carolina in 2010 convicted two former executives at Medical Manager Health Systems Inc. ("MMHS"), a subsidiary of WebMD Corporation from 2000 to 2005, on charges that they conspired to inflate fraudulently MMHS's reported earnings to meet or exceed analysts' expectations. Among the fraudulent practices involved, the defendants used "round-trip" sales with software dealers MMHS sought to buy. With the defendants' participation, MMHS inflated the prices paid to acquire several companies, which had simultaneously agreed to purchase Medical Manager software before the actual acquisitions. The company's associate general counsel awaits trial. Press Release, U.S. Dep't of Justice, Two Former Executives of Medical Manager Found Guilty in Securities Fraud Scheme (Mar. 1, 2010), http://www.justice.gov/opa/pr/2010/March/10-crm-215.html.

5. The SEC has imposed sanctions against corporate counsel for crafting or concealing fraudulent revenue recognition schemes, including "round-trip" transactions. For instance, in 2005, Jonathan Orlick, former general counsel of Gemstar-TV Guide International, Inc. ("Gemstar") paid $305,510.62 in disgorgement, interest, and penalties to settle SEC charges relating to revenue recognition violations at Gemstar. The SEC charges against Orlick included securities fraud, falsifying Gemstar's books and records, aiding and abetting Gemstar's reporting and record-keeping violations, and lying to auditors. According to SEC findings, Orlick directly participated in the recording and reporting of fraudulent revenue and repeatedly signed false management representation letters to Gemstar's auditors. As part of the settlement, the SEC prohibited Orlick from serving as an officer or director of a public company for ten years and suspended him from appearing or practicing before the SEC as an attorney. SEC v. Yuen, Accounting and Auditing Enforcement Release No. 2176, [2003-2006 Transfer Binder] Fed. Sec. L. Rep. (CCH) ¶ 75,838 (Jan. 21, 2005), *available at* http://www.sec.gov/litigation/litreleases/lr19047.htm; *In re* Orlick, Accounting and Auditing Enforcement Release No. 2177, [2003-2006 Transfer Binder] Fed. Sec. L. Rep. (CCH) ¶ 75,839 (Jan. 26, 2005), *available at* http://www.sec.gov/litigation/admin/34-51081.htm.

**On page 565 [omitted from the concise], delete the last citation in the first full paragraph. In November 2009, a federal jury acquitted former HBOC general counsel Jay Lapine on three counts of federal securities fraud. In 2006, another jury acquitted Lapine on a securities fraud conspiracy count, but deadlocked on the remaining charges, and the district court declared a mistrial. *See* Joyce E. Cutler, *Ex-CEO of McKesson Found Guilty, Ex-GC Acquitted in Second Fraud Trial*, 41 Sec. Reg. & L. Rep. (BNA) 2170 (Nov. 23, 2009); *McKesson Case Yields Acquittals and Mistrial*, WALL ST. J., Nov. 4, 2006, at A5.

On page 569 [omitted from the concise], insert the following discussion after the first full paragraph on the page:

**   Commercial lawyers often receive requests for "true sale" opinions in their practices and should develop an understanding of the underlying accounting principles and their complexity. In fact, those principles reached the national news in March 2010, when the examiner in the Lehman Brothers Holding Inc. bankruptcy, the largest in U.S. history, issued a report raising serious questions as to whether the investment bank violated financial accounting rules by using repurchase transactions to move about $50 billion in potentially troubled assets, and related liabilities, off its books at the end of various fiscal periods. Although the notes to the various financial statements disclosed that Lehman treated the repurchase agreements as secured borrowings, the company reported revenues from specifically structured repurchase agreements at the end of quarters.

**   In a typical repurchase transaction, an enterprise sells assets, but agrees to repurchase those same assets. As described in the first paragraph in this note, financial accounting treats such transactions as loans because in substance, the seller receives money, which it agreed to repay with interest-- in Lehman's situation within days. When Lehman swapped assets with a purported value greater than 105 percent of the cash received--the examiner's report suggests that many assets involved suffered from illiquidity and rapidly deteriorating economic conditions, however, the company reported the transactions as outright sales, which reduced assets, liabilities, and reported leverage. Within the firm, these transactions became known as "Repo 105 transactions," or simply "Repo 105s."

**   To qualify for sales treatment, an enterprise must no longer control the assets involved. If the enterprise cannot afford to buy the assets back because their repurchase price greatly exceeds the cash received, the seller arguably no longer controls the assets. (Seemingly, however, the seller still needs to record a liability related to the repurchase obligation, but cash or a marketable security will look better on a balance sheet than an illiquid asset, especially in n economic downturn.) Beginning in 2001, Lehman used the transactions to improve its balance sheet. After the investment bank could not obtain a "true sale" opinion regarding the transactions in the United States, the company contacted a British law firm, which issued the desired opinion, relying on European law. As a result, Lehman transferred assets to Europe to execute the transactions, which the company's auditor, Ernst & Young LLP, presumably acquiesced in, even after a whistleblower raised concerns. The SEC continues to investigate the transactions and has requested information from nineteen financial institutions about their repurchase accounting and disclosures. *See* Steve Burkholder & Malini Manickavasgam, *Lawmakers Blast Regulators for Failure to Uncover Lehman Accounting Irregularities*, 8 Corp. Accountability Rep. (BNA) 412 (Apr. 23, 2010); Michael Corkery, *Lehman Whistle-Blower's Fate: Fired*, WALL ST. J., Mar. 16, 2010; Susanne Craig & Mike Spector, *Repos Played a Key Role in Lehman's Demise*, WALL ST. J., Mar. 13, 2010; Mike Spector et al., *Examiner: Lehman Torpedoed Lehman*, WALL ST. J., Mar. 12, 2010, at A1.

** As this Supplement was going to print, *The Wall Street Journal* published a front page story reporting that in a letter to the SEC in April 2010, Bank of America Corp. ("BofA") admitted to participating in six transactions that incorrectly hid up to $10.7 billion in debt in an effort by a unit to cut the size of its balance sheet and to meet internal financial targets. The article described the transactions as "dollar roll" trades in which the bank transferred mortgage-backed securities to a trading partner and simultaneously agreed to repurchase similar securities from the same partner soon after the fiscal period ended. In its letter, BofA admitted that the bank erroneously treated some short-term repurchases as sales, rather than as borrowings, at the ends of fiscal quarters from 2007 to 2009. Such transactions illustrate so-called "window dressing," in which an enterprise acquires assets or sheds debt before an accounting period comes to an end in an effort to paint a better picture in the financial statements. *See* Michael Rapoport, *BofA Admits Hiding Debt*, WALL ST. J., July 10, 2010, at A1.

** Knowledgeable observers have concluded that inadequate financial reporting about QSPEs and other "off-balance sheet" entities, their activities and investments in troubled loans, and their risks to the sponsoring enterprise contributed to the credit crisis and resulting economic downturn, very likely even more than the highly publicized fair value accounting rules. Regardless, the credit crisis placed pressure on the rulemakers and regulators to clarify SFAS No. 140, now codified in FASB ASC Topic 860, *Transfers and Servicing*. After all, the crisis resulted, in large part, from lenders packaging subprime mortgages into securities sold to other financial institutions and investors, with borrowers subsequently defaulting on the mortgages. When asset values in the QSPEs deteriorated, the sponsoring financial institutions often bore some liability for the decline.

Financial accounting rules have continued to matter throughout the crisis. As more borrowers faced foreclosure, the lenders hesitated to modify the loan terms in fear that any such modifications would violate the sale accounting criteria then found in SFAS No. 140. As described earlier, transferors needed to surrender economic control of the assets transferred to qualify for favorable sale treatment under those rules. Even though such modifications would benefit both the struggling homeowners and the holders of the securities backed by the subprime mortgages, lenders worried that altering the terms of the loans that they had "sold" for financial accounting purposes would demonstrate continued control. In such circumstances, the financial accounting rules seemingly required the lenders to include the troubled mortgages on their balance sheets and at a reduced valuation.

Various members of Congress, hoping to prevent a further rise in foreclosures by allowing banks to make such modifications, requested guidance from the SEC on the proper application of SFAS No. 140, again now codified in FASB ASC Topic 860, under the circumstances. The SEC concluded that loan modifications made when loan default appears "reasonably foreseeable" would not require lenders to bring the loans back on to their balance sheets. Christopher Cox, Chairman of the SEC, Letter to Congressman Barney Frank, Chairman of the House Committee on Financial Services (July 24, 2007), http://www.house.gov/apps/list/press/ financialsvcs_dem/sec_response072507.pdf. Congressional leaders applauded the SEC's flexible approach which encourages lenders to help troubled borrowers, but commentators questioned if the guidance truly aligned with SFAS No. 140. In another controversial step, Senator Charles Schumer sent a letter to the Big Four accounting firms requesting that they remind their audit clients about this SEC guidance and encourage their clients to modify any subprime loans approaching default. Commentators criticized Schumer's advice for violating auditor independence principles. Steve Burkholder, *Schumer Suggests Big Four Urge Audit Clients to Modify Troubled Loans*, 39 Sec. Reg. & L. Rep. (BNA) 1411 (Sept. 17, 2007).

** In June 2009, FASB issued SFAS No. 166, *Accounting for Transfers of Financial Assets–an amendment of FASB Statement No. 140,* which ASU No. 2009-16 later codified in FASB Topic 860, and completed a project designed to simplify the rules on accounting for transfers of financial assets to improve consistency and transparency in financial reporting. Effective at the beginning of an enterprise's first annual reporting period that begins after November 15, 2009 and for interim and annual reporting periods ending after that date, FASB ASC Topic 860 now eliminates the exceptions which exempted QSPEs from the consolidation requirements and which allowed sale accounting for certain securitizations when the transferor has not surrendered control over the transferred financial assets. As a result, many transferred assets that the enterprise could have derecognized, or moved "off-balance sheet," no longer qualify for such treatment. During the credit crisis, these off-balance-sheet vehicles contributed hundreds of billions in dollars of losses at financial institutions. Beginning with the effective date, enterprises must reevaluate former QSPEs for possible consolidation according to then applicable rules. The new rules also enhance the information that the financial statements and related notes provide to supply greater transparency about transfers of financial assets and the risks arising from a transferor's continued involvement, if any, with the transferred assets. *See* TRANSFERS AND SERVICING (TOPIC 860), ACCOUNTING FOR TRANSFERS OF FIN. ASSETS, Accounting Standards Update No. 2009-16 (Fin. Accounting

Standards Bd. 2009) (codified at FASB ASC Topic 860, *Transfers and Servicing*).

Along with the new rules on the consolidation of variable interest entities, described on pages 121 to 122, *infra*, the new rules on transfers of financial assets will enlarge the balance sheets of the nation's banks and financial institutions by forcing QSPEs—and their underlying assets and liabilities—onto the banks' balance sheets. Under existing banking regulations, various banks will need to dedicate or obtain more capital, potentially reducing liquidity in the credit markets, in response to these new financial accounting rules. After the "stress tests" of nineteen large banks that the Federal Reserve conducted in early 2009, the Fed announced that it used assumptions consistent with the new rules in assessing participating banks' capital adequacy. *See New FASB Rules for Securitizations Portend Big Changes to Bank Ledgers*, 41 Sec. Reg. & L. Rep. (BNA) 1179 (June 22, 2009); David Reilly, *Look Under the Banks' Hoods*, WALL ST. J., Feb. 29, 2008, at C1.

b. EXCEPTIONS TO THE EXCHANGE TRANSACTION REQUIREMENT

On page 586 [omitted from the concise], replace the carryover paragraph at the bottom of the page with the following text:

Realizing that financial statement users need "realism," generally accepted accounting principles authorize several exceptions to the exchange transaction requirement for revenue recognition. First, in an effort to provide more relevant information, the FASB has begun to implement a movement to "fair value" accounting. Under a fair value system, enterprises measure certain assets and liabilities at fair value, or market value, rather than at historical cost as GAAP has traditionally required. At each financial statement date, enterprises report changes in fair value in earnings even though no exchange of these assets and liabilities has occurred. To assist the transition to such a system, the board recently released a new standard establishing a unified approach to measuring fair values. As the unabridged fourth edition explains on pages 587 through 596 [pages 376-85 in the concise], GAAP already required most enterprises to use fair value accounting to report investments in certain debt and marketable equity securities. In limited circumstances, an enterprise must include unrealized holding gains and losses on the income statement without an exchange transaction. More commonly, an enterprise's net unrealized holding gain and loss appeared in "other comprehensive income" when computing "comprehensive income." Another recent pronouncement from the FASB, however, grants entities an option to record more assets and liabilities at fair value and expands the unrealized holding gains and losses that enterprises can report on the income statement without an exchange transaction. Second, if changing circumstances impair an asset's value, conservatism requires the enterprise to recognize an immediate loss for any non-temporary decline in value. Both the "fair value" rules and the requirement to recognize a loss when an asset has suffered an other-than-temporary impairment ("OTTI") have attracted considerable attention and generated significant controversy during the credit crisis. Finally, the accounting profession has used current fair market values on personal financial statements for many years.

On page 587, change the heading for section (1) and insert the following text. The text under the current "Investments in Securities" section beginning on this page will become subsection (a) [on page 376 of the concise, in the section on exceptions to the bona fide transaction requirement, note the following developments regarding fair value accounting].

(1) *Fair Value Accounting*

Both FASB and IASB currently endeavor to develop a comprehensive scheme for incorporating fair value measurements into financial reporting. This new approach stands in contrast with the historical-cost principal and exchange transaction requirement for revenue recognition. Financial statement users can benefit from fair value reporting, which provides more timely and relevant asset and liability valuation data. As the credit crisis powerfully illustrates, however, fair value reporting also increases volatility in reported earnings and amounts shown on the balance sheet. Reporting at fair value also comes at the cost of reliability and comparability if companies use different sources and methods for measuring the current values of assets and liabilities. To address these concerns, in 2006 the FASB issued SFAS No. 157, *Fair Value Measurements*. Those rules, now codified in FASB ASC Topic 820, *Fair Value Measurements and Disclosures*, define fair value, establish a unified framework for measuring fair value, and expand disclosures about fair value measurements.

FASB ASC Topic 820 defines "fair value" as the "exit price," meaning "the price that would be received to sell an asset or paid to transfer a liability in an orderly transaction between market participants at the measurement date." The standard establishes a three-tier "hierarchy" for inputs used to determine fair value. First, a quoted price in an active market typically provides the most reliable evidence of fair value. Hence, only "quoted prices (unadjusted) in active markets for identical assets or liabilities" that the reporting entity can access at the measurement date qualify as "Level 1 inputs," which explains the expression "mark-to-market." Next, the hierarchy recognizes other directly or indirectly observable inputs as "Level 2 inputs." These second-tier inputs include quoted market prices for similar assets or liabilities in active markets; quoted prices for identical or comparable assets in inactive markets; interest rates and yield curves observable at commonly quoted intervals; and other market-corroborated inputs. By comparison, FASB ASC Topic 820 defines "Level 3 inputs" as "unobservable inputs for the asset or liability," including the reporting entity's own analysis of the underlying data that market participants would factor into the pricing of the asset or liability. As a result, most commentators refer to those valuations based on Level 2 or Level 3 inputs as "mark-to-model," although some individuals refer to valuations based on Level 2 inputs as "mark-to-comparables." To enhance transparency, the disclosure rules in FASB ASC section 820-10-50 require enterprises to explain their use of significant unobservable inputs from Level 3 and the corresponding effect on earnings.

As originally issued, SFAS No. 157 (now in FASB ASC Topic 820, *Fair Value Measurements and Disclosures*) applied to financial statements issued for fiscal years beginning after November 15, 2007, and interim periods within those years, with early adoption permitted. As a result, the pronouncement required companies using the calendar year for financial accounting purposes to adopt the new rules no later than the first quarter in 2008. Subsequently, FASB approved a one-year partial deferral for fair value measures of non-financial assets and non-financial liabilities, noting challenges arising in implementation. Non-financial assets include goodwill and other intangible assets, while contingencies and asset retirement obligations exemplify non-financial liabilities. FASB ASC ¶¶ 820-10-65-1, 820-10-15-1A, 820-10-50-8A, 820-10-55-23A to -23B (codifications of EFFECTIVE DATE OF FASB STATEMENT NO. 157, FASB Staff Position No. FAS 157-2 (Fin. Accounting Standards Bd. 2008).

Critics feared that granting leeway to managers in measuring the fair values of assets without readily-available market prices potentially invited manipulation and fraud similar to Enron's deceitful accounting practices. At Enron, managers used favorable internal valuation models and data to overvalue energy contracts and artificially boost earnings. Given the use of management's analysis in Level 3 valuations, some commentators have continued to refer to fair value accounting as "mark-to-management," or more skeptically, "mark-to-myth." In promulgating the rules on fair value measurements, however, FASB concluded the expanded disclosure requirements provide financial statement users with better information on the inputs that management used to measure fair value. The board emphasized that a single definition and framework for measuring fair value also enhanced consistency and comparability.

The debate over the merits of fair value accounting and the fair value option intensified as the subprime mortgage crisis spread to other credit markets. Investment banks, which adopted the fair value measurement rules early, struggled to value their holdings as markets for securities and derivatives connected to American subprime mortgages crashed. Commentators feared that businesses would turn to outdated or inaccurate Level 3 inputs for fair value estimates. In October 2007, the Center for Audit Quality, an AICPA affiliate, issued a white paper, *Measurements of Fair Value in Illiquid (or Less Liquid) Markets*, to assist in fair value calculations. The white paper emphasized that firms must look to markets first, even when illiquid or thinly-traded. The measurement rules, the paper reminded, generally did not permit the use of Level 3 inputs when markets offer relevant data. Ctr. for Audit Quality, Am. Inst. of Certified Pub. Accountants,

Measurements of Fair Value in Illiquid (or Less Liquid) Markets (Oct. 3, 2007), http://www.aicpa.org/caq/download/WP_ Measurements_of_FV_in_Illiquid_Markets.pdf; *see also* Steve Burkholder, *CAQ Circulating Advice to Look to Market in Valuing Financial Assets in Subprime Crisis*, 39 Sec. Reg. & L. Rep. (BNA) 1461 (Sept. 24, 2007). In the fall of 2007, the SEC warned public companies that the agency would carefully scrutinize Level 3 valuations and disclosures. The agency subsequently launched several investigations into valuations and the timeliness of disclosures of subprime risks.

As the crisis continued and deepened, Wall Street's largest investment banks took multi-billion dollar write-downs on subprime-related instruments. Critics of fair value accounting blamed the new standards for exacerbating the credit crunch. As banks wrote down investments, regulatory capital requirements limited the banks' ability to lend money. Some investors and executives faulted fair value accounting for exaggerating losses, thereby causing market downturns. A "domino effect" resulted, they argued, with market downturns triggering further writedowns. Many executives felt forced to recognize current losses on holdings they did not intend to sell in the near-term. In April 2008, an International Monetary Fund report implicated fair value as a contributor to the global credit crisis, noting that the heavy discounting of instruments during a crisis produces fair values much lower than the expected future cash flows would imply. Int'l Monetary Fund, Global Financial Stability Report: Containing Systemic Risks and Restoring Financial Soundness 65-66 (Apr. 2008), http://www.imf.org/External/Pubs/FT/GFSR/2008/01/pdf/text.pdf. Analysts acknowledged that fair value accounting increased volatility and reduced comparability from quarter to quarter. David Reilly, *Wave of Write-Offs Rattles Market*, WALL ST. J., Mar. 1, 2008, at A1. At the core, however, no one trusted the financial statements and the numbers that enterprises used for fair values. The market capitalizations at many banks fell below their tangible book values.

Nevertheless, most investors and leaders in the accounting community have continued to defend fair value accounting as part of the solution to the credit crisis, not part of the problem. In their view, misguided lending decisions and the creation of complex instruments based on subprime loans caused the crisis, not accounting rules. Even under the historical-cost system, GAAP required enterprises to write bad loans down to fair value, the amount expected to be recovered in the future. These supporters also observe that international regulators increasingly demand fair value information to reduce the uncertainty in valuations. Proponents emphasize that fair values provide more relevant and helpful information for investment decision-making. Numerous commentators have observed that when management enjoys the latitude to "mark" assets and liabilities, most surprises have been—and will likely continue to be—on the downside. One analyst noted that Lehman Brothers Holding Inc.'s insolvency approximated $150 billion, while Enron's liabilities did not exceed its assets by any more than $70 billion. Advocates of fair value accounting also point to the savings-and-loans crisis of the 1980's, which resulted partly from banks carrying loans at historical cost when the loans had sharply declined in value.

Recall that the definition of fair value explicitly requires "an orderly transaction." In contrast to a forced transaction, such as a distressed sale or rushed liquidation, an orderly transaction "assumes exposure to the market for a period prior to the measurement date to allow for marketing activities that are usual and customary for transactions involving such assets." As the financial crisis expanded, numerous banks and other financial institutions contended that regulators or rulemakers should repeal, or at least suspend, fair value accounting because the crisis had frozen many markets.

Under intense political pressure to dump or suspend "mark-to-market" accounting as then set forth in SFAS No. 157, especially as applied to banks and other financial institutions, FASB provided additional guidance on issues related to fair value accounting and disclosures on multiple occasions. The guidance included two pronouncements on inactive markets and distressed transactions.

Even though the House of Representatives voted against the original "bail-out" bill in September 2008, the legislation contained a provision that would have authorized the SEC to suspend the application of SFAS No. 157, now codified in FASB ASC Topic 820, *Fair Value Measurements and Disclosures*, to any issuer or with respect to any class or category of transaction. In an effort to respond to the criticism that fair value had exacerbated the financial crisis, the SEC's Office of the Chief Accountant and the FASB's staff issued a joint press release, using a question and answer format, to provide immediate guidance and clarification on certain issues involving fair value measurements. Perhaps most significantly, the guidance recognized that unobservable Level 3 inputs might more appropriately determine fair value than observable Level 2 inputs, especially when the underlying circumstances required significant adjustments to available observable inputs. Earlier, the announcement explicitly stated that management could use estimated and discounted future cash flows to measure fair value when an active and orderly market did not exist, as long as the calculation reflected the expectations of market participants, as opposed to management. The press release also emphasized that because fair value measurements require significant judgments, investors need clear and transparent disclosures to understand those judgments and their effects on the financial statements. Finally, the statement announced that FASB was preparing to propose additional interpretative guidance on fair value later in the week. Press Release, SEC Office of the Chief Accountant & FASB Staff Clarifications on Fair Value Accounting (Sept. 30, 2008), http://www.sec.gov/news/press/2008/2008-234.htm.

** After immediately adding a "fast-track" project to its agenda, FASB issued guidance on determining the fair value of a financial asset in an inactive market. The guidance followed a short comment period that lasted less than a week, but produced more than 100 written responses. Using an example that sought to illustrate key considerations in determining the fair value of a financial asset in an inactive market, the guidance, now codified in FASB ASC Subtopic 820-10, *Fair Value Measurements and Disclosures, Overall*, recognized that when a market become inactive such that the enterprise must apply significant adjustments using unobservable inputs to previously used observable inputs, the resulting and appropriate valuation would fall within the Level 3 category. In addition, the Board approved the use of a discounted, present value technique, as long as it incorporated the expectations of market participants. Among other factors indicating an inactive market, the guidance identified a significant widening in the spread between bid and ask prices, a decrease in volumes, stale prices, and prices that vary substantially either over time or among market makers. FASB ASC ¶¶ 820-10-35-15A, -55A, -55B, 820-10-65-2 (codifications of DETERMINING THE FAIR VALUE OF A FINANCIAL ASSET WHEN THE MARKET FOR THAT ASSET IS NOT ACTIVE, FASB Staff Position No. FAS 157-3 (Fin. Accounting Standards Bd. 2008)).

**   In the meantime, President Bush signed EESA into law on October 3, 2008. Section 133 of that legislation mandated that the SEC conduct, in consultation with the Board of Governors of the Federal Reserve and the Secretary of the Treasury, a study on mark-to-market accounting standards then set forth in SFAS No. 157 and submit a report to Congress within ninety days. On December 30, 2008, the SEC submitted its 211-page report. The report recommended against suspending fair value accounting, but suggested several improvements to existing practice, including developing additional guidance for determining fair value in inactive markets, reconsidering the accounting for impairments, assessing whether fair value accounting should seek to separate declines related to changes in credit risk and probable credit losses from changes in liquidity, and enhancing disclosure requirements related to the effect of fair value in the financial statements. The report noted that enterprises generally cannot include recoveries in value that might follow an impairment loss in income until the enterprise sells the underlying asset. As key findings, the report found that investors generally believe that fair value accounting increases transparency and facilitates better investment decisions; that fair value accounting did not appear to cause the bank failures that occurred in 2008; and that suspending fair value accounting to return to historical cost-based financial reports would likely increase investor uncertainty. Office of the Chief Accountant & Div. of Corp. Fin., U.S. Sec. & Exch. Comm'n, Report and Recommendations Pursuant to Section 133 of the Emergency Economic Stabilization Act of 2008: Study on Mark-To-Market Accounting (2008), http://www.sec.gov/news/studies/2008/marktomarket123008.pdf.

As described in the discussion on losses on page 124, *infra*, shortly after the SEC transmitted its report, FASB issued additional guidance on other-than-temporary impairments. About a month later, and in response to the recommendations contained in the SEC report and input from constituents, FASB added three new projects on fair value measurements and disclosures to its agenda, including an effort to offer additional guidance on inactive markets and distressed transactions.

During a Congressional hearing on March 12, 2009, both Democratic and Republican members of the House Financial Services Subcommittee on Capital Markets, Insurance, and Government Sponsored Entities essentially gave FASB Chairman Robert Herz an ultimatum to issue additional guidance within the month or Congress would suspend fair value accounting.

** Within days, FASB again expedited its process and soon issued three staff positions on April 9, 2009, two involving fair value accounting and disclosures and the third related to accounting for impaired securities, such as mortgage-backed securities. The pronouncements provide guidelines for making fair value measurements more consistent with the principles now codified in FASB ASC Topic 820, *Fair Value Measurements and Disclosures*, seek more consistency in financial reporting by increasing the frequency of fair value disclosures, and include guidance to improve clarity and consistency in recording and presenting impairment losses on securities. All three staff positions took effect with 2009 second-quarter financial reporting for enterprises using the calendar year for financial accounting purposes. The pronouncements, however, allowed enterprises to adopt the guidance, in its entirety, for the first quarter.

** With regard to fair value accounting, the first staff position addressed how to determine fair values when no active market exists or where the relevant price inputs represent distressed sales. In short, the new rules, now codified in sections 820-10-35 and 820-10-50 of the Codification, sought to dispel the notion that the measurement rules imposed a "last price" model. In essence, the guidance affirms the need for management to use judgment when evaluating whether a market has become inactive and tries to both expand and guide that judgment. In addition, the new rules require an enterprise to disclose changes in valuation techniques and related inputs for fair value measurements in both interim and annual periods. FASB ASC §§ 820-10-35, -50 (codifications of DETERMINING FAIR VALUE WHEN THE VOLUME AND LEVEL OF ACTIVITY FOR THE ASSET OR LIABILITY HAVE SIGNIFICANTLY DECREASED AND IDENTIFYING TRANSACTIONS THAT ARE NOT ORDERLY, FASB Staff Position No. FAS 157-4 (Fin. Accounting Standards Bd. 2009)).

** FASB ASC section 820-10-35 states that fair value measurements seek to reflect how much the enterprise would sell the asset for in an orderly transaction—as opposed to a distressed or forced transaction—at the date of the financial statements under current market conditions. The Codification proceeds to list numerous factors that enterprises should evaluate to ascertain whether a formerly active market has become inactive. If the market has become inactive, an enterprise must next evaluate whether any observed prices or broker quotes obtained represent distressed transactions. The circumstances that may indicate disorderly transactions include inadequate exposure to the market before the measurement date to allow usual and customary marketing activities, marketing to only a single market participant, a need to sell to meet regulatory or legal requirements, or a transaction price that falls outside other recent prices for the same or similar asset or liability. In inactive or disorderly markets, the Codification proceeds to recognize that management could use a discounted cash flow model to estimate fair value, as long as fair value measurement includes "a risk premium reflecting the amount market participants would demand because of the risk (uncertainty) in the cash flows [in an orderly transaction at the measurement date under current market conditions]." FASB ASC ¶¶ 820-10-35-36, -48, -51A to -53, 820-10-50-2, -5 (codifications of FSP No. FAS 157-4).

** The second staff position on fair value, now codified in FASB ASC section 825-10-50, addresses disclosures regarding any financial instruments that the enterprise does not report on the balance sheet at fair value. The previous rules only required enterprises to disclose fair values once a year. The new rules require such disclosures on a quarterly basis. As a result, commercial banks must now disclose information about the fair value of their loans outstanding each quarter. FASB ASC ¶ 825-10-50-10 (a codification of INTERIM DISCLOSURES ABOUT FAIR VALUES OF FIN. INSTRUMENTS, FASB Staff Position No. FAS 107-1 & APB 28-1 (Fin. Accounting Standards Bd. 2009)).

** Seeking to reduce ambiguity and to improve consistency in applying the rules for measuring liabilities at fair value, FASB issued ASU No. 2009-05, *Measuring Liabilities at Fair Value*, to amend FASB ASC Subtopic 820-10, *Fair Value Measurements and Disclosures--Overall*, in August 2009. The amendments to the Codification clarify that when an enterprise cannot obtain a quoted price in an active market for the identical liability, the enterprise should, as usual, look to the views of marketplace participants and use one or more acceptable valuation techniques. Suitable means for measuring liabilities include techniques that use a quoted price for the identical liability when traded as an asset or quoted prices for similar liabilities or similar liabilities when traded as assets. In addition, other techniques consistent with the principles set forth in FASB ASC Topic 820, *Fair Value Measurements and Disclosures*, qualify. For example, both an income approach or a market approach would satisfy those principles. Under an income approach, an enterprise would use a present value technique to calculate the liability's fair value, while a market approach would try to determine the amount that the enterprise would pay to transfer the liability or would receive to enter into the identical liability. This new guidance applies to all reporting periods beginning after August 26, 2009.

** In response to continued calls from investors for additional information regarding fair value measurements, the FASB issued ASU 2010-6, *Improving Disclosures About Fair Value Measurements*, in January 2010. The amendments, again to Subtopic 820-10, seek to increase transparency in financial reporting by mandating additional information and clarifying existing disclosures. The rules require enterprises to make new disclosures about significant transfers in and out of Level 1 and Level 2 categories and activity in Level 3 fair value measurements. In the reconciliation for changes in amounts for Level 3, an enterprise should present information about purchases, sales, issuances, and settlements on a gross basis. The amendments clarify the level of disaggregation required and address disclosures about inputs and valuation techniques. An enterprise should provide disclosures about fair value measurements for each class of assets and liabilities. A class refers to a subset of assets or liabilities within a line item on the balance sheet. For fair value measurements that fall within Level 2 or Level 3, an enterprise should describe the inputs and techniques used to determine both recurring or nonrecurring measurements. The amendments apply to interim and annual reporting periods beginning after December 15, 2009, except for the Level 3 reconciliation disclosures, which become effective for fiscal years beginning after December 15, 2010, including interim periods within those years.

** FASB also continues to work on several joint projects with IASB regarding fair value, including efforts on fair value measurement and accounting for financial instruments, such as investments, derivatives, loans, and long-term receivables. As a long-term goal, both Boards aspire to require enterprises to measure all financial instruments at fair value, with realized and unrealized gains and losses reported in earnings in the period in which they occur. Banks and other financial institutions have resisted the ultimate objective. In any event, these comprehensive projects seek to converge international measurement, recognition, and impairment standards for financial instruments, to provide greater transparency, and to reduce complexity. In May 2010, FASB issued an exposure draft on financial instruments, including hedging activities. The comment period closes on September 30, 2010. Accounting for Financial Instruments and Revisions to the Accounting for Derivative Instruments and Hedging Activities, Proposed Accounting Standards Update (Fin. Accounting Standards Bd. May 26, 2010), *available via* http://www.fasb.org/cs/ContentServer?c=Page&pagename= FASB%2FPage%2FSectionPage&cid=1175801893139; Fin. Accounting Standards Bd., Project Update, Accounting for Financial Instruments (formerly Financial Instruments: Improvements to Recognition and Measurement and including the Accounting for Hedging Activities Project)—Joint Project of the IASB and FASB (July 2, 2010). In June 2010, the IASB and FASB issued separate exposure drafts seeking to develop common fair value measurement guidance. The comment periods on the exposure drafts close on September 7, 2010. According to their memorandum of understanding, the Boards plan to issue final standards on both projects before June 30, 2011. Amendments for Common Fair Value Measurements and Disclosure Requirements in U.S. GAAP and IFRSs, Proposed Accounting Standards Update (Fin. Accounting Standards Bd. June 29, 2010), *available via* http://www.fasb.org/cs/ContentServer?c=Page&pagename= FASB%2FPage%2FSectionPage&cid=1175801893139; Fin. Accounting Standards Bd., Project Update, Fair Value Measurement—Joint Project of the IASB and FASB (June 29, 2010). Interested readers can monitor developments on both projects via <http://www.fasb.org/jsp/FASB/Page/SectionPage&cid=1218220137074>.

When reading financial statements containing "fair value" amounts and disclosures, law students and lawyers should pay special attention to the percentage of assets and liabilities shown in Level 3 and disclosures about those assets and liabilities. How have those percentages changed from period to period? How has the amount of unrealized gains and losses in Level 3 assets changed? Does the firm explain fully the methods used to value Level 3 assets and liabilities? Has the firm changed its valuation methods? If so, how do any changes affect reported results? For public companies, readers should also study the portions of MD&A addressing fair value measurements and disclosures.

On pages 605 and 606 [pages 391 and 392 of the concise], please change the various references to "FIN 46" to "FIN 46(R)" to reflect the December 2003 revision to that pronouncement.

a) INVESTMENTS IN SECURITIES

On page 606, insert the following discussion and new subsection before "(2) Losses" [on page 392 of the concise, before section c. LOSSES, note these developments regarding FIN 46(R) and fair value accounting]:

** In response to the substantial losses that banks, investors, and other financial institutions incurred during the credit crisis from off-balance-sheet affiliates, particularly in the subprime residential mortgage industry, FASB completed two projects in June 2009. In addition to the project described above to revise SFAS No. 140, now codified in FASB ASC Topic 860, *Transfers and Servicing*, FASB completed a project to amend the consolidation rules that now appear in FASB ASC Topic 810, *Consolidation*. Until ASU No. 2009-17 amended the Codification, SFAS No. 167, *Amendments to FASB Interpretation No. 46(R)*, contained the amendments. The new rules eliminate the exception that allowed QSPEs to avoid consolidation; replace the quantitative-based "risk and rewards model" described on page 140 of the unabridged fourth edition [page 113 of the concise fourth edition] for determining which enterprise, if any, must consolidate a variable interest entity ("VIE") with a qualitative test; and require additional disclosures about an enterprise's involvement in VIEs. FASB believes these changes will improve transparency by providing more relevant and timely information about an enterprise's involvement with other controlled entities that may contain significant risk.

** Transactional lawyers in particular should understand that the new criteria in FASB ASC Topic 810 will undoubtedly lead to consolidation of more financial assets and liabilities. Starting with an enterprise's first annual reporting period that begins after November 15, 2009, which means January 1, 2010 for enterprises using the calendar year for financial accounting purposes, and applying to interim and annual reporting periods ending after that date, enterprises must consolidate entities that previously qualified for off-balance sheet treatment as QSPEs. The new rules may also require an enterprise to consolidate previously unconsolidated VIEs. In lieu of the "risks and rewards model," Topic 810 now contains a primarily qualitative approach for identifying which enterprise holds the power to direct a VIE's activities that most significantly affect the entity's economic performance and (1) the obligation to absorb the entity's losses or (2) the right to receive benefits from the entity. In addition, enterprises holding interests in VIEs must periodically assess whether the enterprise has become the VIE's primary beneficiary, such as to require consolidation. Finally, the new consolidation rules require additional disclosures about an enterprise's involvement in VIEs, which will enhance the information provided to users of financial statements. Again, the new rules apply to calendar-year companies beginning January 1, 2010. *See* FASB ASC ¶¶ 810-10-25-37 to -38G, 810-10-35-4, 810-10-50 (a codification of SFAS No. 167).

b) FAIR VALUE OPTION FOR OTHER ASSETS AND LIABILITIES

FASB ASC Topic 825, *Financial Instruments*, which codified SFAS No. 159, *The Fair Value Option for Financial Assets and Financial Liabilities*, grants enterprises the option to expand fair value reporting beyond investments in securities. The rules permit the reporting of many financial assets and financial liabilities at fair value with unrealized gains and losses included in income, an exception to the exchange transaction principle. Simply stated, financial assets involve contractual rights to receive cash; financial liabilities involve contractual obligations to pay cash. FASB ASC § 825-10-20 (a codification of SFAS No. 159, ¶ 6). For instance, financial assets include accounts receivable, but not fixed assets like buildings; financial liabilities include bonds payable, but not loss contingencies for pending or threatened litigation. Companies choosing the fair value option: (1) may apply the option selectively, instrument by instrument; (2) cannot revoke the option once elected; and (3) must apply the option to whole instruments, not parts of instruments. FASB ASC ¶ 825-10-25-2 (a codification of SFAS No. 159, ¶ 5). The new rules affect financial statements issued for fiscal years starting after November 15, 2007, the same timetable as SFAS No. 157, with early adoption permitted. The FASB viewed these rules as the culmination of the first phase of a comprehensive fair value project. Subsequently, the Board abandoned the second phase of the project which originally planned to consider expansion of the fair value option to non-financial assets and liabilities. Fin. Accounting Standards Bd., Project Updates, Fair Value Option (Oct. 22, 2007).

Controversy and lengthy debate has accompanied the movement toward fair value accounting. Two members of the FASB dissented from the "fair value option" rules, explaining that selective, instrument-by-instrument fair value reporting increases complexity, distorts evaluation of entities' economic exposures, and reduces the relevance of earnings. The dissenters favored a comprehensive fair value requirement instead of a fragmented, optional approach. Other critics decried the new standard for arbitrarily allowing managers to select the financial assets and liabilities measured at fair value, providing an opportunity for earnings management. The FASB, in defense, emphasized that the standard requires extensive disclosures on management's selection of the fair value option. The board highlighted that the fair value option reduces volatility in earnings that can result from the mismatch in reporting some assets and liabilities at historical cost and other related assets and liabilities at fair value. The new standard also achieves further convergence with International Accounting Standards, which already provided a fair value option for financial instruments.

(2) Losses

On pages 606 and 607 [pages 392 and 393 of the concise], replace the first two paragraphs under this heading with the following discussion:

As mentioned in Chapter I and repeated earlier in this chapter, conservatism generally requires an enterprise to recognize expenses and losses immediately. As we have already seen in this chapter and will see again in later chapters, this general rule regarding losses applies to investments, accounts receivable, inventory and long-lived assets. In the previous section, we mentioned that GAAP requires an enterprise to treat any "other than temporary" decline in an investment's value as a loss.

**   As early as 1985, the SEC's staff expressed its belief that the phrase "other than temporary" does not mean permanent. Accounting for Noncurrent Marketable Equity Securities, Staff Accounting Bulletin No. 59 (Sept. 5, 1985), *reprinted in* 7 Fed. Sec. L. Rep. (CCH) ¶ ¶ 75,522, 75,721 at Topic 5–M (May 28, 2003). Today, FASB ASC Topic 320, *Investments—Debt and Equity Securities*, which codified FSP FAS 115-1 & 124-1, *The Meaning of Other-Than-Temporary Impairment and Its Application to Certain Investments*, addresses the steps that an enterprise must follow to determine whether circumstances have impaired an investment, whether the impairment qualifies as temporary, and the how to measure any other-than-temporary impairment loss. The Codification concludes that an investment becomes impaired when its fair value falls below its cost. In determining whether an investment has experienced a non temporary decline, the enterprise must consider various factors originally set forth in SAB No. 59 and other pronouncements, including the length of time and the extent to which fair value has remained less than cost, the enterprise's intent and ability to hold the investment for such time as to allow for any anticipated recovery in fair value, and the investee's financial condition and near-term prospects. If an investment has suffered a non-temporary decline, the enterprise must write down the investment to its fair value and may not recognize any partial recoveries subsequent to that date through the income statement. In other words, the investment's then-fair value becomes its new cost basis from which the enterprise determines any future other-than-temporary impairments. In addition, the enterprise must sell the investment to recognize income from any subsequent increase in value after the write-down. FASB ASC ¶¶ 320-10-35-17 to -34 (codifications of FSP FAS 115-1 & FAS 124-1).

As mentioned earlier on page 116, *supra*, in 2008 the SEC's Office of the Chief Accountant and the FASB's staff jointly issued a press release regarding various issues involving fair value measurements and the credit crisis. Relevant to this discussion, the statement acknowledged that existing GAAP did not provide safe harbors or bright-line rules for exercising judgments about other-than-temporary impairments. The release reiterated, however, that generally speaking, "the greater the decline in value, the greater the period of time until anticipated recovery, and the longer the period of time that a decline has existed," the greater the evidence necessary to conclude that the decline remains temporary. SEC Office of the Chief Accountant & FASB Staff, Clarifications on Fair Value Accounting (Sept. 30, 2009), http://www.sec.gov/news/press/2008/2008-234.htm.

Early in 2009 and on an expedited basis, FASB issued a staff position retaining the other-than-temporary assessment guidance and required disclosures now found in FASB ASC Subtopic 325-40, *Investments—Other, Beneficial Interests in Securitized Financial Assets,* which codified FSP EITF 99-20-1, *Amendments to the Impairment Guidance of EITF Issue No. 99-20.* In an other-than-temporary impairment analysis, an enterprise seeks to determine whether it will probably realize some portion of the unrealized loss on an impaired security. Such a loss realization could occur because either the enterprise will not collect all of the contractual or estimated cash flows, considering both the timing and amount, or the enterprise lacks the intent and ability to hold the security until its value recovers. The pronouncement cautioned that an enterprise cannot automatically conclude that a security has not suffered an other-than-temporary impairment simply because the enterprise has received all of the scheduled payments to date. At the same time, the guidance observed that not every decline in fair value represents an other-than-temporary impairment. Although other-than-temporary assessments require analysis and judgment, the longer or more severe the decline in fair value, the more persuasive the evidence that management needs to overcome the premise that the enterprise will not collect all of the contractual or estimated cash flows. When FASB issued the staff position during the credit crisis, two board members dissented on the grounds that financial accounting standards should serve the needs of investors and the investor community did not request and did not support the guidance, especially on an expedited basis with limited due process. FASB ASC ¶¶ 325-40-35-3, -4, -10A, -10B (codifications to FSP EITF 99-20-1).

Most recently, in April 2009, FASB released guidance now contained in FASB ASC Topics 320, *Investments—Debt and Equity Securities,* and 325-40, *Investments—Other—Beneficial Interests in Securitized Financial Assets,* which codified FSP FAS 115-2 & 124-2, *Recognition and Presentation of Other-Than-Temporary Impairments,* that enables enterprises to avoid taking impairment charges against current earnings on certain investments in debt securities. The new rules, however, bring more consistency to the recognition of impairments and provide more information to investors about the credit risk and illiquidity components of impaired debt securities that the enterprise does not expect to sell until their maturity. Notably, the guidance could change when and where an enterprise records a write-down for held-to-maturity and available-for-sale debt securities. Under previous rules, an enterprise need not reduce net income for a temporary impairment as long as the enterprise could and planned to hold the security until its fair value recovered. Under the new rules, an enterprise need not record an impairment charge as long as the enterprise does not intend to sell the security and evidence indicates on a "more likely than not" basis that regulatory requirements, legal obligations, or other circumstances will not compel the enterprise to sell the security before recovering its remaining basis. Next, the guidance changed the presentation of an impairment charge, splitting it into two components. First, the amount of the impairment related to credit losses will appear on the income statement and will reduce net income. Second, enterprises will show the amount of the impairment related to other factors, such as illiquidity, in other comprehensive income in the equity section of the balance sheet. An enterprise, however, must present the total other-than-temporary impairment on the income statement, with an offset for the portion recognized in other comprehensive income. Last, the guidance now requires interim disclosures about impairments for both debt and equity, including the aging of securities with unrealized losses. Previously, enterprises only provided such disclosures annually. *See* FASB ASC §§ 320-10-35, 320-10-65-1, 325-40-35 (codifications of FSP FAS 115-2 & FAS 124-2).

As part of the joint project on financial instruments, FASB has been considering whether to amend U.S. GAAP to allow an enterprise to recover, through the income statement, a previously recognized other-than-temporary impairment loss on certain debt securities when evidence emerges that the impairment loss has reversed, as allowed under IFRS. The inability to recognize recoveries of an other-than temporary impairment through the income statement arises from a bias toward conservatism in financial reporting, but also places significant pressure on the decision to recognize an impairment loss. *See* Accounting for Financial Instruments and Revisions to the Accounting for Derivative Instruments and Hedging Activities, Proposed Accounting Standards Update ¶ BC193 (Fin. Accounting Standards Bd. May 26, 2010), *available via* http://www.fasb.org/cs/ContentServer?c=Page&pagename=FASB%2FPage%2FSectionPage&cid=1175801893139. Interested readers can monitor developments on the joint project via <http://www.fasb.org/jsp/FASB/Page/SectionPage&cid=1218220137074>.

2. EARNINGS PROCESS SUBSTANTIALLY COMPLETE

a. GENERAL RULES

(3) Nonmonetary Transactions

On page 616, insert the following text after the paragraph ending on the top of the page [on page 395 of the concise, insert the following text above Problem 6.3]:

Under these principles, if an enterprise cannot determine the value of the asset or service relinquished, the enterprise should not record revenue. Mere formalities, such as "swapping" checks of equal value, do not provide an acceptable indicator of value. To illustrate: in 2003, the SEC imposed a cease-and-desist order on an Internet company, MaxWorldwide, Inc, formerly known as L90, Inc. ("L90"), for improper accounting regarding barter transactions involving advertising. In a barter transaction, a type of nonmonetary exchange, two or more enterprises exchange goods or services, but not money. In the transactions at issue, L90 exchanged advertising on its website for similar advertising on another company's website; L90 then "swapped" checks of identical amounts with the other company, sometimes using intermediaries. L90 improperly recorded revenue from these barter transactions based on the check amounts. *In re* MaxWorldwide, Inc., Accounting and Auditing Enforcement Release No. 1760, [2003-2006 Transfer Binder] Fed. Sec. L. Rep. (CCH) ¶ 75,420 (Apr. 23, 2003), *available at* http://www.sec.gov/litigation/admin/34-47727.htm.

Enterprises must account for barter transactions based on the fair value of the assets or services involved under FASB ASC Topic 845, *Nonmonetary Transactions*, which codified APB Opinion No. 29, as amended by SFAS No. 153. FASB ASC Subtopic 605-20, *Revenue Recognition—Services*, which codified EITF Issue No. 99-17, *Accounting for Advertising Barter Transactions*, specifically addresses the proper accounting for advertising barter transactions involving check swaps. Under Subtopic 605-20, enterprises can recognize revenue and expense from an advertising barter transaction only if they can determine the fair value of the advertising surrendered based on their own historical practice. FASB ASC ¶¶ 605-20-25-14 to -18 (a codification of EITF Issue No. 99-17, ¶ 4). Check swaps do not evidence the fair value of the transaction. Where an enterprise cannot determine the fair value of the advertising surrendered, the enterprise records the barter transaction based on the carrying amount of the advertising surrendered, likely zero. The enterprise should still disclose the volume and type of the advertising surrendered and received. Since L90 could not properly determine the fair value of the advertising surrendered, the company could not recognize revenue based solely on the "check swap." FASB ASC ¶¶ 605-20-25-14 to -18, 605-20-50-1 (codifications of EITF Issue No. 99-17, ¶¶ 4, 80).

(4) Software Revenue Recognition

On page 617 [omitted from the concise], insert the following sentence at the end of the carryover paragraph at the top of the page:

These revenue recognition rules seemingly caused Apple Inc. in early 2007 to charge some customers who bought new Macs $1.99 to download a software enhancement that would enable them to use Wi-Fi technology. Without the charge, Apple feared the rules would preclude the company from recognizing any revenue from the computer sales until it shipped such enhancements and that its auditors could have required the company to restate revenue from previous accounting periods. David Reilly, *Apple Gets a Bruise by Blaming a $1.99 Fee on Accounting Rules*, WALL ST. J., Jan. 20, 2007, at B3.

**In October 2009, the FASB concurrently issued two new rules on related revenue recognition issues that have changed how technology, biotech, medical device, auto, and appliance companies account for sales of products that bundle software, hardware, and services. Previous rules usually required companies to defer the majority of the revenues from such sales, gradually recognizing those revenues over time, rather than immediately upon sale. The new rules allow enterprises to recognize revenue sooner.

**   ASU 2009-13, *Multiple-Deliverable Revenue Arrangements*, amended FASB ASC Topic 605, *Revenue Recognition*, to enable vendors to account for products or services, referred to as "deliverables," separately rather than as a combined unit. Under previous rules, an enterprise could recognize revenue from such arrangements only if the vendor could show vendor-specific objective evidence or third-party evidence as to any undelivered elements' selling price. Under the so-called residual method, the vendor could allocate the residual amount in the arrangement to the delivered element. As a result, the residual method allocated any discount in selling prices from the combined transaction entirely to the delivered elements. The new rules eliminate the residual method. By comparison, the relative selling price method allocates any discount in the arrangement proportionately to each deliverable, which enables enterprises to recognize all the expected revenue from the completed parts of the transaction.

**   The guidance also removes the previous rules that required management to obtain vendor-specific objective evidence or third-party evidence of fair value for each deliverable in an arrangement with multiple elements or the enterprise could not immediately recognize revenue from that deliverable. Now, when an enterprise cannot obtain such evidence, management nevertheless can estimate the proportion of the selling price attributable to each deliverable. The revised rules, however, require additional disclosures about how a vender allocates revenue to deliverables, the significant judgments involved and any changes to those judgments in allocating revenue, and how those judgments affect when the enterprise reports revenue and its amount.

**   ASU 2009-14, *Certain Revenue Arrangements That Include Software Elements*, changes FASB ASC Topic 985, *Software*, and addresses concerns that constituents had expressed about the accounting for transactions that contained tangible products and software. Investors and vendors had argued that the previous rules forced them to delay recognizing revenue for certain products, such as Apple Inc.'s iPhone, that bundled tangible products and software. Previously, Apple recognized iPhone revenue over a two-year period, the time it expected the customer to use the device. The new rules remove tangible products from the scope of the software revenue recognition guidance. *See* Michael Rapoport, *FASB, as Expected, Approves Accounting Change That Benefits Tech Companies*, WALL ST. J., Sept. 24, 2009, at C6.

**   The new rules apply prospectively for arrangements entered into or materially modified in fiscal years beginning on or after June 15, 2010, with earlier adoption permitted. If an enterprise elects early adoption, however, the enterprise must apply the guidance retrospectively from the beginning of its fiscal year.

C.   THE MATCHING PRINCIPLE FOR EXPENSES

2. ACCRUAL OF EXPENSES AND LOSSES

b. THE PROBLEM OF UNCOLLECTIBLE ACCOUNTS

On page 667, add the following discussion to the bottom of the page [on page 431 of the concise, add the following before the PROBLEMS section]:

The current financial crisis has reignited the debate among investors, regulators, standard-setters, and executives about how enterprises, especially banks and other financial institutions, should calculate their reserves for loan losses—similar to the allowance for doubtful accounts at a retailer or wholesaler—and the appropriate time to increase those reserves. During the crisis, many companies, especially banks and thrifts, have suffered huge losses from bad loans. As the economic downturn began and credit quality started to deteriorate, some companies anticipated more defaults and increased their bad-loan reserves, thereby lowering reported earnings. Other companies preferred to rely on their historical experience and did not increase their reserves, which kept current profits high. *See, e.g.*, Peter Eavis, *New Threat: Loan Losses*, WALL ST. J., Apr. 22, 2008, at C3; Robin Sidel & David Reilly, *No Worries: Banks Keeping Less Money in Reserve*, WALL ST. J., Feb. 27, 2007, at C7.

**   In early 2007, the FASB launched a new project to improve disclosures that a creditor provides about the allowance for credit losses and the credit risks inherent in its loan portfolio. Proposed new disclosures include information about the credit characteristics in the enterprise's portfolio of financing receivables, such as loans, finance leases, and trade receivables with terms that exceed one year. Fin. Accounting Standards Bd., Project Updates, Disclosures about Credit Quality and the Allowance for Credit Losses (June 14, 2010). Interested readers can access project updates via <http://www.fasb.org/jsp/FASB/Page/SectionPage&cid=1218220137074>.

** Among the recommendations in the plan that the Obama administration announced in June 2009 to overhaul the financial regulatory system, the administration urged accounting standard setters, specifically FASB, IASB, and the SEC, to improve accounting standards for reserves for loan losses before the end of 2009 without compromising the transparency of financial statements. (FASB missed this deadline, but plans to issue an accounting standards update in the third quarter of 2010, completing the project described in the previous paragraph.) The document advocated that these standard setters require enterprises to use "more forward-looking loan loss provisioning practices" and to consider factors that would cause loan losses to differ from recent historical experience. Such practices would likely result in enterprises recording larger provisions earlier in the credit cycle, while at the same time providing transparency to users of financial statements about changes in credit trends. U.S. DEP'T OF TREASURY, FINANCIAL REGULATORY REFORM: A NEW FOUNDATION 18, 30-31 (2009), http://www.financialstability.gov/docs/regs/FinalReport_web.pdf.

D.   DRAFTING AND NEGOTIATING AGREEMENTS AND OTHER LEGAL DOCUMENTS CONTAINING TERMINOLOGY IMPLICATING THE INCOME STATEMENT

On page 686, replace the text beginning at (c) with the following [on page 438 of the concise, note the following update on stock options and uncertain tax positions, lettered for the unabridged edition]:

(c) *Stock options.* In a so-called "share-based payment" transaction, which often refers to a "stock option," an enterprise issues certain ownership interests in exchange for services. FASB ASC Topic 718, *Compensation—Stock Compensation*, which codified SFAS No. 123R, *Share-Based Payment* (now in), requires companies to treat the fair value of any such awards, determined on the grant date, as an expense, which would reduce net income. Enterprises must select and apply a valuation model for this purpose. The new rules generally became effective for public companies at the start of the first annual reporting period beginning after December 31, 2005. FASB ASC § 718-10-30 (a codification of SFAS No. 123R). Even before many companies began issuing financial statements adopting the new rules, *The Wall Street Journal* published a front-page, Pulitzer prize-winning story that exposed widespread scandals involving backdated stock options. Charles Forelle & James Bandler, *The Perfect Payday*, WALL ST. J., Mar. 18, 2006, at

A1. To date, the scandals have led to at least eighty restatements, civil and criminal government investigations, dozens of executive dismissals, and numerous private lawsuits. Mark Maremont & John Hechinger, *Brocade Settles Suit for $160 Million*, WALL ST. J., June 3, 2008, at B4; Mark Maremont & Charles Forelle, *Bosses' Pay: How Stock Options Became Part of the Problem*, WALL ST. J., Dec. 27, 2006, at A1.

** (d) *Uncertain tax positions.* In June 2006, the FASB issued a new promulgation on uncertain income taxes, which applies to public companies for fiscal years beginning after December 15, 2006 and has established consistent criteria for reporting uncertain tax positions. Nonpublic enterprises could wait until the first annual period beginning after December 15, 2008 to adopt the new rules. Prior to the pronouncement, diverse accounting practices for income tax reserves provided opportunities for earnings management, and few companies disclosed details on the nature or amount of the reserves.

** FASB ASC Subtopic 740-10 (a codification of FASB Interpretation No. 48, *Accounting for Uncertainty in Income Taxes (an Interpretation of FASB Statement No. 109)* requires enterprises to examine each open tax position that constitutes a "unit of account," a judgment based on how the enterprise prepares its tax return and how the enterprise believes the taxing authority will approach the return. A two-step process then applies to analyze each uncertain tax position. The first step involves recognition: the enterprise can recognize only those tax benefits "more likely than not" sustainable, on their technical merits, upon examination. The enterprise must presume taxing authorities with full knowledge of all relevant information will examine the position. The second step focuses on measurement: the enterprise measures tax positions meeting the recognition criteria at the largest amount of benefit "more likely than not" realizable upon ultimate settlement. The enterprise makes measurements in light of the facts, circumstances, and information available at the reporting date. The rules include disclosure requirements to provide more information for financial statement users regarding an enterprise's uncertain tax positions, including descriptions regarding positions for which unrecognized tax benefits will reasonably possibly and significantly increase or decrease within the next twelve months. For public entities, the disclosures include a tabular reconciliation of the total amount of unrecognized tax benefits at the beginning and end of the period. FASB ASC ¶¶ 740-10-25-6 to -7, -13, 740-10-30-7, 740-10-50-15, 740-10-50-15A (codifications of FIN 48, ¶¶ 5-8, 21, as amended by ASU 2009-06, *Implementation Guidance on Accounting for Uncertainty in Income Taxes and Disclosure Amendments for Nonpublic Entities*).

If the uncertain tax benefit fails to meet the recognition criteria, the enterprise must establish a liability for "unrecognized tax benefits," with a corresponding increase in tax expense. The liability, often referred to as a "reserve," reflects tax benefits claimed on tax returns but not allowed for financial reporting purposes. In 2007, a Credit Suisse Group study examined the financial reporting consequences at 361 large companies. The resulting research report found that those companies had recognized a combined $141 billion in tax liabilities under the new interpretation. Jesse Drucker, *Lifting the Veil on Tax Risk*, WALL ST. J., May 25, 2007, at C1. Management's assessment of these estimated liabilities over time, as facts and circumstances change, can increase the volatility of earnings.

The FASB designed the new required disclosures to provide investors with more information about the uncertainty in income tax assets and liabilities. Tax authorities, predictably, will also read these new disclosures carefully, as this Supplement discusses in the materials updating Chapter VII on pages 146 and 147, *infra*.

** (e) *Securitizations and Consolidations.* As discussed earlier on pages 111 to 112 and 121 to 122, *supra*, amendments to FASB ASC Topic 810, *Consolidation*, and Topic 860, *Transfers and Servicing*, which codified new rules in SFAS No. 166, *Accounting for Transfers of Financial Assets[–]an amendment of FASB Statement No. 140*, and SFAS No. 167, *Amendments to FASB Interpretation No. 46(R)*, have enlarged the balance sheets of the nation's banks and financial institutions by forcing QSPEs—and their hundreds of billions of dollars in underlying assets and liabilities—onto the banks' balance sheets. The new rules, which FASB issued in June 2009, apply to companies using the calendar year for financial reporting purposes effective January 1, 2010. Discover Financial Services Inc., for example, disclosed that the rules would require it to bring $21 billion in assets onto its books and to increase its loss reserves by $2.1 billion, which would result in a $1.3 billion after-tax reduction in shareholders' equity in 2010's first quarter. J.P. Morgan Chase & Co. estimated that the rule would require it to consolidate about $145 billion in assets. Aparajita Saha-Bubna, *Discover Financial Plans New Accounting Rule*, WSJ.com, Mar. 12, 2010; Susan Pulliam, *Banks Try to Stiff-Arm New Rule*, WALL. ST. J., June 4, 2009, at C1. In addition to requiring additional regulatory capital to support the larger balance sheets, the new financial accounting requirements will affect leverage and coverage ratios in loan agreements and other contracts.

** In 2004, the IASB and FASB agreed that they should undertake a joint project to try to converge accounting standards governing consolidation. *See* Fin. Accounting Standards Bd., Project Update, Consolidation: Policy and Procedures--Joint Project of the IASB and FASB (Apr. 26, 2010). Generally speaking, IFRS recognizes de facto control over an investee as a basis for consolidation. Apart from VIEs, GAAP does not, focusing principally on majority ownership. Although the joint project does not currently enjoy priority status, interested readers can access project updates via <http://www.fasb.org/jsp/FASB/Page/SectionPage&cid=1218220137074>.

CHAPTER VII

CONTINGENCIES

B.   THE FINANCIAL ACCOUNTING RULES

On pages 695-704 [pages 444-453 of the concise], please note that FASB ASC Topic 450, *Contingencies*, codified SFAS No. 5, *Accounting for Contingencies*. In the quoted material in paragraphs 8(a), 11, 34, 35, and 36 from SFAS No. 5 on pages 697, 698, 702 and 703 [pages 446, 447, 451, and 452 of the concise], recent amendments to the rules for so-called "subsequent events," now generally set forth in FASB ASC Topic 855, *Subsequent Events*, which codified SFAS No. 165, *Subsequent Events*, change the cut-off point from "issuance of the financial statements" to the time the financial statements "are issued or are available to be issued (as discussed in Section 855-10-25)."

On pages 705 and 706, replace the discussion that follows the heading (ii) with the following text [in the concise, please observe the changes in the quoted language below arising from FASB ASC Topic 855, *Subsequent Events*, which codified SFAS No. 165, in note 2 on page 454]:

**   (ii) Period in which the underlying cause that gave rise to the litigation, claim or assessment ("the underlying event") occurred. FASB ASC Subtopic 450-20, *Loss Contingencies,* provides that an enterprise can accrue an amount related to a loss contingency only if information available before the financial statements "are issued or are available to be issued," indicates that the underlying event or events that gave rise to the contingency had impaired an asset or created a liability *at the date of the financial statements.* FASB ASC ¶ 450-20-55-17, which codified ACCOUNTING FOR CONTINGENCIES, Statement of Fin. Accounting Standards No. 5, ¶ 34 (Fin. Accounting Standards Bd. 1975), as amended by SUBSEQUENT EVENTS, Statement of Fin. Accounting Standards No. 165, ¶ B3 (Fin. Accounting Standards Bd. 2009). As a result, events that occur after the balance sheet date and that provide additional evidence about conditions that existed at the date of the balance sheet, such as notice of a claim, can change the appropriate accounting and reporting until the enterprise has issued the financial statements or, in the case of certain private enterprises, the financial statements "are complete in a form and format that complies with GAAP and all approvals necessary for issuance have been obtained." For example, management, the board of directors, the significant shareholders, or some combination of these groups may need to approve the financial statements, such that they qualify as "available to be issued." In such a circumstance, either the financial statements or the related notes must disclose the date through which the enterprise has evaluated subsequent events and whether that date represents the date the financial statements were issued or were available to be issued. FASB ASC §§ 855-10-20 (glossary), 855-10-50-1 (codifications of SFAS No. 165, ¶¶ 5-6, 12).

** At the same time, keep in mind that an enterprise cannot accrue any amount for a loss contingency when the underlying event or condition occurred after the date of the financial statements, but before the enterprise issues, or, in the case of certain private entities, at least approves, the financial statements. For example, FASB ASC Subtopic 450-20, *Loss Contingencies*, precludes an accrual for a lawsuit seeking damages resulting from an accident that occurred *after* the date of the financial statements. FASB ASC ¶ 450-20-55-17 (a codification of SFAS No. 5, ¶ 34, as amended by SFAS No. 165, ¶ B3). But, the disclosure rules regarding loss contingencies may require the enterprise to disclose the existence of a potential loss incurred from a so-called "subsequent event" to keep the financial statements from being misleading. FASB ASC ¶ 450-20-50-9 (a codification of SFAS No. 5, ¶ 11, as amended by SFAS No. 165, ¶ B3.b.).

** Please also observe that the rules governing loss contingencies may require an enterprise to accrue an amount related to a loss contingency involving a lawsuit, claim or assessment when the underlying cause occurred on or before the date of the enterprise's financial statements, even though the enterprise does not learn about the existence or possibility of the lawsuit, claim or assessment until after the date of the financial statements. FASB ASC ¶ 450-20-55-11 (a codification of SFAS No. 5, ¶ 35). Because the underlying event or condition occurred on or before the date of the financial statements, any information available prior to the completion and dissemination of the financial statements can affect the proper accounting treatment.

On page 707, delete the first full paragraph and insert the following text at the end of the carryover paragraph at the top of the page [on page 455 of the concise, replace the first paragraph with the following]:

**Returning full circle, for purposes of IAS 37, *Provisions, Contingent Liabilities and Contingent Assets*, the IASB interprets "probable" as meaning "more likely than not." PROVISIONS, CONTINGENT LIAB. & CONTINGENT

ASSETS, Int'l Accounting Standard No. 37, ¶ 23 (Int' l Accounting Standards Bd. 2008), *reprinted in* INT'L ACCOUNTING STANDARDS BD., INT'L FIN. REPORTING STANDARDS (AS ISSUED AT 1 JANUARY 2010), at A816 (2010). Based on comment letters and discussions at the 2005 public roundtable on the FASB's project on uncertain income taxes, FASB concluded that constituents do not consistently apply the confidence level that the term "probable" expresses. ACCOUNTING FOR UNCERTAINTY IN INCOME TAXES–AN INTERPRETATION OF FASB STATEMENT NO. 109, FASB Interpretation No. 48, ¶ B32 (Fin. Accounting Standards Bd. 2006).

On page 708 [omitted from the concise], replace the first sentence and related citation that follows the heading (i) with the following:

**   (i) Accrual of loss contingencies. FASB ASC Subtopic 450-20, *Loss Contingencies*, both requires and allows an enterprise to accrue an estimated loss only if both: (a) information available prior to the financial statements being issued or being available to be issued indicates that the enterprise probably, or at least more likely than not, incurred a liability or suffered the impairment of an asset before the date of the financial statements; and (b) the enterprise can reasonably estimate the loss. FASB ASC ¶ 450-20-25-2 (a codification of SFAS No. 5, ¶ 8, as amended by SFAS No. 165, ¶ B3.a.).

On page 711, at the end of the discussion on gain contingencies at the top of the page, insert the following example [on page 458 of the concise, add the following example to Note 8]:

To illustrate the possible legal issues arising from gain contingencies, the SEC filed civil charges in 2007 against Meridian Holdings, Inc. and two senior executives for allegedly using a $30 million default judgment award to inflate earnings fraudulently when they, and therefore, the company "had no reasonable basis to believe the judgment was collectible." SEC v. Meridian Holdings, Inc., Litigation Release No. 20318 (Oct. 1, 2007), http://www.sec.gov/litigation/litreleases/2007/lr20318.htm.

On page 712, insert the following text after the carryover paragraph ending on the top of the page [on page 458 of the concise at the end of Note 6 insert the following update regarding Merck, and also note the developments related to the FASB project on SFAS No. 5]:

**   In November 2007, Merck settled the principal Vioxx litigation for $4.85 billion, which the company treated as an expense during the fourth quarter. Throughout that year, Merck spent $616 million on legal defense costs related to Vioxx cases and also increased the related reserve by $280 million. At year-end, Merck's total "*Vioxx* Reserve" stood at $5.372 billion, reflecting the settlement amount and $522 million in reserve for future legal defense costs. Merck & Co., Annual Report (Form 10-K), at 78 (Feb. 28, 2008). During

2008, Merck spent about $305 million on legal defense costs worldwide related to Vioxx litigation, recorded a $62 million charge for future legal defense costs, and paid $750 million pursuant to the settlement, which left the "Vioxx Reserve" at approximately $4.379 billion on December 31, 2008. Merck & Co., Annual Report (Form 10-K), at 35 (Feb. 27, 2009). During 2009, Merck paid $4.1 billion into various settlement funds, spent approximately $244 million in legal defense costs worldwide related to Vioxx litigation, and recorded a $75 million charge for future legal defense costs, which left the "Vioxx Reserve" at approximately $110 million on December 31, 2009. Merck & Co., Annual Report (Form 10-K), at 102 (Mar. 1, 2010). Merck indicated that it "will continue to monitor its legal defense costs and review the adequacy of the associated reserves and may determine to increase the *Vioxx* Reserve at any time in the future if . . . it believes it would be appropriate to do so." *Id.* Other than a reserve established in connection with the resolution of certain shareholder derivative lawsuits, Merck has not established any reserves for any potential liability related to ongoing Vioxx product liability lawsuits or investigations because, among other reasons, the company "cannot reasonably estimate the possible loss or range of loss with respect to the *Vioxx* Lawsuits not included in the Settlement Program." *Id.*

Interestingly, the first paragraph in Note 12 to the Merck's financial statements, entitled "Contingencies and Environmental Liabilities," provides:

> The Company records accruals for contingencies when it is probable that a liability has been incurred and the amount can be reasonably estimated. These accruals are adjusted periodically as assessments change or additional information becomes available. For product liability claims, a portion of the overall accrual is actuarially determined and considers such factors as past experience, number of claims reported and estimates of claims incurred but not yet reported. Individually significant contingent losses are accrued when probable and reasonably estimable.

Id. at 143.

**4. In June 2008, the FASB issued a controversial exposure draft presenting proposed amendments to SFAS No. 5, now codified in FASB ASC Topic 450, *Contingencies*, to enhance the disclosure requirements for loss contingencies. DISCLOSURE OF CERTAIN LOSS CONTINGENCIES–AN AMENDMENT OF FASB STATEMENTS NO. 5 AND 141(R), Proposed Statement of Fin. Accounting Standards (Fin. Accounting Standards Bd. June 5, 2008). As no surprise, the organized bar, financial statement preparers, and auditors submitted strong objections during the comment period. In response, FASB decided to try to develop an alternative model and to conduct field testing before redeliberating the project.

** After completing redeliberations in April 2010, the Board announced that it would issue a revised exposure draft for a thirty-day comment period. The project summary that the FASB's staff periodically updates sets forth a disclosure object, disclosure principles, a disclosure threshold, mandatory qualitative and quantitative disclosures for all contingencies that meet the disclosure threshold, and a tabular reconciliation for public entities. Defense lawyers fear that the heightened disclosures will waive the attorney-client privilege and attorney work product protection. Both litigators and corporate counsel would do well to stay abreast of developments on this project.

**   The Board's staff has articulated the project's disclosure objective as follows: "An entity should disclose qualitative and quantitative information about loss contingencies to enable financial statement users to understand [the contingencies'] nature, potential timing, and potential magnitude." In addition, the staff has identified the following disclosure principles to help enterprises formulate disclosures appropriate to their individual facts and circumstances. During a contingency's early stages, an enterprise should disclose information to help users understand the contingency's nature and potential magnitude. As additional information becomes available, the enterprise should provide more extensive disclosures. An enterprise may aggregate disclosures about similar contingencies, but should disclose the basis for aggregation.

Disclosure Objective

Disclosure principles

**   As to the disclosure threshold, the Board has tentatively decided to retain the existing requirement that enterprises disclose asserted claims and assessments considered at least "reasonably possible" to give rise to a loss. At the same time, the Board now recognizes that certain remote loss contingencies also merit disclosure given their nature, potential timing, or potential magnitude. When assessing a loss contingency's materiality, an enterprise should not consider possible insurance recoveries or other indemnification arrangements.

Disclosure threshold

**   Perhaps most significantly, the Board has tentatively concluded that public entities should provide a tabular reconciliation about any accrued loss contingencies by class for each period for which the entity presents an income statement. The disclosure should contains: (1) the amount of any accruals at the beginning and end of the period; (2) any increases in the accruals for new loss contingencies during the period; (3) any changes in estimates for loss contingencies accrued in prior periods; and (4) any decreases for cash payments or other settlements during the period. Nonpublic entities need not provide such a tabular reconciliation.

Public Entities: Tabular reconciliation re: accrued loss contingencie

**   Any new guidance would presumably apply to fiscal years ending after December 15, 2010, and interim and annual periods in subsequent fiscal years, subject to an exception for nonpublic entities. Under that exception, the rules would not apply to such enterprises until the first annual period beginning after December 15, 2010. Following that first applicable annual period, the rules would also apply to interim periods in any subsequent fiscal year. Fin. Accounting Standards Bd., Project Updates, Disclosures of Certain Loss Contingencies (Apr. 26, 2010). Interested readers can access project updates via <http://www.fasb.org/jsp/FASB/Page/SectionPage&cid=1218820137074>.

**5. FASB ASC Topic 805, *Business Combinations*, which codified SFAS No. 141(R) on that same subject, generally requires an enterprise to recognize the assets acquired and liabilities assumed in a business combination, including litigation contingencies, at their fair market values on the acquisition date. *See* FASB ASC ¶ 805-20-30-1 (a codification of SFAS No. 141(R) ¶ 20). Following SFAS No. 141(R)'s issuance, preparers, auditors, and lawyers expressed concerns that the requirement to determine a legal contingency's fair market value could prejudice the underlying legal dispute. Responding to those concerns, FASB announced a return to the rules in the original SFAS No. 141. Under the original, and now again applicable, rules codified in FASB ASC Subtopic 805-20, *Identifiable Assets and Liabilities, and Any Noncontrolling Interest*, an enterprise only recognizes an acquired contingency at fair market value if the enterprise can determine that amount during the measurement period, which typically ends no later than one year after the transaction's closing. Otherwise, enterprises would follow the rules contained in FASB ASC Subtopic 450-20, *Loss Contingencies*, and originally set forth in SFAS No. 5 and FIN 14. As a result, an acquirer typically will not recognize the liability as of the acquisition date. FASB ASC ¶¶ 805-20-25-19 to -20B & 805-20-30-9, -23 (codifications of ACCOUNTING FOR ASSETS ACQUIRED AND LIABILITIES ASSUMED IN A BUS. COMBINATION THAT ARISE FROM CONTINGENCIES, FASB Staff Position No. FAS 141(R)-1, at ¶¶ 7-9 (Fin. Accounting Standards Bd. 2009).

C.   SECURITIES DISCLOSURE ISSUES

On page 723 [omitted from the concise], insert the following discussion at the end of the carryover paragraph:

In 2006, the SEC issued an administrative cease-and-desist consent order against Ashland Inc. and its former director of environmental remediation for improperly reducing the company's reserves for environmental cleanup costs at more than fifty chemical and refinery sites around the country. Cumulatively, these reserves ranged from $152 million to $178 million during 1998 to 2005. The reductions allowed the company to overstate its net income from 1999 to 2001. Although three whistleblowers raised questions about the reserves, an internal audit failed to discover most of the improper reductions. Among other things, the company agreed to strengthen its policies and internal controls for determining and documenting environmental reserves; to conduct an annual best practices review with its outside auditor on such policies and controls; and to retain a consultant to review its policies, procedures, and internal controls regarding environmental reserves and complaints from whistleblowers. *In re* Ashland Inc., Accounting and Auditing Enforcement Release No. 2518 (Nov. 29, 2006), http://www.sec.gov/litigation/admin/2006/34-54830.pdf.

**On page 727, insert the following note after Note 4 [on page 466 of the concise, insert the following note after Note 2, numbered for the unabridged version:

4A. Changing accounting rules, political administrations, disclosure requirements, and attitudes regarding environmental stewardship increasingly challenge businesses that must record or disclose environmental liabilities and their lawyers. For an accessible article discussing the issues and challenges, see Bernie Hawkins et al., *Disclosing Environmental Liabilities*, BUS. LAW TODAY, July/Aug. 2009, at 61-64.

On page 728 [page 467 of the concise], before the examples of press reports and securities filings documenting that public companies continue to record accruals for estimated amounts necessary to resolve pending or expected litigation, please insert the following more recent examples:

**   •In March 2010, Wachovia Bank, a subsidiary of Wells Fargo & Co., reached a $160 million settlement with the Justice Department to resolve allegations that the bank allowed Mexican drug traffickers to launder their profits. Anticipating the legal liability the larger bank would assume as Wachovia's corporate parent, Wells Fargo established a litigation reserve of approximately $160 million when acquiring the smaller bank. Press Release, Wells Fargo & Co., Wachovia Bank, N.A. Settles Previously Disclosed Compliance Matters (March 17, 2010), *available at* https://www.wellsfargo.com/press/2010/20100317_Wachovia; *see also* Evan Perez & Carrick Mollenkamp, *Wachovia Settles Money-Laundering Case*, WALL ST. J., Mar. 18, 2010, at C3.

**   • Only a few days earlier, UBS AG released its 2009 annual report, which describes probable liability arising from, among various other legal matters, the bank's management of third-party funds during the Madoff investment fraud, underwriting practices during the credit crisis, and cross-border wealth management services. UBS AB, Zurich and Basel, 2009 Annual Report, at 303-05 (2010). As of December 31, 2009, UBS had established a litigation reserve of nearly 2.3 billion Swiss francs to meet these expected legal liabilities. *Id.* at 303; *see also* Goran Mijuk, *UBS Sees Turnaround in 2010*, WSJ.com, Mar. 15,2010.

**   •In February 2010, State Street Corp. entered into settlement agreements with the SEC and the Commonwealth of Massachusetts to terminate their investigations into charges that State Street misled investors about their exposure to subprime mortgaged-backed-securities during the credit crisis. Press Release, State Street Corp., State Street Enters into Settlements with Regulatory Authorities to Resolve Inquiry into Losses by Certain Active SSGA Fixed-Income Strategies During 2007 (Feb. 4, 2010), *available at* http://phx.corporate-ir.net/phoenix.zhtml?c=78261&p=irol-newsArticle&ID=1383271. After these settlements, State Street had exhausted the $673 million litigation reserve that the company had maintained. State Street Corp., Quarterly Report (Form 10-Q), at 58 (May 7, 2010). More than two years earlier and during the fourth quarter in 2007, the company established a $625 million reserve. State Street Corp., Annual Report (Form 10-K), at 46 (Feb. 27, 2009); *see also State Street to Pay More Than $300M in Settlements Over Sub-Prime Investments*, 42 Sec. Reg. & L. Rep. (BNA) 218 (Feb. 8, 2010); Jennifer Levitz, *State Street Sees Shortfall in Legal Fund*, WALL ST. J., Aug. 11, 2009, at C3.

• In February 2009, GlaxoSmithKline plc ("GSK") reported that its profit attributable to shareholders for the 2008 fourth quarter fell to £982 million from £1,057 million during the previous year, adversely affected by a £517 million legal charge related to a Colorado investigation into GSK's market practices. The company's earnings release also disclosed that GSK's aggregate provision for legal and other disputes (not including tax matters) stood at £1.9 billion on December 31, 2008. Press Release, GlaxoSmithKline plc, GSK delivers EPS of 104.7p before major restructuring[;] Dividend increased 8% to 57p, at 16, 21 (Feb. 5, 2009), http://www.gsk.com/investors/reports/q42008/q42008.pdf; *see also* Jeanne Whalen, *Glaxo Net Falls 7.1%; Job Cuts Planned*, WALL ST. J., Feb. 6, 2009, at B5.

• Late in 2008, Regions Financial Corporation ("Regions") announced that it had reached an agreement with the IRS, which established the amount of Regions' federal income tax liabilities through 2006. The agreement enabled Regions to record about a $275 million reduction in income tax expense for the fourth quarter, which increased the company's earnings by the same amount. Press Release, Regions Financial Corporation, Regions Reaches Agreement With IRS (Dec. 22, 2008), http://phx.corporate-ir.net/phoenix.zhtml?c=65036&p=irol-newsArticle_print&ID=1238567&highlight=.

• In March 2008, Citigroup Inc. ("Citigroup") reached an agreement with the Enron Bankruptcy Estate to resolve bankruptcy and fraud claims that the Estate had filed against Citigroup after Enron's collapse. Citigroup agreed to pay $1.66 billion to the Estate and to withdraw certain claims in the bankruptcy proceeding. In also announcing a separate settlement with the holders of Enron credit-linked notes, the company's press release stated: "Both settlements are fully covered by Citi's existing litigation reserves." Press Release, Citigroup Inc., Citi Settles Enron Estate Litigation for $1.66 Billion (Mar. 26, 2008), http://www.citigroup.com/citigroup/press/2008/080326a.htm.

• Earlier that same month, *The Wall Street Journal* reported that BP p.l.c. ("BP") had set aside $2.13 billion—an amount significantly higher than the previously disclosed $1.6 billion—to settle lawsuits arising from a 2005 accident at a Texas refinery that killed fifteen workers. Benoit Faucon, *BP Sets Aside $2.13 Billion to Settle Texas Refinery Accident Claims*, WALL ST. J., Mar. 4, 2008, at A12. BP's 2007 annual report reveals that the profit attributable to BP shareholders for 2005, 2006, and 2007 included charges in respect of the Texas refinery accident of $700 million, $925 million, and $500 million for those years, respectively. BP P.L.C., 2007 ANNUAL REPORT AND ACCOUNTS 46–47 (2008). In note 37 to the financial statements entitled "Provisions," BP states that "within the [$3,487 million] litigation and other category at 31 December 2007 are provisions for litigation of $1,737 million." *Id.* at 151. That same note quantifies the provision as of December 31, 2007 "in respect of the Texas City incident, of which, disbursements to claimants in 2007 were $314 million (2006 $863 million)" at $456 million. *Id.*

• In February 2007, Merck & Co., Inc. announced that it had reached an agreement to settle previously disclosed tax disputes with the IRS arising from examinations covering the period 1993-2001 at a net cash cost to Merck approximating $2.3 billion. The company's press release states: "Merck has previously reserved for these items and this settlement is not expected to have any material impact on the Company's annual earnings for 2007." Press Release, Merck & Co., Merck Settles Tax Dispute with Internal Revenue Service (Feb. 14, 2007), http://www.merck.com/newsroom/press_releases/corporate/2007_0214.html.

• In November 2006 and in connection with the closing of Google Inc.'s acquisition of YouTube, Google announced that it had placed "12.5% of the [$1.65 billion in] equity issued and issuable in the transaction . . . [in] escrow for one year to secure certain indemnification obligations." Press Release, Google Inc., Google Closes Acquisition of YouTube (Nov. 13, 2006), http://investor.google.com/releases/20061114.html. The press release at least hints that Google held back approximately $206.25 million "to cover expenses related to copyright-infringement lawsuits or content-licensing fees that YouTube already has agreed to pay, or may be forced to pay, in the future." *YouTube Deal Is Completed With Set-Aside for Suits, Fees*, WALL ST. J., Nov. 15, 2006, at B10.

• In August 2006, Xerox Corp. announced that Congress's Joint Committee on Taxation had approved an unexpected tax benefit exceeding $400 million after an IRS audit. Because the company had previously treated that amount as an expense, the resolution would enable Xerox to record more than $400 million in additional net income, arising from reduced income tax expense, during its third quarter. William Bulkeley, *Xerox Will Fund More Job Cuts With Tax Benefit*, WALL ST. J., Aug. 7, 2006, at B4.

See also Alison Johansen, *Loss Contingency Disclosures*, 6 Corp Accountability Rep. (BNA) 970 (Sept. 12, 2008) (listing information gathered from selected SEC filings by companies including Broadcom Corp., Caterpillar, Inc., Dell Inc., FedEx Corp., and United Technologies Corp.). Please also recall that a 2007 Credit Suisse Group study found that 361 large companies recognized a combined $141 billion in tax liabilities when they adopted FIN 48, now codified in FASB ASC Subtopic 740-10, *Income Taxes—Overall*). See page 130, *supra*.

D.   AUDIT INQUIRIES AND RELEVANT PROFESSIONAL STANDARDS

**On page 739 [page 477 of the concise], insert the following note before Note 1:

0. The new Codification affects audit response letters because the ABA Statement of Policy and the illustrative response letters refer to SFAS No. 5, which now appears in FASB ASC Topic 450, *Contingencies*. Although the ABA Section of Business Law's Committee on Audit Responses believes that readers should construe any references to SFAS No. 5 in either the Statement of Policy or a response letter to encompass the corresponding material in the Codification, the Committee suggests that lawyers consider whether to reference FASB ASC Subtopic 450-20, *Loss Contingencies*, in their responses regarding fiscal periods ending after September 15, 2009. For example, lawyers could either: (1) add the appropriate reference to the Codification after any mention of SFAS No. 5, or (2) refer to the Codification rather than to SFAS No. 5, perhaps with an explanation that the Codification replaces prior accounting pronouncements, including SFAS No. 5, as generally accepted accounting principles for financial statements for periods ending after September 15, 2009. *See* Comm. on Audit Responses, A.B.A., *Statement of the Effect of the FASB Codification on Audit Response Letters*, 65 BUS. LAW. 491 (2010).

On page 741, insert the following note after Note 3 [on page 479 of the concise, insert the following note after Note 2, numbered for the unabridged edition]:

4. In a post-SOx world, lawyers increasingly complain that auditors unnecessarily request privileged information from an enterprise's counsel, especially in the context of section 404(b)'s requirement that the auditor also express an opinion regarding the enterprise's internal control over financial reporting. Auditors respond that the PCAOB's auditing standard on audit documentation forces them to request such information.

For its part, the ABA adopted a resolution in 2006 urging the SEC, PCAOB and AICPA to develop standards and practices to ensure the preservation of the attorney-client privilege and work product protections throughout the audit process. The ABA's Task Force on the Attorney-Client Privilege proposed that auditors access privileged information only "where it is clearly necessary for purposes of the audit and not . . . where it merely would be convenient or would provide additional confirmation or comfort." The auditor's access "should be limited to factual information that is not available from other sources or, solely when relied on by the client to justify its financial reporting position, applicable legal advice and opinions." ABA Task Force on the Attorney-Client Privilege, Report on Audit Issues (Aug. 2006), http://www.abanet.org/buslaw/attorneyclient/materials/hod/0806_report.pdf.

The on-going controversy raises questions about the future viability of the 1975 accord between the legal and accounting professions, which only addressed year-end audit letters, now that SOx imposes additional obligations on auditors and the PCAOB, rather than the AICPA, regulates the accountants that audit public companies. Malini Manickavasagam, *Attorneys Say Auditors Do Not Need Privileged Information to Provide Attestation*, 6 Corp. Accountability Rep. (BNA) 362 (Apr. 11, 2008); David Schwartz, *Experts Discuss Growing Trend of Auditors Seeking Privileged Documents*, 5 Corp. Accountability Rep. (BNA) 272 (Mar. 16, 2007).

E.   DISCOVERY ISSUES

1.   AUDIT INQUIRY LETTERS

On page 752 [page 484 of the concise], in the last paragraph [first full paragraph of the concise] please notice that the Sixth, Seventh, and Ninth Circuits have joined the Second, Third, Fourth, Eighth, and D.C. Circuits in adopting some version of the "because of" standard. *See* United States v. Roxworthy, 457 F.3d 590, 593 (6th Cir. 2006); *In re* Grand Jury Subpoena, 357 F.3d 900, 907 (9th Cir. 2004).

On page 753 [page 484 of the concise], insert the following discussion after the first full paragraph:

In *United States v. Textron Inc.*, 577 F.3d 21 (1st Cir. 2009) (en banc), *cert. denied*, 78 U.S.L.W. 3687 (May 24, 2010), a majority of the First Circuit, sitting en banc, created and applied a "prepared *for use* in possible litigation" standard when determining whether tax accrual workpapers qualified for work product protection. In holding that the work product doctrine did not protect workpapers, which Textron's attorneys had prepared, from an IRS summons, the First Circuit vacated a district court order refusing to enforce the summons. Previously, the en banc court had granted the government's petition for rehearing en banc, vacated a 2-1 panel decision affirming the district court order, and obtained additional briefs from the parties and interested amici. Because Textron's lawyers prepared the workpapers "to support a financial statement and the independent audit of it," the 3-2 decision concluded that the lawyers did not prepare the documents for potential use in litigation if and when it might arise. *Id.* at 27, 29, 30. In essence, the court focused on the document's function rather than its subject matter or content.

Although the *Textron* decision involved tax accrual workpapers, the court's reasoning potentially applies to any document not prepared "for" litigation but related to a subject that might occasion litigation. Consequently, the new "prepared *for use* in possible litigation" standard has emerged as an alternative to both the majority "because of anticipated litigation" and the "primary motivating purpose" tests that offer work product protection to so-called "dual purpose" documents. You may recall that *United States v. Adlman*, 134 F.3d 1194 (2d Cir. 1998), discussed on page 752 of the unabridged fourth edition [page 484 of the concise version] and applied in at least eight circuits, set forth the "because of anticipated litigation" test. In contrast, *United States v. El Paso Co.*, 682 F.2d 530, 542 (5th Cir. 1982), formulated the previously more restrictive "primary motivating purpose" test that *United States v. Gulf Oil Corp.*, 760 F.2d 292 (Temp. Emer. Ct. App. 1985), which appears as a principal case on pages 748-751 of the unabridged fourth edition [only briefly discussed on page 483 of the concise version], applied. If extended beyond tax accrual workpapers, the *Textron* decision's reasoning could enable litigants to discover documents relating to an opponent's litigation reserves, legal analyses created to assist with SEC reporting requirements, or information provided to an independent auditor. *See, e.g.*, Robert W. Pommer III, *First Circuit Reverses Course in Closely Watched Work Product Cases; Establishes Broad New Standard That Could Extend Outside Tax Area*, 41 Sec. Reg. & L. Rep. (BNA) 2050 (Nov. 9, 2009); Nancy T. Bowen et al., *Newly Minted 'For Use in Possible Litigation' Test of* Textron *May Have Far-Reaching Implications for Taxpayers*, 7 Corp. Accountability Rep. (BNA) 1272 (Oct. 23, 2009); Michelle M. Henkel, *Textron Eviscerates the 60-Year Old Work Product Privilege*, 125 TAX NOTES 237 (Oct. 12, 2009).

2.   ACCOUNTANT-CLIENT PRIVILEGE

On page 770 [omitted from the concise], insert the following discussion after the first full paragraph:

Numerous leaders in the business and legal communities criticized such prosecutorial tactics for creating a "culture of waiver" endangering the attorney-client privilege. The ABA's Task Force on the Attorney-Client Privilege spearheaded efforts for reform, resulting in several key developments. In 2006, the U.S. Sentencing Commission voted to remove language from the Federal Sentencing Guidelines addressing consideration of privilege waivers. On August 28, 2008, the U.S. Department of Justice announced revisions to its Principles of Federal Prosecution of Business Organizations to state that credit for cooperation will not depend on the organization's waiver of attorney-client privilege or work product protection, but rather on disclosure of relevant facts. Dept. of Justice, Press Release, Justice Department Revises Charging Guidelines for Prosecuting Corporate Fraud (Aug. 28, 2008), http://www.usdoj.gov/opa/pr/2008/August/08-odag-757.html; *see also* Dept. of Justice, Principles of Federal Prosecution of Business Organizations §§ 9-28.710 to .760, http://www.usdoj.gov/opa/documents/corp-charging-guidelines.pdf. The guidelines do not bind other federal agencies, including the SEC.

On page 771 [omitted from the concise], in the carryover paragraph at the top of the page, add the following sentence after the citation to *United States v. Massachusetts Institute of Technology*:

The Supreme Court denied certiorari in a petition that sought review of a Tenth Circuit decision that refused to apply "selective waiver" to protect privileged documents that a public company provided to the Justice Department and the SEC during criminal and civil investigations. *In re* Qwest Commc'ns Int'l Inc., 450 F.3d 1179 (10th Cir. 2006), *cert. denied*, 127 S. Ct. 584 (2006).

On page 771 [omitted from the concise], delete the last three sentences and the related citation at end of the carryover paragraph ending on the page:

On September 19, 2008, President Bush signed Public Law 110-322, 122 Stat. 3537 (2008), which amends the Federal Rules of Evidence by adding Rule 502 to address the waiver of the attorney-client privilege and the work product doctrine, primarily as to inadvertent waivers. The legislation mirrors the proposed language that the Judicial Conference of the United States approved and transmitted to Congress in September 2007. The House Judiciary Committee requested an addendum to the explanatory note accompanying the legislation to caution that Rule 502 "does not provide a basis for a court to enable parties to agree to a selective waiver of the privilege, such as to a federal agency conducting an investigation, while preserving the privilege as against other parties seeking the information." 154 Cong. Rec. H7817, H7818-19 (Sept. 8, 2008) (statement of Rep. Jackson-Lee).

On page 776 [omitted from the concise] after the carryover sentence at the top of the page, insert the following text:

Some courts, including federal courts, have developed a common-law privilege to limit the discovery of tax returns in nontax civil litigation between private parties. This privilege varies from jurisdiction to jurisdiction, and sometimes even within a particular jurisdiction, typically depending upon the policy reasons articulated for the privilege, which have included privacy concerns, the desire to encourage complete and accurate turns, and an unwillingness to force litigants to disclose their tax returns as a price for bringing or defending litigation. *See* Nancy T. Bowen, *Strategies for Defending Against Discovery Requests for Tax Returns*, 122 TAX NOTES 217 (Jan. 12, 2009).

**On pages 776-77 [omitted from the concise], replace the carryover sentence and the rest of the carryover paragraph with the following text:

**In 2006, the federal government brought the first case under the new policy and sought to enforce a summons against Textron Inc., seeking the company's tax accrual workpapers. In an en banc 3-2 decision, the First Circuit vacated a district court order refusing to enforce the summons after withdrawing a panel decision affirming the order. As discussed more fully on pages 143-144, *infra*, the en banc majority concluded that work product protection only applies to documents "prepared *for use* in possible litigation" and does not reach documents created to comply with financial reporting rules. United States v. Textron Inc., 577 F.3d 21, 27, 29, 30 (1st Cir. 2009) (en banc), *cert. denied*, 78 U.S.L.W. 3687 (May 24, 2010).

** During the Textron litigation, the IRS lost another case involving tax accrual workpapers and the work product doctrine. The IRS appealed the decision to the Eleventh Circuit, but then moved to dismiss the appeal after the parties settled the case. Regions Fin. Corp. v. United States, No. 2:06-CV-00895-RDP, 2008 WL 2139008 (N.D. Ala. May 8, 2008), *appeal dismissed*, No. 08-13866 (11th Cir. Dec. 30, 2008). The IRS reportedly obtained the workpapers in the settlement. Amy S. Elliott, *Hochman Downplays Significance of Regions Settlement Despite Textron Appeal*, 2009 Tax Notes Today 7-5 (Jan. 13, 2009).

** In another important development related to tax accrual workpapers, FASB ASC Subtopic 740-10, *Income Taxes—Overall*, originally promulgated as FASB Interpretation No. 48 ("FIN 48"), *Accounting for Uncertainty in Income Taxes*, described at pages 130-131, *supra*, now requires enterprises to recognize liabilities for certain "unrecognized tax benefits," with changes in such liabilities treated as part of tax expense, and to disclose additional information regarding these items. As a result, enterprises have been documenting uncertain tax positions and providing additional disclosures in the financial statements. Tax-paying enterprises subject to these new rules have feared that the compliance work performed will provide a "roadmap" for the IRS to investigate a company's questionable tax positions. In 2007, the IRS announced plans to apply the traditional "policy of restraint" in seeking workpapers prepared to follow the new financial accounting rules for determining income tax expense. The IRS, however, advised its agents to review the publicly available disclosures in the financial statements to identify areas of potential noncompliance. *See* John Keenan et al., *Tax Accrual Workpapers: Caught Between a Rock and a Hard Place*, Daily Tax Rep. (BNA) No. 7, at J-1 (Jan. 11, 2008); *see also* Alison Bennett, *IRS Unlikely to Reopen Audits Due to FIN 48 Disclosures, Official Says*, Daily Tax Rep. (BNA) No. 92, at G-2 (May 13, 2008) (noting that the IRS will continue to analyze the new disclosures to find areas of potential compliance risk but generally does not plan to reopen an audit based upon those disclosures).

**   Notwithstanding this general "policy of restraint," in early 2010, the IRS announced plans to require certain large businesses to attach a new tax schedule, tentatively called "Schedule UTP," to their federal income tax returns. The schedule would require the taxpayer to describe each uncertain tax position and to provide an estimate of the taxpayer's maximum exposure on the item. The taxpayer would not need to provide risk assessments or the amount of any tax reserve attributable to any position. The rules would generally apply to corporations with both uncertain tax positions and at least $10 million in assets, starting with returns for calendar year 2010 or fiscal years beginning in 2010. The IRS believes that this information will enable it to identify returns for audit and to prioritize issues upon audit. Uncertain Tax Positions -- Policy of Restraint, I.R.S. Announcement 2010-9, 2010-7 I.R.B. 408; Draft Schedule and Instructions for Uncertain Tax Positions Proposal, I.R.S. Announcement 2010-30, 2010-19 I.R.B. 668.

CHAPTER VIII

INVENTORY

B. DETERMINING ENDING INVENTORY

2. HOW TO PRICE INVENTORY

a. FLOW ASSUMPTIONS

(2) Critique and Basis for Selection

c) LAST-IN, FIRST-OUT

(ii) Disadvantages

On page 825, in the middle of the page and after the first full paragraph, insert the following new text [on page 518 of the concise, insert the following after the paragraph beginning "As previously noted, . . . "]:

**   To further illustrate LIFO's effects, consider Exxon Mobil Corporation's 2007, 2008, and 2009 financial results. When oil prices increased rapidly during 2007, LIFO increased Exxon Mobil's costs, and therefore, reduced its income before taxes, by about $9.5 billion. If Exxon Mobil had used replacement cost, rather than LIFO, to value its ending inventory, its income before income taxes would have increased from a then-record $70.5 billion to about $80 billion. The notes to Exxon Mobil's 2007 financial statements quantified the company's LIFO reserve, or the cumulative difference between the inventory's current replacement cost and its carrying amount on the balance sheet, at $25.4 billion. Exxon Mobil Corp., Annual Report (Form 10-K), at 50, 56 (Feb. 28, 2008); *see also* David Reilly, *Big Oil's Accounting Methods Fuel Criticism*, WALL ST. J., Aug. 8, 2006, at C1 (providing the LIFO reserve and an estimated net profit for 2005). By comparison, when oil prices fell during the second half of 2008, Exxon Mobil's LIFO reserve fell to $10.0 billion at December 31, 2008, which means that LIFO actually added $15.4 billion to the company's reported $81.75 billion in income before taxes during 2008. Exxon Mobil Corp., Annual Report (Form 10-K), at 58, 64 (Feb. 27, 2009). Then, when oil prices rose gradually during 2009, LIFO increased the company's costs and reduced its income before taxes for 2009 by about $7.1 billion to $34.8 billion. At the end of 2009, Exxon Mobil's LIFO reserve stood at $17.1 billion. Exxon Mobil Corp., Annual Report (Form 10-K), at 62, 69 (Feb. 26, 2010).

** Given the proposed transition to IFRS, which do not allow the LIFO method, and the rapidly expanding federal deficit and mounting national debt, LIFO's future looks increasingly doubtful. The tax benefits that companies with LIFO reserves currently enjoy seem unlikely to survive. Unless Congress eliminates the conformity requirement, the IASB decides to allow LIFO, or the SEC permits registrants to continue to use LIFO, a transition to IFRS would preclude taxpayers from using LIFO for federal income tax purposes and could generate as much as $100 billion, but after the economic downturn more recently estimated at about $60 billion, in additional federal income taxes over ten years. Even before the SEC announced its proposed roadmap for switching to IFRS, influential members of Congress from both major political parties sponsored legislation to repeal LIFO, first in 2005 for oil and gas companies, and more recently, for all businesses. President Obama's two budget proposals to date have contained provisions that would repeal the LIFO inventory accounting method for taxable years beginning after December 31, 2011, require taxpayers to write up their beginning LIFO inventory to its FIFO value in the first taxable year beginning after that date, and tax the income resulting from the change ratably over an eight-year period starting with that taxable year. *See* Thomas Jaworski, *LIFO Repeal: Would the New Revenue Be Worth the Corporate Resistance?*, 127 TAX NOTES 253 (Apr. 19, 2010); Lauren Gardner, *Move from GAAP to IFRS Could Spell Big Changes for Companies Using LIFO*, 6 Corp. Accountability Rep. (BNA) 964 (Sept. 12, 2008); Edward D. Kleinbard et al., *Is It Time to Liquidate LIFO?*, 113 TAX NOTES 237 (Oct. 16, 2006).

On page 835, insert the following note after the principal case, *United States v. Ingredient Technology Corp.* [on page 522 of the concise, insert the following above section c.]:

NOTE

Unscrupulous individuals can also use LIFO liquidations to manipulate income to meet earnings targets. In 2007, Nicor, Inc., a natural gas distributor, agreed to pay a $10 million penalty to settle civil charges that the company engaged in improper transactions, made material misrepresentations, and failed to disclose material information regarding its gas inventory that enabled it to meet earnings targets and increase its revenues under a performance-based rate plan that the Illinois Commerce Commission administered. The complaint alleges that the company used a series of improper transactions to shift inventory off of its books so that it could access a substantial portion of its low-cost LIFO layers of inventory. As a result, Nicor inflated its reported income for 2000 and 2001. In addition, Nicor failed to disclose, in either the Management's Discussion & Analysis sections of its securities filings, or in its financial statements contained in those filings, that it had recognized material, non-recurring income from those LIFO liquidations. SEC v. Nicor, Inc., Litigation Release No. 20060 (Mar. 29, 2007), http://www.sec.gov/litigation/litreleases/2007/lr20060.htm.

CHAPTER IX

LONG-LIVED ASSETS AND INTANGIBLES

B. CLASSIFICATION OF EXPENDITURES: ASSETS VS. EXPENSES

On page 872 [page 540 of the concise], replace the full paragraph with the following text:

**   Prior to 2007, GAAP required enterprises to expense certain IPR&D acquired in a business combination. FASB ASC Topic 805, *Business Combinations*, which codified the new rules promulgated in SFAS No. 141(R) in 2007 in an effort to promote further convergence with international accounting standards, now requires acquirers to recognize and measure this IPR&D at acquisition-date fair value, to treat the intangible as indefinite-lived, and to periodically test the asset for impairment, until the acquirer completes or abandons the research and development efforts. FASB ASC ¶¶ 805-20-25-1, 805-20-30-1, 805-20-35-5 (codifications of SFAS No. 141(R), ¶¶ 66, B149–50).

**   Although FASB originally planned to consider whether consistency requires applying FASB ASC Topic 805's recognition provisions to IPR&D acquired outside of business combinations, such as asset acquisitions, the FASB Chairman removed the project from the Board's agenda in early 1999 so that the EITF could address the issue. Although the EITF reached a tentative conclusion that enterprises should capitalize all tangible and intangible research and development assets obtained in an asset acquisition, the Task Force could not reach the necessary consensus-for-exposure and recommended that the FASB Chairman remove the project from the EITF agenda, which he did. Following that decision, the FASB staff recommended that the FASB Chairman not add the issue to the Board's agenda. Interested readers can use FASB's web site to monitor future developments regarding this issue. For now, the current recap appears at <http://www.fasb.org/jsp/FASB/Page/SectionPage&cid=1218220137528#09-2>.

On page 873, insert the following note after Note 3 [on page 542 of the concise, note the following as to the discussion in Note 1]:

3A. In September 2006, FASB issued guidance on the accounting for planned major maintenance activities, very common in the airline, chemical, oil and gas, and shipping industries, but also prevalent in other businesses. Effective with the first fiscal year beginning after December 15, 2006, the FASB staff position allows enterprises to choose among three permissible methods to account for costs related to planned major maintenance. The permissible accounting ranges from expensing these costs as incurred to capitalizing such costs and amortizing them over the accounting periods until the date of the next expected overhaul. Enterprises, of course, must disclose the method of accounting used. ACCOUNTING FOR PLANNED MAJOR MAINTENANCE ACTIVITIES, FASB Staff Position No. AUG AIR-1 (Fin. Accounting Standards Bd. 2006) (codified at FASB ASC ¶¶ 360-10-25-5, 360-10-45-1).

C. ALLOCATION OF CAPITALIZED COSTS

1. COSTS TO ACQUIRE AND RETIRE THE ASSET

b. SPECIAL ISSUES IN ASSET ACQUISITIONS

(3) Lump-Sum Purchases

On page 880, replace the last sentence in this section with the following text [on page 548 of the concise, replace the first paragraph with the following]:

By comparison, if ABC purchases the four assets for any amount which exceeds their $100,000 cumulative fair value in a transaction that qualifies as a "business combination," a term which we will discuss later in the unabridged version on pages 904 to 908 [pages 569 to 578 of the concise], the excess represents goodwill, which we will also describe in that same discussion.

On page 563 of the concise [no adjustment needed in the unabridged version], replace the chart at the bottom of the pages with the following:

	Financial Accounting Purposes	Tax Purposes
Income Before Depreciation and Taxes	$7,500	$7,500
Depreciation	2,500	4,000
Income Before Taxes	$5,000	$3,500
Income Taxes	2,000	1,400
Net Income	$3,000	$2,100

On page 566 of the concise [no adjustment needed in the unabridged version], the amount in the ninth line under the heading "Inter-Period Tax Allocation" should be $1,400 (rather than $600).

On page 567 of the concise [no adjustment needed in the unabridged version], the Financial Accounting column in the chart at the bottom of page reversed the amounts for income taxes and net income. The amount for income taxes should be $200,000 (rather than $300,000), while the net income should be $300,000 (rather than $200,000).

D. DEPLETION

1. COST COLLECTION METHODS

On page 902, replace the last textual sentence and related citations with the following to reflect recent amendments to the SEC's reporting requirements [omitted from concise]:

**Effective January 1, 2010, the SEC has announced revisions to its almost three-decades-old oil and gas reporting and disclosure requirements in an effort to give investors more information about the reserves that oil and gas companies hold. The SEC will continue to allow both the full cost and successful efforts methods, but has updated the disclosure requirements to align them with current industry practices and changes in technology. In particular, the amendments allow companies to disclose their probable and possible reserves, rather than only their proved reserves under the existing rules; permit companies to use reliable technologies to calculate reserves under certain circumstances; and require companies to report oil and gas reserves using a twelve-month average price, rather than the current single day, year-end price. The amendments also align the full cost accounting rules with the revised disclosures. Modernization of Oil and Gas Reporting, Financial Reporting Release No. 78, 74 Fed. Reg. 2158 (Jan. 14, 2009), *available at* http://www.sec.gov/rules/final/2009/33-8995fr.pdf. Subsequently, the SEC staff issued SAB No. 113 to provide updated guidance on how the staff interprets accounting rules for the oil and gas industry. Staff Accounting Bulletin No. 113, 74 Fed. Reg. 57,062 (Nov. 4, 2009), *available at* http://www.sec.gov/interps/account/sab113.htm.

** In early 2010, FASB issued ASU 2010-03 to align the estimation and disclosure requirements in FASB ASC Topic 932, *Extractive Activities--Oil and Gas*, which codified SFAS No. 19, as amended by SFAS No. 69, with the SEC's new rule. The amendments expand the definition of "oil- and gas-producing activities" to include the extraction of saleable hydrocarbons from nonrenewable natural resources, such as oil sands, shale, and coalbeds, that an enterprise intends to upgrade into synthetic oil or gas. The new rules also require disclosures about equity method investments to provide the same detail as necessary for consolidated investments. The new requirements apply to annual reporting periods ending on or after December 31, 2009, but if the expanded definition reaches an enterprise for the first time, the enterprise can elect to apply the disclosure requirements in annual periods beginning after December 31, 2009.

E.   INTANGIBLE ASSETS AND GOODWILL

On page 905, replace the paragraph starting on the bottom of the page with the following discussion [on pages 570-72 of the concise, please note]:

By comparison, an enterprise must capitalize the costs to acquire any intangible asset acquired from third parties, whether individually or with a group of other assets. The rules for initially recognizing and recording purchased intangibles depend upon whether the acquisition involved a business combination. FASB ASC Topic 805, *Business Combinations*, which codified SFAS No. 141 as revised in 2007 on that same topic, defines a business combination as a transaction or other event in which an acquirer obtains control of one or more businesses. The Codification explains control generally as "the direct or indirect ability to determine the direction of management and policies through ownership, contract, or otherwise." FASB ASC § 805-10-20 (a codification of SFAS No. 141(R), ¶ 3).

On page 906, please replace the second full paragraph with the following discussion [on pages 570-72 of the concise, please again note]:

If the acquisition involves a business combination, FASB ASC Topic 805, which you may recall codified the rules in SFAS No. 141(R) on business combinations, generally requires an enterprise to recognize the assets acquired and liabilities assumed at their acquisition-date fair values. Enterprises must then recognize any remaining portion of the purchase price as goodwill, which the standard defines as the excess of the consideration transferred in the acquisition over the fair values of the assets acquired and liabilities assumed.

On page 906, add the following text to the end of the third full paragraph [on page 576 of the concise, note the following development related to determining the useful lives of intangible assets as described in the second full paragraph]:

FASB ASC Topic 350, *Intangibles—Goodwill and Other*, which codified SFAS No. 142 and related promulgations, offers additional guidance to assist enterprises in determining the useful life of intangible assets. In particular, the Codification lists the factors enterprises should use to develop assumptions about renewals or extensions related to the useful life of recognized intangible assets. FASB ASC ¶ 350-30-35-3 (a codification of DETERMINATION OF THE USEFUL LIFE OF INTANGIBLE ASSETS, FASB Staff Position No. FAS 142-3 (Fin. Accounting Standards Bd. 2008)).

On page 907, add the following sentence at the end of the second full paragraph [on page 572 of the concise, add the following to the end of the carryover paragraph ending on the top of the page]:

Lawyers should keep in mind that any write-downs reduce equity and could cause an enterprise to violate a covenant in a loan agreement. *See, e.g.,* Michael Rapoport, *Expedia Might Trip Debt Covenant*, WALL ST. J., Oct. 12, 2006, at C3 (discussing potential consequences if the accounting rules require Expedia Inc. to write off any of its $5.86 billion in goodwill).

On page 924, replace Notes 8 and 9 with the following discussion [on pages 540-41 of the concise, replace the carryover paragraph with the text in Note 8 below]:

**8. Even before then SEC Chairman Arthur Levitt highlighted "merger magic" as one of five "illusions" in accounting practice in 1998, see page 540 [page 332 of the concise], *supra*, FASB had begun to consider additional standards on accounting for purchased intangibles, including purchased in-process research and development ("IPR&D"). As described in more detail on page 155, *supra*, prior to 2007, GAAP required enterprises to expense certain IPR&D acquired in a business combination. Today, FASB ASC Topic 805, *Business Combinations*, which codified the new rules promulgated in 2007 in SFAS No. 141(R), requires acquirers to recognize and measure this IPR&D at acquisition-date fair value, to treat the intangible as indefinite-lived, and to test the asset periodically for impairment, until the enterprise completes or abandons the research and development efforts. FASB ASC ¶¶ 805-20-25-1, 805-20-30-1, 805-20-35-5 (codifications of SFAS No. 141(R), ¶¶ 66, B149–50).

**9. As part of their joint project on business combinations, the FASB and IASB concluded that enterprises should not treat acquisition-related costs, such as legal, consulting, and due diligence costs, as includible in goodwill. The FASB and IASB believed that the consideration related to the underlying business combination does not include acquisition-related costs. Instead, such costs reflect separate transactions where the buyer pays for the services received. Under FASB ASC Topic 805, *Business Combinations*, which codified SFAS No. 141(R), enterprises now recognize all acquisition-related costs as expenses as incurred, except for any costs to issue debt or equity securities. FASB ASC ¶ 805-10-25-23 (a codification of SFAS No. 141(R), ¶¶ 59, B365–66.

**10. Transactional lawyers in particular should understand how the new rules on business combinations, now codified in FASB ASC Topic 805, affect how entities negotiate and structure mergers and acquisitions. The new rules apply to any "business combination," defined as any transaction in which an acquirer obtains control of one or more "businesses." FASB ASC ¶ 805-10-15-3. The standards define "business" broadly as "[a]n integrated set of activities and assets that is capable of being conducted and managed for the purpose of providing a return." FASB ASC § 805-10-20. This expansive definition encompasses a wide variety of transactions.

**   In many mergers and acquisitions, the acquirer will issue equity interests, such as stock, options, or warrants, as part or all of the consideration in the transaction. The new rules can pose difficulties in estimating the purchase price when the acquirer uses equity-based consideration. The acquirer now measures the consideration transferred, including equity interests, at fair value on the "acquisition date." FASB ASC ¶ 805-30-30-7. The "acquisition date" refers to the date the acquirer obtains control of the acquiree, generally the closing date of the transaction. FASB ASC ¶¶ 805-10-25-6 to -7. The acquirer's stock price can change between the date the acquirer announces the transaction and the actual closing date. Therefore, the purchase price recorded could differ from the initial estimate of the purchase price based on the value of the acquirer's shares on the announcement date. Lawyers can expect acquirers concerned with minimizing such volatility to increase the use of cash consideration or to negotiate a "collar," a cap and floor on pricing, in the acquisition agreement.

**   The new standards could also impact how acquirers structure "earn outs." In a typical earn out, the acquirer agrees to pay additional consideration after the closing if the acquiree satisfies specified criteria, such as a target level of sales or earnings, within a set time frame. The acquirer and acquiree typically negotiate an earn out when the parties cannot agree on a purchase price that properly values the acquiree. Using the terminology of the business combinations standards, earn outs constitute "contingent consideration." The acquirer must recognize the fair value of any contingent consideration on the acquisition date regardless of the likelihood of the acquiree satisfying the earn out criteria. FASB ASC ¶ 805-30-25-5. Determining the fair value of contingent consideration can involve considerable complexity. The acquirer must determine the likelihood that the acquiree will meet the earn out requirements and discount the required payments appropriately.

**   The acquirer generally will classify earn outs requiring payment of cash as a liability and those involving share-based payments as equity. FASB ASC ¶ 805-30-25-6. The acquirer must remeasure contingent consideration classified as a liability at fair value at each reporting date until the resolution of the contingency, with changes in fair value recognized in earnings. Contingent consideration classified as equity does not require remeasurement; the acquirer accounts for the subsequent settlement within equity. FASB ASC ¶ 805-30-35-1. Cash earn outs, then, will subject the acquirer to considerable earnings volatility as the acquirer remeasures the contingent consideration liability at each reporting date. Lawyers can anticipate that acquirers seeking to minimize post-acquisition earnings volatility will avoid the use of earn outs, negotiate for a shorter earn out period, or use equity-based consideration in the earn out.

** The new standards could also impact how acquirers plan due diligence for proposed and pending transactions. As mentioned in the previous note, acquirers must now expense acquisition-related costs in the period incurred. Such costs include professional fees for lawyers, bankers, accountants, and other advisors. FASB ASC ¶ 805-10-25-23. Acquirers must expense these costs in the period incurred, even if the acquirer announces or closes the transaction in a future period. Observers might anticipate an upcoming deal when an acquirer discloses acquisition-related costs without the formal announcement of a transaction. Lawyers can expect acquirers seeking to avoid early revelation of a potential upcoming transaction to delay the start of due diligence or to compress the time frame for completing such diligence to ensure that acquisition-related costs will appear in the same period as the announcement of the deal.

F. LEASE ACCOUNTING

2. TREATMENT

On page 929, insert the following text after the carryover paragraph ending on the top of the page [on page 580 of the concise, insert the following text after the first full paragraph]:

** In July 2006, the FASB voted to begin a comprehensive reconsideration of lease accounting as a joint project with the IASB. The project aims to ensure that enterprises recognize the assets and liabilities arising from lease contracts on the balance sheet. In preliminary decision-making, the rulemakers have favored a "right-of-use" accounting model over the current "all-or-nothing" approach where lessees can keep lease obligations off the balance sheet by qualifying for classification as an operating lease. By comparison, the "right-of-use" model focuses on the entitlements to future economic benefits arising from the lease rather than ownership. Lessees would record an asset for the right to use the leased item during the lease term and a liability for the obligation to make lease payments. Requirements to return the equipment in a specified condition or other obligations at the lease's termination could constitute additional liabilities for the lessee. Under this proposed approach, lessees will unquestionably report more leases on the their balance sheets than under the current rules. In contrast, lessors would recognize an asset for the right to receive payments over the lease term and a liability for the performance obligation under the lease. In March 2009, the FASB and IASB issued a joint discussion paper detailing their preliminary views regarding the project. The Boards hope to complete a final standard before June 30, 2011. Fin. Accounting Standards Bd., Project Update, Leases—Joint Project of the IASB and FASB (June 22, 2010). Interested readers can use FASB's website to access project updates via <http://www.fasb.org/jsp/FASB/Page/SectionPage&cid=1218220137074>.

G.   WRITE–DOWNS AND THE "BIG BATH"

2.   THE NEW RULES

b.   GENERAL RULES ON DISPOSAL ACTIVITIES

On page 943 [page 590 of the concise], in the first paragraph under this heading, please omit the passage "to exit activities that involve an entity newly acquired in a business combination." As described below, FASB ASC Topic 805, *Business Combinations* applies the criteria in FASB ASC Topic 420, *Exit or Disposal Cost Obligations,* to exit activities that involve an entity acquired in a business combination. The sentence in the text, therefore, should read as follows: "These rules, however, do not apply to costs to terminate a capital lease."

On page 945, replace the full paragraph with the following [on page 591 of the concise, replace the last paragraph with the following]:

** Under FASB ASC Topic 805, *Business Combinations*, which codified SFAS No. 141(R), enterprises must apply these same rules to exit activities that arise from business combinations. Acquirers may recognize liabilities for exit or restructuring costs related to the business acquired only if those liabilities meet the recognition criteria in FASB ASC Topic 420, *Exit or Disposal Cost Obligations,* which codified SFAS No. 146, *Accounting for Costs Associated with Exit or Disposal Activities,* at the acquisition date. As suggested on page 938 of the unabridged fourth edition [page 590 of the concise], that pronouncement concluded that an enterprise's commitment to an exit plan does not, by itself, create a present obligation to others that meets the definition of a liability. When an enterprise actually incurs a liability for a cost associated with an exit or disposal activity, the enterprise must recognize and measure the cost at fair value. FASB ASC ¶¶ 420-10-25-1 to -3, 420-10-30-1 (a codification of SFAS No. 146). Amounts that the acquirer expects, but is not obligated, to incur do not meet the recognition criteria, and the enterprise should account for such costs separately in the post-combination financial statements, usually as expenses when incurred. The new standard, in essence, levels the playing field for restructuring costs, whether originating from an existing operating activity or an acquisition. FASB ASC ¶ 805-20-25-2 (a codification of SFAS No. 141(R), ¶ 13). The new rule would presumably preclude companies like Cendant Corp., which allegedly intentionally overstated merger reserves and then reversed those amounts in later periods to overstate pretax operating income by more than $500 million between 1995 and 1997, from using acquisition reserves to hide subsequent poor performance from investors. Lingling Wei, *Merger Loophole May Be Plugged*, WALL ST. J., Aug. 13, 2004, at C3.

APPENDIX B

PRESENT AND FUTURE VALUE TABLES

Table I: Future Value of $1.00

$f = p(1 + r)^n$, where r = interest rate; n = number of compounding periods; $p = \$1.00$.

Periods = n	1%	2%	3%	4%	5%	6%	7%	8%	9%	10%	12%	15%
1	1.01000	1.02000	1.03000	1.04000	1.05000	1.06000	1.07000	1.08000	1.09000	1.10000	1.12000	1.15000
2	1.02010	1.04040	1.06090	1.08160	1.10250	1.12360	1.14490	1.16640	1.18810	1.21000	1.25440	1.32250
3	1.03030	1.06121	1.09273	1.12486	1.15763	1.19102	1.22504	1.25971	1.29503	1.33100	1.40493	1.52087
4	1.04060	1.08243	1.12551	1.16986	1.21551	1.26248	1.31080	1.36049	1.41158	1.46410	1.57352	1.74901
5	1.05101	1.10408	1.15927	1.21665	1.27628	1.33823	1.40255	1.46933	1.53862	1.61051	1.76234	2.01136
6	1.06152	1.12616	1.19405	1.26532	1.34010	1.41852	1.50073	1.58687	1.67710	1.77156	1.97382	2.31306
7	1.07214	1.14869	1.22987	1.31593	1.40710	1.50363	1.60578	1.71382	1.82804	1.94872	2.21068	2.66002
8	1.08286	1.17166	1.26677	1.36857	1.47746	1.59385	1.71818	1.85093	1.99256	2.14359	2.47596	3.05902
9	1.09369	1.19509	1.30477	1.42331	1.55133	1.68948	1.83846	1.99900	2.17189	2.35795	2.77308	3.51788
10	1.10462	1.21899	1.34392	1.48024	1.62889	1.79085	1.96715	2.15892	2.36736	2.59374	3.10585	4.04556
11	1.11567	1.24337	1.38423	1.53945	1.71034	1.89830	2.10485	2.33164	2.58043	2.85312	3.47855	4.65239
12	1.12683	1.26824	1.42576	1.60103	1.79586	2.01220	2.25219	2.51817	2.81266	3.13843	3.89598	5.35025
13	1.13809	1.29361	1.46853	1.66507	1.88565	2.13293	2.40985	2.71962	3.06580	3.45227	4.36349	6.15279
14	1.14947	1.31948	1.51259	1.73168	1.97993	2.26090	2.57853	2.93719	3.34173	3.79750	4.88711	7.07571
15	1.16097	1.34587	1.55797	1.80094	2.07893	2.39656	2.75903	3.17217	3.64248	4.17725	5.47357	8.13706
16	1.17258	1.37279	1.60471	1.87298	2.18287	2.54035	2.95216	3.42594	3.97031	4.59497	6.13039	9.35762
17	1.18430	1.40024	1.65285	1.94790	2.29202	2.69277	3.15882	3.70002	4.32763	5.05447	6.86604	10.76126
18	1.19615	1.42825	1.70243	2.02582	2.40662	2.85434	3.37993	3.99602	4.71712	5.55992	7.68997	12.37545
19	1.20811	1.45681	1.75351	2.10685	2.52695	3.02560	3.61653	4.31570	5.14166	6.11591	8.61276	14.23177
20	1.22019	1.48595	1.80611	2.19112	2.65330	3.20714	3.86968	4.66096	5.60441	6.72750	9.64629	16.36654
22	1.24472	1.54598	1.91610	2.36992	2.92526	3.60354	4.43040	5.43654	6.65860	8.14027	12.10031	21.64475
24	1.26973	1.60844	2.03279	2.56330	3.22510	4.04893	5.07237	6.34118	7.91108	9.84973	15.17863	28.62518
26	1.29526	1.67342	2.15659	2.77247	3.55567	4.54938	5.80735	7.39635	9.39916	11.91818	19.04007	37.85680
28	1.32129	1.74102	2.28793	2.99870	3.92013	5.11169	6.64884	8.62711	11.16714	14.42099	23.88387	50.06561
30	1.34785	1.81136	2.42726	3.24340	4.32194	5.74349	7.61226	10.06266	13.26768	17.44940	29.95992	66.21177
32	1.37494	1.88454	2.57508	3.50806	4.76494	6.45339	8.71527	11.73708	15.76333	21.11378	37.58173	87.56507
34	1.40258	1.96068	2.73191	3.79432	5.25335	7.25103	9.97811	13.69013	18.72841	25.54767	47.14252	115.8048
36	1.43077	2.03989	2.89828	4.10393	5.79182	8.14725	11.42394	15.96817	22.25123	30.91268	59.13557	153.1519
38	1.45953	2.12230	3.07478	4.43881	6.38548	9.15425	13.07927	18.62528	26.43668	37.40434	74.17966	202.5433
40	1.48886	2.20804	3.26204	4.80102	7.03999	10.28572	14.97446	21.72452	31.40942	45.25926	93.05097	267.8635
50	1.64463	2.69159	4.38391	7.10668	11.46740	18.42015	29.45703	46.90161	74.35752	117.3909	289.0022	1,083.66
100	2.70481	7.24465	19.21863	50.50495	131.5013	339.3021	867.7163	2,199.76	5,529.04	13,780.6	83,522.3	1.17 mil.

Table II: Future Value of Annuity of $1.00 in Arrears

$$F = [(1 + r)^n - 1]/r, \text{ where } r = \text{interest rate}; \ n = \text{number payments.}$$

No. of Payments = n	1%	2%	3%	4%	5%	6%	7%	8%	9%	10%	12%	15%
1	1.00000	1.00000	1.00000	1.00000	1.00000	1.00000	1.00000	1.00000	1.00000	1.00000	1.00000	1.00000
2	2.01000	2.02000	2.03000	2.04000	2.05000	2.06000	2.07000	2.08000	2.09000	2.10000	2.12000	2.15000
3	3.03010	3.06040	3.09090	3.12160	3.15250	3.18360	3.21490	3.24640	3.27810	3.31000	3.37440	3.47250
4	4.06040	4.12161	4.18363	4.24646	4.31013	4.37462	4.43994	4.50611	4.57313	4.64100	4.77933	4.99338
5	5.10101	5.20404	5.30914	5.41632	5.52563	5.63709	5.75074	5.86660	5.98471	6.10510	6.35285	6.74238
6	6.15202	6.30812	6.46841	6.63298	6.80191	6.97532	7.15329	7.33593	7.52333	7.71561	8.11519	8.75374
7	7.21354	7.43428	7.66246	7.89829	8.14201	8.39384	8.65402	8.92280	9.20043	9.48717	10.08901	11.06680
8	8.28567	8.58297	8.89234	9.21423	9.54911	9.89747	10.25980	10.63663	11.02847	11.43589	12.29969	13.72682
9	9.36853	9.75463	10.15911	10.58280	11.02656	11.49132	11.97799	12.48756	13.02104	13.57948	14.77566	16.78584
10	10.46221	10.94972	11.46388	12.00611	12.57789	13.18079	13.81645	14.48656	15.19293	15.93742	17.54874	20.30372
11	11.56683	12.16872	12.80780	13.48635	14.20679	14.97164	15.78360	16.64549	17.56029	18.53117	20.65458	24.34928
12	12.68250	13.41209	14.19203	15.02581	15.91713	16.86994	17.88845	18.97713	20.14072	21.38428	24.13313	29.00167
13	13.80933	14.68033	15.61779	16.62684	17.71298	18.88214	20.14064	21.49530	22.95338	24.52271	28.02911	34.35192
14	14.94742	15.97394	17.08632	18.29191	19.59863	21.01507	22.55049	24.21492	26.01919	27.97498	32.39260	40.50471
15	16.09690	17.29342	18.59891	20.02359	21.57856	23.27597	25.12902	27.15211	29.36092	31.77248	37.27971	47.58041
16	17.25786	18.63929	20.15688	21.82453	23.65749	25.67253	27.88805	30.32428	33.00340	35.94973	42.75328	55.71747
17	18.43044	20.01207	21.76159	23.69751	25.84037	28.21288	30.84022	33.75023	36.97370	40.54470	48.88367	65.07509
18	19.61475	21.41231	23.41444	25.64541	28.13238	30.90565	33.99903	37.45024	41.30134	45.59917	55.74971	75.83636
19	20.81090	22.84056	25.11687	27.67123	30.53900	33.75999	37.37896	41.44626	46.01846	51.15909	63.43968	88.21181
20	22.01900	24.29737	26.87037	29.77808	33.06595	36.78559	40.99549	45.76196	51.16012	57.27500	72.05244	102.2436
22	24.47159	27.29898	30.53678	34.24797	38.50521	43.39229	49.00574	55.45676	62.87334	71.40275	92.50258	137.6316
24	26.97346	30.42186	34.42647	39.08260	44.50200	50.81558	58.17667	66.76476	76.78981	88.49733	118.1552	184.1678
26	29.52563	33.67091	38.55304	44.31174	51.11345	59.15638	68.67647	79.95442	93.32398	109.1818	150.3339	245.7120
28	32.12910	37.05121	42.93092	49.96758	58.40258	68.52811	80.69769	95.33883	112.9682	134.2099	190.6989	327.1041
30	34.78489	40.56808	47.57542	56.08494	66.43885	79.05819	94.46079	113.2832	136.3075	164.4940	241.3327	434.7451
32	37.49407	44.22703	52.50276	62.70147	75.29883	90.88978	110.2182	134.2135	164.0370	201.1378	304.8477	577.1005
34	40.25770	48.03380	57.73018	69.85791	85.06696	104.1838	128.2588	158.6267	196.9823	245.4767	384.5210	765.3654
36	43.07688	51.99437	63.27594	77.59831	95.83632	119.1209	148.9135	187.1021	236.1247	299.1268	484.4631	1,014.35
38	45.95272	56.11494	69.15945	85.97034	107.7095	135.9042	172.5610	220.3159	282.6298	364.0434	609.8305	1,343.62
40	48.88637	60.40198	75.40126	95.02552	120.7998	154.7620	199.6351	259.0565	337.8824	442.5926	767.0914	1,779.09
50	64.46318	84.57940	112.7969	152.6671	209.3480	290.3359	406.5289	573.7702	815.0836	1,163.91	2,400.02	7,217.72
100	170.4814	312.2323	607.2877	1,237.62	2,610.03	5,638.37	12,381.70	27,484.50	61,422.70	137,796	696,011	7.83 mil.

Table III: Present Value of $1.00

$p = f/(1 + r)^n$, where r = discount (interest) rate; n = number of periods until payment; f = $1.00.

Periods = n	1%	2%	3%	4%	5%	6%	7%	8%	9%	10%	12%	15%
1	.99010	.98039	.97087	.96154	.95238	.94340	.93458	.92593	.91743	.90909	.89286	.86957
2	.98030	.96117	.94260	.92456	.90703	.89000	.87344	.85734	.84168	.82645	.79719	.75614
3	.97059	.94232	.91514	.88900	.86384	.83962	.81630	.79383	.77218	.75131	.71178	.65752
4	.96098	.92385	.88849	.85480	.82270	.79209	.76290	.73503	.70843	.68301	.63552	.57175
5	.95147	.90573	.86261	.82193	.78353	.74726	.71299	.68058	.64993	.62092	.56743	.49718
6	.94205	.88797	.83748	.79031	.74622	.70496	.66634	.63017	.59627	.56447	.50663	.43233
7	.93272	.87056	.81309	.75992	.71068	.66506	.62275	.58349	.54703	.51316	.45235	.37594
8	.92348	.85349	.78941	.73069	.67684	.62741	.58201	.54027	.50187	.46651	.40388	.32690
9	.91434	.83676	.76642	.70259	.64461	.59190	.54393	.50025	.46043	.42410	.36061	.28426
10	.90529	.82035	.74409	.67556	.61391	.55839	.50835	.46319	.42241	.38554	.32197	.24718
11	.89632	.80426	.72242	.64958	.58468	.52679	.47509	.42888	.38753	.35049	.28748	.21494
12	.88745	.78849	.70138	.62460	.55684	.49697	.44401	.39711	.35553	.31863	.25668	.18691
13	.87866	.77303	.68095	.60057	.53032	.46884	.41496	.36770	.32618	.28966	.22917	.16253
14	.86996	.75788	.66112	.57748	.50507	.44230	.38782	.34046	.29925	.26333	.20462	.14133
15	.86135	.74301	.64186	.55526	.48102	.41727	.36245	.31524	.27454	.23939	.18270	.12289
16	.85282	.72845	.62317	.53391	.45811	.39365	.33873	.29189	.25187	.21763	.16312	.10686
17	.84438	.71416	.60502	.51337	.43630	.37136	.31657	.27027	.23107	.19784	.14564	.09293
18	.83602	.70016	.58739	.49363	.41552	.35034	.29586	.25025	.21199	.17986	.13004	.08081
19	.82774	.68643	.57029	.47464	.39573	.33051	.27651	.23171	.19449	.16351	.11611	.07027
20	.81954	.67297	.55368	.45639	.37689	.31180	.25842	.21455	.17843	.14864	.10367	.06110
22	.80340	.64684	.52189	.42196	.34185	.27751	.22571	.18394	.15018	.12285	.08264	.04620
24	.78757	.62172	.49193	.39012	.31007	.24698	.19715	.15770	.12640	.10153	.06588	.03493
26	.77205	.59758	.46369	.36069	.28124	.21981	.17220	.13520	.10639	.08391	.05252	.02642
28	.75684	.57437	.43708	.33348	.25509	.19563	.15040	.11591	.08955	.06934	.04187	.01997
30	.74192	.55207	.41199	.30832	.23138	.17411	.13137	.09938	.07537	.05731	.03338	.01510
32	.72730	.53063	.38834	.28506	.20987	.15496	.11474	.08520	.06344	.04736	.02661	.01142
34	.71297	.51003	.36604	.26355	.19035	.13791	.10022	.07305	.05339	.03914	.02121	.00864
36	.69892	.49022	.34503	.24367	.17266	.12274	.08754	.06262	.04494	.03235	.01691	.00653
38	.68515	.47119	.32523	.22529	.15661	.10924	.07646	.05369	.03783	.02673	.01348	.00494
40	.67165	.45289	.30656	.20829	.14205	.09722	.06678	.04603	.03184	.02209	.01075	.00373
50	.60804	.37153	.22811	.14071	.08720	.05429	.03395	.02132	.01345	.00852	.00346	.00092
100	.36971	.13803	.05203	.01980	.00760	.00295	.00115	.00045	.00018	.00007	.00001	.00000

Table IV: Present Value of Annuity of $1.00 in Arrears

$P = (1 - 1/[1 + r]^n)/r$, where r = discount (interest) rate; n = number of payments.

No. of Payments = n	1%	2%	3%	4%	5%	6%	7%	8%	9%	10%	12%	15%
1	.99010	.98039	.97087	.96154	.95238	.94340	.93458	.92593	.91743	.90909	.89286	.86957
2	1.97040	1.94156	1.91347	1.88609	1.85941	1.83339	1.80802	1.78326	1.75911	1.73554	1.69005	1.62571
3	2.94099	2.88388	2.82861	2.77509	2.72325	2.67301	2.62432	2.57710	2.53129	2.48685	2.40183	2.28323
4	3.90197	3.80773	3.71710	3.62990	3.54595	3.46511	3.38721	3.31213	3.23972	3.16987	3.03735	2.85498
5	4.85343	4.71346	4.57971	4.45182	4.32948	4.21236	4.10020	3.99271	3.88965	3.79079	3.60478	3.35216
6	5.79548	5.60143	5.41719	5.24214	5.07569	4.91732	4.76654	4.62288	4.48592	4.35526	4.11141	3.78448
7	6.72819	6.47199	6.23028	6.00205	5.78637	5.58238	5.38929	5.20637	5.03295	4.86842	4.56376	4.16042
8	7.65168	7.32548	7.01969	6.73274	6.46321	6.20979	5.97130	5.74664	5.53482	5.33493	4.96764	4.48732
9	8.56602	8.16224	7.78611	7.43533	7.10782	6.80169	6.51523	6.24689	5.99525	5.75902	5.32825	4.77158
10	9.47130	8.98259	8.53020	8.11090	7.72172	7.36009	7.02358	6.71008	6.41766	6.14457	5.65022	5.01877
11	10.36763	9.78685	9.25262	8.76048	8.30641	7.88687	7.49867	7.13896	6.80519	6.49506	5.93770	5.23371
12	11.25508	10.57534	9.95400	9.38507	8.86325	8.38384	7.94269	7.53608	7.16073	6.81369	6.19437	5.42062
13	12.13374	11.34837	10.63496	9.98565	9.39357	8.85268	8.35765	7.90378	7.48690	7.10336	6.42355	5.58315
14	13.00370	12.10625	11.29607	10.56312	9.89864	9.29498	8.74547	8.24424	7.78615	7.36669	6.62817	5.72448
15	13.86505	12.84926	11.93794	11.11839	10.37966	9.71225	9.10791	8.55948	8.06069	7.60608	6.81086	5.84737
16	14.71787	13.57771	12.56110	11.65230	10.83777	10.10590	9.44665	8.85137	8.31256	7.82371	6.97399	5.95423
17	15.56225	14.29187	13.16612	12.16567	11.27407	10.47726	9.76322	9.12164	8.54363	8.02155	7.11963	6.04716
18	16.39827	14.99203	13.75351	12.65930	11.68959	10.82760	10.05909	9.37189	8.75563	8.20141	7.24967	6.12797
19	17.22601	15.67846	14.32380	13.13394	12.08532	11.15812	10.33560	9.60360	8.95011	8.36492	7.36578	6.19823
20	18.04555	16.35143	14.87747	13.59033	12.46221	11.46992	10.59401	9.81815	9.12855	8.51356	7.46944	6.25933
22	19.66038	17.65805	15.93692	14.45112	13.16300	12.04158	11.06124	10.20074	9.44243	8.77154	7.64465	6.35866
24	21.24339	18.91393	16.93554	15.24696	13.79864	12.55036	11.46933	10.52876	9.70661	8.98474	7.78432	6.43377
26	22.79520	20.12104	17.87684	15.98277	14.37519	13.00317	11.82578	10.80998	9.92897	9.16095	7.89566	6.49056
28	24.31644	21.28127	18.76411	16.66306	14.89813	13.40616	12.13711	11.05108	10.11613	9.30657	7.98442	6.53351
30	25.80771	22.39646	19.60044	17.29203	15.37245	13.76483	12.40904	11.25778	10.27365	9.42691	8.05518	6.56598
32	27.26959	23.46833	20.38877	17.87355	15.80268	14.08404	12.64656	11.43500	10.40624	9.52638	8.11159	6.59053
34	28.70267	24.49859	21.13184	18.41120	16.19290	14.36814	12.85401	11.58693	10.51784	9.60857	8.15656	6.60910
36	30.10751	25.48884	21.83225	18.90828	16.54685	14.62099	13.03521	11.71719	10.61176	9.67651	8.19241	6.62314
38	31.48466	26.44064	22.49246	19.36786	16.86789	14.84602	13.19347	11.82887	10.69082	9.73265	8.22099	6.63375
40	32.83469	27.35548	23.11477	19.79277	17.15909	15.04630	13.33171	11.92461	10.75736	9.77905	8.24378	6.64178
50	39.19612	31.42361	25.72976	21.48218	18.25593	15.76186	13.80075	12.23348	10.96168	9.91481	8.30450	6.66051
100	63.02888	43.09835	31.59891	24.50500	19.84791	16.61755	14.26925	12.49432	11.10910	9.99927	8.33323	6.66666